Walkabout
NORTHERN
CALIFORNIA
2nd Edition
Hiking Inn to Inn

Tom Courtney

WILDERNESS PRESS ... *on the trail since 1967*

Walkabout Northern California: Hiking Inn to Inn

Second edition, 2019
Copyright © 2019 and 2011 by Tom Courtney
Manufactured in the United States
Distributed by Publishers Group West

Library of Congress Cataloging-in-Publication Data

Names: Courtney, Tom, 1948– author.
Title: Walkabout Northern California : hiking inn to inn / Tom Courtney.
Description: 2nd edition. | Birmingham, AL : Wilderness Press, an imprint
    of AdventureKEEN, [2019] | Includes bibliographical references and index.
Identifiers: LCCN 2018031102 | ISBN 9780899978901 (pbk.)
Subjects: LCSH: Hotels—California, Northern—Guidebooks. | Hiking—California,
    Northern—Guidebooks. | Trails—California, Northern—Guidebooks. | California,
    Northern—Guidebooks.
Classification: LCC F867.5 .C687 2019 | DDC 796.5109794—dc23
LC record available at https://lccn.loc.gov/2018031102

Front cover photos copyright © 2019 by Tom Courtney
Interior photos by Tom Courtney except the following: page 29: Scott Jordan
Maps and cover design: Scott McGrew
Interior design and layout: Adapted from the author's design
Project editor: Kate Johnson
Proofreader: Laura Franck
Indexer: Tom Courtney

Published by 🦅 **WILDERNESS PRESS**
An imprint of AdventureKEEN
2204 First Ave. S., Ste. 102
Birmingham, AL 35233
800-443-7227

Visit wildernesspress.com for a complete listing of our books and for ordering information.
Contact us at our website, at facebook.com/wildernesspress1967, or at twitter.com
/wilderness1967 with questions or comments. To find out more about who we are and
what we're doing, visit blog.wildernesspress.com.

Cover photos: (clockwise from top left) Cabin at the Santa Cruz KOA ("Walkabout
the Monterey Bay," page 108); Pelican Inn ("The Marin Coast," page 12); Olema House
("The Marin Coast," page 12); and Stinson Beach, Bolinas Lagoon, and Bolinas Peninsula
("Circumambulation," page 196)

"Courtney's engaging descriptions include natural and human history and stories of quirky locals. He also provides route information, lodging recommendations, trailhead directions, sources for trail maps, and tips on gear and safety ...The book offers rich experience: car-free rambles rewarded with creature comforts—perfect for aging backpackers, carbon-conscious travelers, and anyone interested in slowing down to appreciate nature and hospitality."

—SUE ROSENTHAL, *Bay Nature*

"Now comes a guide that brings readers both Courtney's savvy knowledge and firsthand experience of exploring 400 miles of California wilderness. Different from other hiking guides, this one provides readers with everything they need to turn their adventure into a true walkabout ... It's a practical guide but also rich in detail. Courtney allows readers to see deep inside the wilderness of each hiking segment. He brings it to life, tempting all those who love the outdoors to see it for themselves."

—ANN TATKO-PETERSON,
Contra Costa Times (now *East Bay Times*)

"Nothing wrong with roughing it, of course, but occasionally a guy likes to soak his weary feet in a hot tub, sip a fine merlot alongside a juicy steak, and sleep in high-thread-count sheets along the way."

—SAM McMANIS, *Sacramento Bee*

"You wake up in your comfy room, eat a delicious breakfast, set off for the day through the beautiful wilds, and make it to the next lodging in time for cocktails. This type of traveling is fairly common in Europe, but not as popular here in the States ... It might seem daunting to plan an inn-to-inn trip yourself, but Courtney offers detailed itineraries, complete with trail notes, suggested stops, lodging recommendations, and the like."

—SUSIE NADLER, *Apartment Therapy*

"[Courtney] fell in love with to-inn walking in England. Now he wants to make it as popular in the United States as it was there."

—JUDITH STONE, *Sunset*

Acknowledgments

I WOULD LIKE TO EXPRESS MY DEEP GRATITUDE:

To the many friends and members of the Walkabout California community who enthusiastically supported and encouraged this project and who have hiked inn to inn through the wilds of California.

To Lynn MacMichael, a one-person marketing tornado, who read every word of this volume and improved it with her insights.

To Scott Jordan, longtime friend and inn-to-inn hiking buddy, who joined me on walkabouts through Lassen and the Sierra, always ready for adventure. His editorial advice was invaluable.

To my daughter, Emily Courtney, Walkabout California's business manager. Her deep knowledge and steady hand launched the venture and made it flourish. Her passion and support never wavered, and her meticulous editorial advice was priceless.

Finally, to my wife, Heidi. She hiked with me on eight of these walkabouts, from a romantic weekend stroll along the Mendocino Coast to 20-mile treks on the rugged Lost Coast. There is no more delightful companion on the trail. She kept my writing grounded and true. This project would not have happened without her unfaltering enthusiasm and support.

Preface to the Second Edition

WHAT JOY—TO SET OUT ON A TRAIL in the wilds of Northern California, to hike for two to five days, stopping each evening at an inn, B&B, or hostel for a hot shower, a good meal, and a comfortable bed. That was the inspiration for the first edition of this book. I am grateful to Wilderness Press that they share this vision.

Many of us lead hectic, urban lives. Yet we have a primal yearning for a deeper connection to nature and to ourselves. A multiday sojourn in California's wilderness helps us make that connection.

The popularity of distance walking and hiking from inn to inn has grown dramatically. In 1990, fewer than 5,000 pilgrims received their Compostela—accreditation for hiking 100 kilometers or biking 200 kilometers on Camino de Santiago across Northern Spain. That annual number now exceeds 300,000. Likewise, since the first edition of this book, thousands have taken to the trails to hike from inn to inn through California. Thousands more have come to our website, WalkaboutCalifornia.com, to share their insights and experiences of hiking from inn to inn around the world, to ask questions and plan their own adventure, and to find inspiration for outdoor exploration.

There have been many changes since the first edition of this book. Options for transportation and lodging have become more abundant and convenient. Ride-hailing services have blossomed, offering easy rides to the trailhead. Short-term rental services, such as Airbnb and VRBO, have multiplied lodging options. Inns and restaurants have closed, opened, and changed hands. Some trails have become overgrown and impassible. New trails have emerged. There are also two new walk-abouts in this edition: "Sierra Nevada Foothills Along the American River" and "Walkabout Carquinez Strait."

So join us. Explore the rugged Pacific coastline, stopping at seaside villages and quaint inns. Hike the beautiful Sierra Nevada Mountains, staying at lake and riverside resorts. Visit the alpine lakes, raging rivers, and otherworldly hydrothermal landscapes of Lassen Volcanic National Park, and relax in the hot spring–fed pool of a 100-year-old guest ranch. Walk back in history along California's great waterways. Take a Walkabout California, hiking from inn to inn.

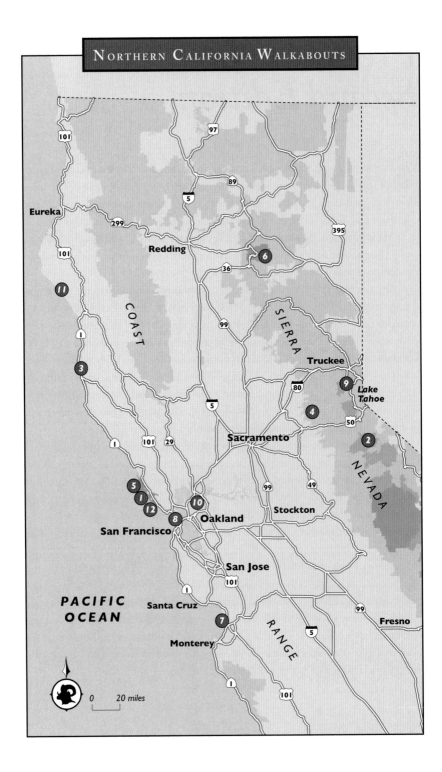

NORTHERN CALIFORNIA WALKABOUTS

101
97
89
5
Eureka
299
395
Redding
6
36
COAST
99
SIERRA
Truckee
11
80
9
1
Lake
Tahoe
3
4
50
5
2
Sacramento
NEVADA
29
101
1
5
99
49
10
Oakland
5
1
Stockton
12
8
San Francisco
San Jose
101
PACIFIC
OCEAN
Santa Cruz
1
99
Fresno
7
RANGE
5
Monterey
101
1

0   20 miles

CONTENTS

The Marin Coast (see page 12)

Introduction

Afoot and light-hearted I take to the open road,
Healthy, free, the world before me,
The long brown path before me leading wherever I choose.

—WALT WHITMAN, "Song of the Open Road"

Never did I think so much, exist so vividly, and experience
so much, never have I been so myself—if I may use
that expression—as in the journeys I have taken alone
and on foot.

—JEAN-JACQUES ROUSSEAU, *The Confessions*

AMERICANS CROSS THE ATLANTIC TO WALK FROM INN TO INN on long-established European trails. They hike the Alps or Southern France, explore the British Isles at 2 miles an hour, or pilgrimage through Northern Spain on the road to Santiago de Compostela, stopping each night at a hostel or inn.

To my delight, I have discovered that in California it is also possible to enjoy dozens of multiday walks from inn to inn. This book will help you plan self-guided hikes along the wild Pacific Coast, through the majestic Sierra Nevada, into the Southern Cascades, through the parklands around San Francisco Bay, and more. Each day ends with a comfortable bed, a glass of wine, a good meal, and perhaps even a therapeutic massage or a soak in hot springs.

Hike the Marin Coast from the Headlands to Point Reyes, stopping each evening in a coastal village where you can explore the pubs and restaurants. Cross the Sierra in the footsteps of the pioneers, and stay in cabins on the shores of clear mountain lakes. Take a romantic stroll along the beautiful Mendocino Coast, and enjoy gourmet cuisine at inns perched on bluffs overlooking the vast Pacific. Walk along the shore of Monterey Bay, and marvel at the abundance of sea and bird life in its protected waters. Hike Lassen, exploring mountain lakes, deep canyons, and otherworldly hydrothermal landscapes, with a visit to a rustic guest ranch, where you will enjoy sumptuous dining and a muscle-soothing soak in hot springs.

The multiday hiker derives a special joy from hiking in the wilderness. The tensions of the workaday world melt away. The mind slows as the miles pass, and your focus shifts to the sights, smells, and sounds of nature. You go not only into the woods but deeper into yourself. A walk in the wilderness is the antidote to the frantic pace of modern life. Leave the car behind to hike for a few days, and you have not only the time to process your to-do list and plan the work that needs to be done when the hike is over but also the time to daydream, to tell your friend a story that might take three days to complete, to contemplate, to meditate. If a pilgrimage is a walk to a sacred site, then perhaps nature's wild places are our cathedrals, and every hike in the wilderness is a pilgrimage both to a place and into one's heart.

Walking in the wild places of California, on the same trails that others have hiked for 10,000 years, one imagines how life must have been: the Sinkyone teenager who looked up at King Peak soaring to the heavens from the Lost Coast and thought, "Tomorrow I will climb to its summit and see the rest of the world." Or the pioneer wife on the Emigrant Trail who, with her family, walked most of the 2,000 miles from their former home in Indiana and, as she was about to ascend West Pass, thought, "Just one more great climb. We will conquer the elephant, and then walk to the fields of gold."

Or the Ohlone children on the Monterey Bay, filling baskets with mussels for the village feast, who have come farther south than ever before when the eldest says, "It is time to go back." A young girl points south, "just to that river." Pelicans and seagulls crowd the sandbar where the river meets the sea. A school of dolphins leaps beyond the breaking surf, and farther out to sea, migrating gray whales surface and spout. The eldest says, "Tomorrow, at low tide, we will cross the river and see what the mussels are like on the other side."

A long hike through the wilderness deepens our connections to those who came before us. We feel the same yearning to climb to the next ridge to see what is on the other side. It also deepens our connection to nature and the need to preserve it. The strongest advocates for protecting the threatened California wilderness are those who hike its trails.

The Walkabout California adventure started with a hike in the Marin Headlands, just across the Golden Gate from San Francisco. For quite some time I had admired the Miwok Trail's grace and beauty as it climbs and winds up Gerbode Valley and through the coastal hills. A map of Golden Gate National Recreation Area revealed that the Miwok connected with a half dozen other trails. If I took Wolf Ridge Trail, I could drop down into Tennessee Valley and take the Coastal Trail to Muir Beach. Did the journey need to stop there? Trails on the western flank of Mount Tamalpais go all the way to Stinson Beach. Could I keep going to Bolinas? I pulled out a Mount Tam map. Yes, I could climb to the Bolinas Ridge, hike through a redwood forest, descend, and stroll into town. Then I got out a Point Reyes map and saw I could keep hiking north all the way to Olema,

38 miles over four hiking days through some of the most breathtakingly beautiful coastline in the world. Along the way I would stay in four coastal villages, each with interesting inns and great dining.

I was hooked. By the time I finished that first walkabout, I wanted more, and I began to search for other inn-to-inn adventures. Were there other hiking routes through the California wilderness where inns, B&Bs, hotels, resorts, or hostels were within a reasonable day's hike? I wanted to stay on trails, but a short stroll on a quiet country lane or even a very short walk on the shoulder of a rural highway would work to connect trails. The result is an exploration of more than 450 miles of California wilderness, nights spent in more than 50 inns, many extraordinary meals, and this book.

In the spring of 2009, my daughter, Emily, and I launched our website, WalkaboutCalifornia.com, with trail guides, some ideas about how to get started on your own walkabout, and an invitation to an online discussion about inn-to-inn hiking. The timing was right—people from around the world were ready to hit the trail on a California walkabout. We posted more hiking guides, and others joined in for discussions of European inn-to-inn hikes, questions and ideas about California walkabouts, restaurant and inn suggestions, and photographs of their journeys.

The Mendocino Coast (see page 44)

Sorensen's Resort (see "Crossing the Sierra on the Emigrant Trail," page 28)

When we started hiking inn to inn in California, innkeepers were stunned that we had not arrived by car. Now, inn-to-inn hikers are no surprise. When we checked into the Bear Valley Cottage on the Point Reyes walkabout, our host, Amanda, rushed into her kitchen and returned with a well-worn copy of one of our Marin Coast guides that a guest had left behind. She offers a 15% discount for guests arriving on foot or by bike. Inn-to-inn hikers have become a regular part of her business.

What is the recipe for a really great inn? A beautiful setting is probably the most important ingredient. Throw in a room that is spacious, quiet, and well lit, with a comfortable bed, and don't forget a gracious innkeeper, one who cares about your comfort as if you were a friend. "Your clothes are wet. Let me throw them in the dryer." "Can we pack you a lunch for tomorrow's hike?"

What makes a good hiking companion? I am lucky to have two who add to the joys of the trail and the pleasures of a good meal at the end of the day. Heidi, my wife, can hike all day. A horticulturist by trade, she is also a naturalist. If time allows, she will stop to study every wildflower. Along the trail my mind wanders, but she brings me back to notice the song of a meadowlark, the fragrance of a bay laurel grove, the intricate beauty of a Douglas iris, or a new constellation peeking over the horizon. My old friend Scott Jordan, a family court judge in Reno, knows the Sierra Nevada Mountains well, tells a great story, appreciates walking quietly for a few miles, and is always eager for an inn-to-inn hike. Spending a few days on the trail together renews and deepens a friendship.

Travel light. A 12- to 15-pound day pack with a book, lunch, and a change of clothes should do it. Is 10 miles a long hike? Not if you have all day. The sun shines for 15 hours on midsummer California days. How about 15 miles? No problem. Enjoy a leisurely breakfast before you set out. Choose a comfortable pace. Stop to rest and read by a woodland stream. Have a swim in a Sierra lake. Take a nap in the shade of a buckeye. You will still arrive in time for happy hour.

Some of the great California inn-to-inn hikes I describe can take a week, but many can be enjoyed over a weekend. Some are challenging, but many are perfect for the casual hiker. Each chapter in this volume describes one or more great California inn-to-inn hikes. At the end of each chapter, you will find a detailed description of the route, transportation alternatives to the trailhead and back, and information about places to stay. Use these to plan your walks. Read the whole section to get a flavor of the countryside; meet some of its denizens, both two- and four-legged; learn a little of its history; and know what villages, inns, and restaurants to expect along the way.

So lace up your hiking boots and strap on a day pack. Leave the car behind and explore some of the most beautiful wilderness in the world. Take a walkabout in Northern California.

PLANNING YOUR WALKABOUT

Best Seasons for Hiking in California

THE CALIFORNIA COAST enjoys a Mediterranean climate with rainy winters and dry summers. In midsummer, hot air from inland valleys rises, often drawing dense banks of fog from the Pacific that can blanket the coastline. The fog is most persistent in the northern part of the state. Spring and fall are the best times to hike the coast, but pay attention to weather reports. It can rain in midsummer, and a heavy fog can feel like rain. Always bring a light rain jacket. Late April–mid-June and the autumn months of September and October are ideal for a coastal inn-to-inn hike. You'll have the best chance for perfect weather and to avoid the summer crowds.

Hiking in the mountains depends upon the intensity and timing of winter snows. High Sierra trails may not open until July. The months from June through mid-October are usually very good, but be prepared for afternoon thunderstorms at any time. Expect water levels to be highest in the early season, making some stream crossings more difficult. Autumn is ideal for the best weather and for having the trails to yourself.

Maps

EACH HIKE INCLUDES a simplified trail map, but it is important to also bring along at least one up-to-date topographical map for most of these hikes. Map suggestions can be found at the end of each hike. Here are some excellent sources:

- ◻ **California State Parks** parks.ca.gov
- ◻ **Map Adventures** mapadventures.com, 800-891-1534
- ◻ **National Park Service** nps.gov
- ◻ **Tom Harrison Maps** tomharrisonmaps.com
- ◻ **U.S. Geological Survey (USGS)** store.usgs.gov
- ◻ **Wilderness Press** wildernesspress.com, 800-443-7227

What to Bring

All the paraphernalia of a journey can be such a hindrance, so I discard most everything, but then sleeping apparel, paper robe, and raincoat, inkstone, brush, and paper, medicine, lunch basket, and so on, wrapping them all up and hoisting them onto my back—legs wobbly and body weak—I felt as if I was being dragged backwards and I barely made any headway at all, feeling nothing but misery.

—MATSUO BASHO, *Knapsack Notebook*

I TRAVEL AS LIGHTLY AS POSSIBLE, with light boots and a large day pack that fits my shoulders and has a hip belt. I try to resist the urge to fill the pack.

Other essentials:

- ◻ Cell phone and charger
- ◻ Compass and maps
- ◻ Extra socks and underwear that can easily be washed and dried overnight
- ◻ Flashlight or headlamp
- ◻ Hat with a brim
- ◻ Hiking clothes (one or two sets of, depending upon the length of the walkabout)

- ☐ Lunch plus some high-energy trail bars or other trail snacks
- ☐ Multitool pocketknife
- ☐ Overshirt for warmth that is nice enough for dinner in a restaurant
- ☐ Minimal toiletries (the inns should provide soap, shampoo, and lotion)
- ☐ Rain jacket small enough to fit into a small stuff sack
- ☐ Sunglasses, sunscreen, and a small first aid kit with moleskin for blisters
- ☐ Swimsuit for the beach, pool, or spa and a small towel
- ☐ Toilet paper
- ☐ Water
- ☐ Waterproof matches or lighter

Optional items:

- ☐ Bandanna
- ☐ Binoculars
- ☐ Camera
- ☐ Extra batteries
- ☐ Gloves or mittens
- ☐ GPS receiver
- ☐ Hiking poles
- ☐ Insect repellent
- ☐ Light sarong for beach lounging and toweling off
- ☐ Lightweight change of clothes for dinner
- ☐ Long, lightweight, moisture-wicking underwear (tops and bottoms) for warmth
- ☐ Paperback book and journal
- ☐ Rain pants
- ☐ Tide table. You can find accurate tables at tidesandcurrents.noaa.gov /tide_predictions
- ☐ Water filter or purification tablets

Safety

THE BEST SAFETY PRECAUTIONS are to stay warm, dry, hydrated, regularly fueled with food, and rested. Taking these precautions will keep you from getting hypothermia and put you in the best position to manage any surprises.

Other safety measures include:

KNOW YOUR ROUTE. Study the maps and read the hike description before you leave. Check in with the park or Forest Service offices before you start to find out if there are any difficulties with your itinerary. Talk to other hikers on the trail.

LEAVE YOUR ITINERARY WITH A FRIEND OR FAMILY MEMBER. Let your innkeepers know that you are coming on foot, and give them a number to call if you don't arrive by a specified time. Call your friend or loved one when you return home to let them know you are safe.

HIKE WITH A PARTNER. OK, I am guilty of violating this one, but it is easier to get out of a jam if you have someone to help you.

BRING RELIABLE MAPS AND A COMPASS. A GPS receiver is also helpful.

TAKE A CELL PHONE. Many of these hikes have coverage for major carriers.

LEARN TO IDENTIFY POISON OAK, AND STAY AWAY FROM IT.

RATTLESNAKES ARE COMMON IN SOME PARTS OF CALIFORNIA. They may be found near streambeds, under driftwood, or basking in the sunshine on a trail. If you hear a rattle, stop and determine the direction. Head the other way.

KEEP AN EYE ON THE OCEAN. Rogue waves will soak your feet or worse. Every year unsuspecting beachgoers get knocked down and dragged out to sea by surprise surges.

PAY ATTENTION TO THE TIDES. Sections of some of the coast hikes can be passed only at low tide. Read the hike description to learn where these spots are, and time your hike to reach them when the tide is out. For tide schedules, go to tidesandcurrents .noaa.gov/tide_predictions.

TAKE CARE WITH STREAM CROSSINGS. If a waterway looks dangerous, take the long route around. Hiking poles are helpful for maintaining balance. Some streams that flow into the ocean are most easily forded at low tide, when a sandbar forms at the mouth.

LIGHTNING CAN BE HAZARDOUS DURING AFTERNOON THUNDERSTORMS IN THE SIERRA. Pay attention to the weather, and head for lower ground if a storm is coming.

ALTITUDE SICKNESS IS RARE BUT POSSIBLE FOR SEA-LEVEL DWELLERS WHO HIKE IN THE MOUNTAINS. The symptoms are shortness of breath, headache,

Spring flowers on the Mendocino Coast (see page 44)

nausea, vomiting, drowsiness, and memory loss. The best preventive measures are to give yourself time to acclimate, load up on carbohydrates before and during your hike, and drink lots of fluids. If you or a member of your party starts to feel the symptoms, head for a lower elevation.

TAKE PRECAUTIONS AGAINST LYME DISEASE. Lyme disease from tick bites is infrequent in Northern California compared to the northeastern United States and the Upper Midwest. But it does occur, mostly in coastal counties. Tuck your shirt into your pants and your pants into your socks, use repellents, and avoid sitting on logs in oak forests.

How to Use This Book

EACH HIKE'S DESCRIPTION gives you a sense of what to expect along the trail. The other sections help you plan and arrange your trip. Each chapter has a map showing the overall route. You will also want to bring topographical maps for most of these hikes; I suggest specific maps for each route. Detailed directions for each hike keep you on track. I have managed to take a wrong turn on most of these walkabouts, but this section will minimize your false steps.

Driving and parking directions help you find out-of-the-way trailheads. Information on public and private transport (taxis and shuttles) will help you to plan how to get back to your starting place or even how to make the trip without a car.

Places to Stay lists contact information for inns, B&Bs, hotels, resorts, and hostels. This list may be partial if there are many lodging options. Prices are also broken into these categories:

LODGING COST			
$ less than $100	$$ $100–$150	$$$ $150–$200	$$$$ more than $200

Lessons from the Trail

In properly developed countries, the inhabitants regard walkers with grave suspicion and have taught their dogs to do the same.

—ALAN BOOTH, *The Roads to Sata: A 2,000-Mile Walk Through Japan*

Caples Lake (see "Crossing the Sierra on the Emigrant Trail," page 28)

HERE ARE SOME LESSONS that I learned on the trail, mostly the hard way:

TRAVEL LIGHT. Your shoulders and legs will thank you.

TAKE GOOD MAPS. Two maps are better than one. Still, don't be surprised if you need to backtrack to find a hidden, unmarked trail.

TAKE A RAIN JACKET that is light and compresses into a small stuff sack.

IF THE POISON OAK LOOKS DIFFICULT TO AVOID, DON'T GO THERE. It will get you. Turn around and take the longer route.

YOU WILL BE ABLE TO WALK ALL DAY if you take rest breaks and stay hydrated and fueled with food.

TURN AROUND AT LEAST EVERY 0.5 MILE and look at where you've come from. Otherwise you'll miss some spectacular scenery.

THE BEST CONDITIONS FOR HIKING ON THE BEACH—flat, firm sand—are usually found during the hours before and after low tide.

WHEN YOU GET UP FROM A REST BREAK OR LUNCH, stop before you walk away to see if you left anything behind. Otherwise you may arrive at your B&B and discover your camera is back on the trail.

STAY IN TOUCH

THE WALKABOUT CALIFORNIA COMMUNITY IS GROWING, and there are so many more inn-to-inn hikes to be discovered in California. I continue to explore, and so do others. Visit WalkaboutCalifornia.com to share your ideas about inn-to-inn hiking, your reviews of restaurants and inns that you enjoyed along the trail, your photos, and any questions about the hikes. Find out about new walkabouts, and share in the adventure.

Walk while ye have the light, lest darkness come upon you.
—JOHN 12:35

"Then it doesn't matter which way you go," said the Cat.
"—so long as I get somewhere," Alice added as an explanation.
"Oh, you're sure to do that," said the Cat, "if you only walk long enough."
—LEWIS CARROLL,
Alice's Adventures in Wonderland

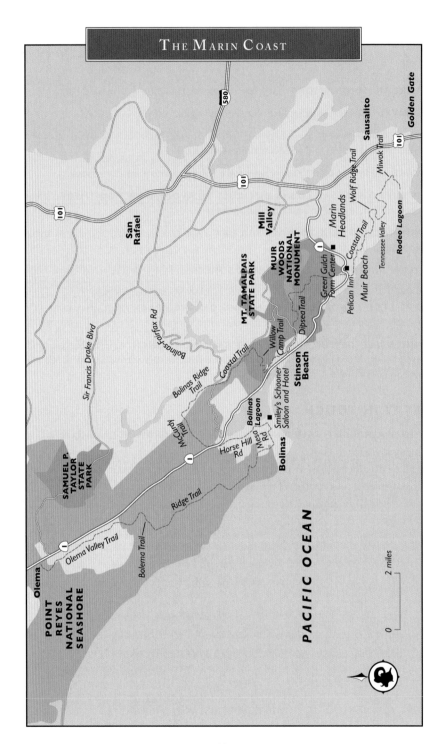

THE MARIN COAST

580

101

101

101

Golden Gate

Sausalito

Wolf Ridge Trail

Miwok Trail

San Rafael

Marin Headlands

Coastal Trail

Rodeo Lagoon

Tennessee Valley

Mill Valley

MUIR WOODS NATIONAL MONUMENT

Green Gulch Farm Center

Pelican Inn

Muir Beach

MT. TAMALPAIS STATE PARK

Bolinas-Fairfax Rd

Sir Francis Drake Blvd

Dipsea Trail

Coastal Trail

Willow Camp Trail

Bolinas Ridge Trail

Stinson Beach

Smiley's Schooner Saloon and Hotel

Bolinas Lagoon

McCurdy Trail

Mesa Rd

Horse Hill Rd

Bolinas

1

SAMUEL P. TAYLOR STATE PARK

Ridge Trail

Bolema Trail

Olema Valley Trail

1

Olema

POINT REYES NATIONAL SEASHORE

PACIFIC OCEAN

0   2 miles

THE MARIN COAST

Marin Headlands to Point Reyes

> *The tradesman, the attorney comes out of the din and craft of the street and sees the sky, the woods, and is a man again.*
>
> —RALPH WALDO EMERSON, "Nature"

View of the Marin Coast from the Coastal Trail

Why not walk in the direction of life, enjoying peace in each moment with every step? There is no need to struggle. Enjoy each step. We have already arrived.

—THICH NHAT HANH, *The Long Road Turns to Joy: A Guide to Walking Meditation*

THIS MODERATE 41.3-MILE HIKE along some of the most beautiful and dramatic coastline in the world starts in the Marin Headlands, a short distance from San Francisco, and ends at Point Reyes National Seashore. The first two days of hiking are easy strolls. The second two are longer with some elevation gain, but still moderate hikes. Along the way, the trail passes through three coastal villages: Muir Beach, Stinson Beach, and Bolinas, each offering interesting places to stay and great dining. Take an extra day or two to relax, explore the beach, and maybe even get a massage. A second, shorter walkabout (see page 24) can be done in a weekend. Walk the trails of the Coast Miwok and a stretch of California's wild and beautiful coast right at the doorstep of the San Francisco Bay Area.

ITINERARY

DAY 1:	Marin Headlands to Muir Beach	**7.0**
DAY 2:	Muir Beach to Stinson Beach	**6.8**
DAY 3:	Stinson Beach to Bolinas	**13.5**
DAY 4:	Bolinas to Olema	**14.0**
TOTAL MILEAGE		**41.3**

Day 1: Marin Headlands to Muir Beach

MIST HOVERS ABOVE THE CALM WATERS of Rodeo Lagoon as the morning sun breaks through the fog. The graceful, winding Miwok Trail climbs through the coastal hills up the western slope of Gerbode Valley past the remains of the Silva dairy ranch, home of Portuguese settlers who worked this land in the 1800s. A broken stone wall, a grove of towering eucalyptus, and perhaps the calla lilies that thrive in the Headlands' marshy lowlands are all that remains of the ranch. As you round the first bend, the sounds of civilization fade, replaced by the trilling of a meadowlark, the high-pitched cry of a red-tailed hawk gliding on an updraft, and the gentle splashing of an unnamed creek hidden from sight in the thick willows.

This journey explores some of the most beautiful country in California, along the hills and valleys of America's western edge. It starts in the Marin Headlands at a trailhead that's a short 10-minute drive from the first freeway exit north of the Golden Gate Bridge. Part of Golden Gate National Recreation Area, the Marin Headlands was once a Nike missile site with nuclear warheads ready to defend against enemy bombers, and now it is hundreds of acres of wild coastal hills and Pacific coastline waiting to be explored.

The first day's hike, a 7-mile stroll to Muir Beach, can be savored at a leisurely pace. No need to hurry. You have all day with nothing to do but walk. At the end of the day, a lovely inn and hearty meal await you.

It was early June when I set out, the start of summer, California's dry season. The hills were turning from green to brown, but stands of yellow monkeyflowers and white hemlock still filled the washes. Gardens of 6-foot-high purple foxgloves and ranging violet peas thrived in moist, protected pockets.

From the ridge, the view is exhilarating: To the south the San Francisco skyline stretches beyond the Golden Gate, and the vast blue Pacific meets the horizon to the west. To the north Mount Tamalpais rises from the ocean to 2,571 feet, and in the distance, your destination, Point Reyes. Breathe deeply of the Pacific's wind. In the coming days this sweet breeze will fill your lungs and refresh every cell down to your marrow.

Take the Wolf Ridge Trail to the Coastal Trail, and drop steeply into the Tennessee Valley. The valley's trail leads to the beach. Waves crash on the rocks and cliffs that form the small, protected Tennessee Cove. It was once called Indian Cove, but its name changed on the foggy night of March 5, 1853, when the SS *Tennessee* made the final leg of its journey from Panama to San Francisco. Captain Mellus felt confident of his position as he worked the ship toward the treacherous entrance of the Golden Gate, but a thick fog engulfed the vessel, and a strong current swept her past the Gate. Around 9 p.m. a steerage passenger standing on the bow spotted breakers ahead and shouted to the wheelhouse. Captain Mellus heard the crashing of waves. The fog lifted briefly, but it was too late. The ship struck the rocks of Indian Cove.

The crew sprang into action. Chief Mate Dowling jumped overboard with a small line tied around his waist. He struggled to shore and pulled a larger cable after him. All night cable or quarter boats ferried the 551 passengers safely to shore without losing a single life, but the SS *Tennessee* broke up by midday and sank. Some people say that even today a severe storm will expose parts of the ship still wedged among the rocks.

Looking north from Wolf Ridge

Heading north, the Coastal Trail winds 3 miles to Muir Beach, up and down the bluffs above waves crashing on ragged cliffs. Muir Beach is formed by Redwood Creek, which flows down Mount Tam, through Muir Woods, and into the crescent bay. Houses perch on the bluffs above the beach's north end. A rocky outcropping divides the long southern section from the smaller north beach, which can be reached at low tide; it's a favorite spot on sunny days for nude sunbathers.

At the entrance road to the state beach stands Pelican Inn, a 16th-century-style English country public house nestled in a wooded valley along Redwood Creek. Only a short drive from San Francisco, it has the feel of a faraway place and time. I settled into a spacious room, furnished with a high canopied bed and Persian rugs, the walls adorned with bawdy prints of 16th-century celebrants at horse races and drunken revelers chasing barmaids.

The Pelican's pub welcomes locals and travelers on CA 1 to a friendly meeting place with whitewashed walls, dark wooden beams, and leaded glass windows. A couple came in, and the fellow said, "Two beers please. I hope $5 will cover it. That's all we got."

"Five dollars will work," said Nick the bartender, with a smile, and handed him two pints of Bass.

We introduced ourselves. A small man dressed in jeans, work boots, and a John Deere cap, Sebastian had a broad smile and too much energy to sit still for long. Maria quietly drank her beer while he paced, studying a photo on the wall of Muir Beach in times past and talked for the two of them. He had grown up in Muir Beach in the 1960s, and now driving down the coast, he wanted to stop for a short visit in his home village.

I ordered us a second round, and we started a game of darts.

"What was it like growing up here?" I asked.

He toed the line, ready for a toss, and paused for a moment, recalling his youth. "It was a hippie community. Us kids felt like we were Tom Sawyer and Huck Finn. The ocean, the river, the mountain were our playground. We ran wild."

"It's quiet around here now," Nick said, "but I heard it was pretty crazy back in the day."

Sebastian said, "I was 15 in '67, the summer of love. There was a club called the Wobbly Rock Inn right above the beach. All the local bands played there—the Grateful Dead, Jefferson Airplane, New Riders. We were too young to get in, but we hung around and caught the music from the beach or the hill in back of the Wobbly.

"One night the Hell's Angels came through. There must have been a hundred Harleys. Everyone else in town stayed home that night, but us kids watched them from the bluffs. They lit bonfires on the beach, drank, and partied all night.

"I remember sitting on the bluff, smokin' a J with my buddies and watching the night Ken Kesey and the Pranksters came out on the bus. They staged an acid test at the Wobbly. The party moved to the beach, and hippies were dancing naked in the moonlight. It was a hell of an education for a kid.

"They eventually condemned the Wobbly Rock and tore it down," he continued. "My mom moved out in '79. Now it's a commuter town. All those houses on the cliffs cost a million dollars."

I bid them goodnight and went to the restaurant. English cuisine is often disparaged, but the Pelican's curried blackened lamb is exquisite with a glass of cabernet by the fireplace after a day's hike. You might want to walk off your dinner with a stroll down to the beach under a starry sky.

Many claim that another traveler, Sir Francis Drake, visited Muir Beach, and it is easy to see why. He could have harbored his ship in the safe bay, traded with the Coast Miwok, and resupplied with freshwater from Redwood Creek and plentiful game from the woods and hillsides of Mount Tamalpais. Walking the beach in the moonlight, it is easy to imagine Miwok children playing in the surf with the *Golden Hinde* anchored in the bay or perhaps the faint chords of the Dead between the crashing waves.

Day 2: Muir Beach to Stinson Beach

IN THE MORNING THE PELICAN sends off its guests with a hearty complimentary breakfast of bacon, eggs, toast, English bangers, fried tomatoes, and fruit. Following Sebastian's directions, I found the hidden public stairs that climb through the village clinging to the cliffs above Muir Beach (see The Route, page 23, for directions). Houses on stilts with picture windows and decks overlook the Pacific. Lush coastal gardens overflow with calla lilies, pride of Madera, and poppies.

After a short walk along CA 1, the Coast View Trail starts its gradual ascent up Mount Tam through grasslands and coyote brush. It climbs 3 miles to 1,200 feet and meets the Dipsea Trail. Below, CA 1 winds along the coast, small boats fish the coastal waters, and massive freighters enter and depart through the Golden Gate. On a clear day the rocky Farallon Islands can be seen on the horizon jutting out of the Pacific 27 miles west.

The Dipsea descends another 3 miles to Stinson Beach, first traversing grassy hillsides and then dropping down into the cool redwood and bay forest of Steep Ravine. Steps have been laid to form the trail that drops into the deep canyon to Webb Creek. Emerging from the woods, the trail opens to the first view of Stinson Beach. Houses poke through the trees climbing up the flank of Mount Tam, and the long beach extends for miles almost to Bolinas, sheltering broad Bolinas Lagoon to the east. After another short trip through the woods, the trail spills out onto CA 1 at the edge of town.

Muir Beach feels like a commuter village. It has no commercial center, and very few people were around on the weekday morning when I passed through. Stinson Beach has a different feel. Commuters are willing to take the longer, winding drive on CA 1, but its population also includes locals and weekenders. It has a commercial center with a grocery store, shops, restaurants, and bars. On the weekends, the town bustles with tourists who have been coming since the mid-1800s, when retired sea captain Alfred Easkoot bought land along the beach and rented out tents to visitors who came on foot, on horseback, and by boat. Easkoot built the town's first house in 1883, and today many houses are more than a century old. Well-established gardens overflow with perennials that thrive in the cool, foggy climate.

After walking 7 miles, you may want to reward yourself with a late lunch of oysters and beer at the Stinson Beach Grill or perhaps explore the beach, bookstore, and neighborhoods of this coastal village. Stinson Beach offers a few good dining options. On the quiet midweek evening of my visit, I joined the locals at the Parkside Cafe for an all-you-can-eat pasta dinner, carbo-loading for the long trail ahead.

Day 3: Stinson Beach to Bolinas

DAY 3 STARTS WITH A SHORT WALK through the neighborhoods of Stinson Beach to reach Willow Camp Trail. This 13.5-mile leg starts with a 2.5-mile,

1,900-foot climb to Bolinas Ridge. Ordinarily the views are breathtaking on the Willow Camp as the coast unfolds with each step, but this day a light rain fell. A surreal cloud engulfed me, and visibility was reduced to only about 20 feet. Even sounds were muted. Thigh-high grass, heavy with rain, bent over the trail and saturated my pants. My rain-resistant jacket soon gave up the fight, and my boots spurted with each step. This was June, not the rainy season. The weather report predicted warm, sunny days. Another victim of global climate change?

I recalled the ecstasy John Muir expressed in *My First Summer in the Sierra* as he hiked in a mountain rainstorm:

> *Happy showers that fall on so fair a wilderness—scarce a single drop can fail to find a beautiful spot.... God's messenger, angel of love sent on its way with majesty and pomp and display of power that make man's greatest shows ridiculous.*

At the ridge take the Coastal Trail north, or hike as I did on the Ridge Road. A biker appeared in the mist, the only other soul I saw that day until I got back to CA 1. As he sailed by, I yelled, "You must be crazy to be out on a day like today!"

"I am," he shouted back and disappeared into the cloud.

The flank of Mount Tamalpais

A wild turkey scurried across the road like a vision in the vapor.

Walk along the ridge 2.5 miles to Bolinas-Fairfax Road. Cross the road and hike the Bolinas Ridge Trail. It starts in serene redwoods, emerges into an open manzanita and oak forest, then reenters redwoods. As you continue along the rolling ridgeline, the forests alternate for 3.5 miles until McCurdy Trail. (For an alternate route, hiking down Bolinas-Fairfax Road, see The Route, Day 3, page 24.)

Descend McCurdy 1.7 miles to CA 1. This is not a well-maintained trail, but it is popular with mountain bikers, who keep it from becoming overgrown. Initially it is steep, but it soon enters the forest and becomes more gradual. Leaving the forest, hike the final mile through beautiful, rolling grasslands, descending into the wooded Olema Valley. You are walking down to the San Andreas Fault.

Turn left on CA 1 for a brief walk on the shoulder. Turn right on Horseshoe Hill Road, a quiet, forested country lane passing by small homesteads. Turn right on Olema Bolinas Road, and hike the walking path into Bolinas along the lagoon past eucalyptus forests, farms, homes, and the site of Gregorio Briones's original 1837 homestead. Gregorio served in the Mexican army and government for 20 years and received the land grant of Rancho Baulenes for his loyal service. This leg of the journey is all on his land, which stretched from Bolinas south to Stinson Beach, east to Bolinas Ridge, and down to the sea.

Bolinas is not Stinson Beach. It doesn't reach out to tourists. In fact, you have to know where it is to even find it. For decades the State of California has put up road signs directing motorists to Bolinas, and they are always torn down.

I spent a day in Bolinas exploring and resting. My wife, Heidi, joined me that evening for the final leg of the journey. After walking in solitude for three days, I welcomed her company. A horticulturist by trade, she is also an amateur naturalist and a great companion for a day on the trail.

We had a slow meal of fresh fish at the Coast Café and finished the night at Smiley's, which claims to be one of the oldest continuously operating saloons in California. Pictures of the bar in the 1800s decorate the walls along with a newspaper article about its 150th anniversary celebration. Smiley's is a gathering place for locals, many of whom came here during the back-to-the-land movement of the 1960s and '70s and stayed. A very local band, composed of three ukuleles and an electric bass, played into the night.

When the band took a break, a short woman with a round face joined us at the bar. Her long blonde curls flowed in all directions as if she'd just returned with the fishing fleet after sailing through a fierce gale.

Ordering a beer and a shot of Jose Cuervo, she stuck out her hand and said, "Hi, I'm Michelle. What brings you folks to Bolinas?"

Heidi said, "He's been hiking for the last three days up from the Marin Headlands. We're walking to Olema tomorrow."

"Walkin'! My God. I've lived here for 35 years and never walked those trails." She called the bartender, "Roy, these folks are hikin' from the Headlands to Olema. You ever done that?"

Roy made his way down the bar. "Hikin'? My truck broke down last week out on Mesa Road, and I had to hike into town. Didn't like it much. How come you don't drive? It's a pretty drive up Highway 1."

Soon half the bar was debating the merits of a good hike. I asked if there was any kind of taxi service that could bring us back in a few days from Olema to pick up our car.

Michelle laughed. "Oh hell, hon, don't bother. I'll pick you up myself. That's if you don't mind ridin' in an old pickup. Call me when you get there." She wrote down her number on a napkin.

When we left, Michelle had joined the other smokers outside. "There's the hikers. Nice to meet you folks. Call me from Olema."

It was a balmy evening, and as we strolled back to our inn, we heard a fellow smoker ask Michelle, "Don't they have a car?"

Day 4: Bolinas to Olema

THE FINAL LEG OF THE JOURNEY is 14 miles, but in early June the days in the Bay Area have 15 hours of sunlight, plenty of time for a relaxed pace. Mesa Road, a quiet country lane, travels through ranchland 4 miles to the trailhead in Point Reyes National Seashore. For the next 5 miles the Ridge Trail gradually climbs to 1,200 feet along the crest of the first range of coastal hills. It travels through spruce, fir, bay, and fern forests, periodically opening to glorious views of the Pacific to the west and the Bolinas Ridge to the east. Filtered sunlight shone through the branches like sunbeams through stained glass cathedral windows, and black-tailed does and fawns wandered through the woodlands, curious and unafraid.

I talked about how relaxing it had been to spend days just walking, and the feeling of getting out of my head and into my body. Heidi, a student of Buddhism, said, "Asian religions say the authentic center of the body is in the abdomen just below the navel. The Japanese call it Hara. Chinese Qigong calls it the Dan Tien. Tibetan Buddhists call it wind horse. They say, if you can bring your energy—your 'wind'—down from your head and into your body, you can ride that wind." That image can carry a hiker on a long journey.

After a few hours on the Ridge Trail, descend the eastern slope, switching back and forth down to Olema Valley, and head north to Five Brooks, a maze of small streams. Two parallel streams separated by only a few hundred feet flow in opposite directions, Olema Creek north to Tomales Bay and Pine Gulch Creek south to Bolinas Lagoon.

The Rift Zone Trail follows the San Andreas Fault, which formed Olema Valley, Tomales Bay, and Bolinas Lagoon. Thirty million years ago this land started its journey in Central California riding the Pacific Plate as it grinds north at a leisurely 2 inches a year, but it jumped 20 feet on April 18, 1906, the day of the great San Francisco earthquake.

Leaving the park, the trail enters Vedanta Society land. The Hindu society acquired this ranch, with beautiful forests and pasture land, in 1946 and opened this section to hikers and its retreat center to seekers of all faiths. They lease a portion of the land to a local cattle rancher—a contradiction perhaps. The Mount Tamalpais walkabout (page 196) describes a visit to the Vedanta Society Retreat. The final 5 miles of the trek climbs up forested hills and down into valleys before reaching Olema. It took us 8 hours to hike the final day.

The Ridge Trail

This trip is a mix of short, leisurely days and days of harder hiking. Each village you visit has its own personality: Muir Beach, a bedroom community; Stinson Beach, weekend homes and ready for tourists; Bolinas, many old-timers and happy to stay off the tourists' radar. Walking through some of the most beautiful wilderness in California and enjoying elegant inns with wonderful dining—what a great way to get to know the Marin Coast.

THE ROUTE

All mileages listed for a given day are cumulative.

Day 1: Marin Headlands to Muir Beach

Starting at eastern end of Rodeo Lagoon, take Miwok Trail to Wolf Ridge Trail, and turn left to Coastal Trail. Descend to Tennessee Valley.   **4.0 miles**

Continue on Coastal Trail to Muir Beach. Walk up the beach entrance road to Pelican Inn or up the valley on Middle Green Gulch Trail to Green Gulch Farm Zen Center.

total miles 7.0

Day 2: Muir Beach to Stinson Beach

Walk west on the beach entrance road, and take the road that angles right just before the parking lot. Continue past the PRIVATE ROAD sign. This road is open to walkers. Opposite the first house on the left, a paved driveway on the right leads to a cluster of houses with a stairway at the top. Walk up the driveway (a public pathway), and take the stairs. Cross the first street. Continue on the stairs and path past Muir Beach Community Center. Walk left on Seascape Drive to Muir Beach Overlook and CA 1. Walk north on the broad shoulder of CA 1 for 0.5 mile. The wide Coast View Trail is on the right side of the road. Take it to the Dipsea Trail.   **4.1 miles**

Follow the Dipsea Trail to Stinson Beach.

total miles 6.8

Day 3: Stinson Beach to Bolinas

To reach Willow Camp Trailhead from CA 1, walk east on Calle Del Mar, turn left on Buena Vista, left on Lincoln Avenue, left on Belvedere Avenue, and right on Avenida Farrolone to the trailhead. Hike Willow Camp Trail to Coastal Trail, a steep climb to 1,900 feet.   **2.1 miles**

Turn left on Coastal Trail to Bolinas-Fairfax Road.   **5.3 miles**

Cross Bolinas-Fairfax Road and continue on Bolinas Ridge Trail to McCurdy Trail. **8.8 miles**

Take McCurdy Trail to CA 1. **10.5 miles**

Turn left and walk the shoulder of CA 1 for 0.6 mile to Horseshoe Hill Road and turn right. **11.1 miles**

Turn right on Olema-Bolinas Road. **12.6 miles**

Hike into Bolinas.

total miles 13.5

Day 3: Alternate Route

Reaching Bolinas-Fairfax Road at 5.3 miles, you can hike down this quiet winding road to CA 1. **9.6 miles**

Cross CA 1 and walk Olema-Bolinas Road into Bolinas.

total miles 11.5

Day 4: Bolinas to Olema

Return 0.2 mile on the road into Bolinas to Mesa Road. Turn left on Mesa Road to reach Ridge Trail Trailhead. **4.0 miles**

Follow Ridge Trail to Bolema Trail. **8.8 miles**

Turn east on Bolema Trail to Olema Valley Trail. **9.9 miles**

Turn north (left) on Olema Valley Trail to Rift Zone Trail. Continue north on Rift Zone Trail to Olema.

total miles 14.0

Alternate Trek: An Inexpensive Option

Day 1

Hike from San Francisco over the Golden Gate Bridge to the Marin Headlands Hostel (415-331-2777) on Coastal Trail.

Day 2

Hike to Muir Beach, take Green Gulch Trail, and stay at Green Gulch Farm Zen Center.

Day 3

Hike to Stinson Beach, stay a night, or take the Western Stagecoach bus back to the Golden Gate Bridge.

TRANSPORTATION

Flying into the Bay Area

FROM SFO TAKE BART to Embarcadero Station ($8.95), and follow the public transportation directions below. From Oakland International Airport take the BART Shuttle to the Oakland Coliseum BART Station ($6). Take BART to the San Francisco Embarcadero Station ($4.20), and follow the public transportation directions below.

Public Transportation from San Francisco to the Marin Headlands

VISIT 511.ORG for easy public transportation trip planning.

The Golden Gate Transit Bus 76X goes from San Francisco to the Marin Headlands, but only on weekends. Take BART to downtown San Francisco and exit at the Embarcadero Station. Walk up Market Street a few blocks and catch the 76X at the corner of Sutter and Sansome. The bus will drop you off at the Marin Headlands Visitor Center.

You can take a ferry from the San Francisco Ferry Building to Sausalito any day of the week and then take a taxi to the trailhead. The Society of American Travel Writers ranked this beautiful ferry ride as the second best in the world, next to Hong Kong's Star Ferry. Take BART to downtown San Francisco and exit at the Embarcadero Station. The Ferry Building is at the foot of Market Street, a short walk from the BART station. Find ferry schedules at goldengateferry.org. The ferry ride to Sausalito costs $12. Taxi fare from Sausalito to the trailhead is approximately $25. Contact Sausalito Taxi at 415-332-5356.

Returning to the Marin Headlands by Public Transportation

THE WEST MARIN STAGECOACH provides bus service from Olema, Bolinas, and Stinson Beach. Contact them at 415-526-3239 or marintransit.org. There are two routes that can drop you off at Marin City, Sausalito, or San Rafael. Taxi fare from Sausalito to Rodeo Beach is approximately $25. Contact Sausalito Taxi at 415-332-5356.

If you take the south route from Bolinas or Stinson Beach and you would like a nice 6-mile hike back into the Headlands, get off at Tam Junction, and hike south on CA 1 for a short distance to Tennessee Valley Road. Turn right on Tennessee Valley Road, walk 0.8 mile, and turn left on Oakwood Valley Trail, which takes you to the Bobcat Trail, which in turn returns you to Rodeo Lagoon.

Pelican Inn

Returning to San Francisco by Public Transportation

IF YOU ARE RETURNING TO SAN FRANCISCO from Bolinas or Stinson Beach, take the West Marin Stagecoach 61 to Marin City ($2). If you are returning to San Francisco from Olema, take the West Marin Stagecoach 68 to the San Rafael Transit Center ($2). Golden Gate Transit Buses will take you into downtown San Francisco from both locations. Go to 511.org to plan your trip.

Driving Directions to the Marin Headlands

FROM SAN FRANCISCO TAKE CA 101 NORTH across the Golden Gate Bridge, and exit immediately at Alexander Avenue. Stay right to get on Alexander Avenue, take the first left, and proceed through the tunnel. If you are driving from the north, take the last exit before the Golden Gate Bridge, turn right, go under the highway, take the first left, and proceed through the tunnel. Continue on Bunker Road, following the signs to Rodeo Beach. Miwok Trail starts at the eastern end of Rodeo Lagoon.

MAPS

THE NATIONAL PARK SERVICE provides free downloadable maps at nps.gov. *Marin Headlands* and *Golden Gate National Recreation Area* are good for Days 1 and 2.

National Geographic's *Mount Tamalpais, Point Reyes Trail Map* ($11.95) at shop.nationalgeographic.com is an excellent map.

Map Adventures also publishes good maps for this walkabout: *Mount Tam Hiking and Biking Trail Map* ($10.95) and *Point Reyes Hiking and Biking Trail Map* ($10.95). Visit mapadventures.com.

PLACES TO STAY

LODGING COST

$ *less than $100* $$ *$100–$150* $$$ *$150–$200* $$$$ *more than $200*

Muir Beach

PELICAN INN $$$$ • 10 Pacific Way at CA 1 • 415-383-6000 • pelicaninn.com
• Includes a hearty breakfast. Fun 16th-century English country–style inn. Nice pub and restaurant.

GREEN GULCH FARM ZEN CENTER $–$$$$ • 1601 Shoreline Hwy.
• 415-383-3134 • sfzc.org/green-gulch • Three delicious vegetarian meals included. Single and double rooms in a beautiful, contemplative setting. A short walk up the valley from Muir Beach.

Stinson Beach

SANDPIPER LODGING AT THE BEACH $$–$$$$ • 1 Marine Way • 415-868-1632 • sandpiperstinsonbeach.com

REDWOODS HAUS B&B $$–$$$ • 1 Belvedere and CA 1 • 415-868-1034
• redwoodhaus.com • Breakfast included.

Bolinas

SMILEY'S SCHOONER SALOON AND HOTEL $$–$$$ • 41 Wharf Road
• 415-881-1851 • smileyssaloon.com

ELEVEN $$–$$$ • 11 Wharf Road • 415-868-1133 • 11wharfroad.com

GRAND HOTEL $ • 15 Brighton Ave. • 415-868-1757

Olema

OLEMA HOUSE (formerly The Lodge at Point Reyes) **$$$$** • 10021 CA 1
• 415-663-9000 • olemahouse.com

ROBIN'S RETREAT AND HONEYBEE COTTAGE $$–$$$ • 10210 Shoreline Hwy.
• 415-663-1288 • robinsretreat.com

INN AT ROUNDSTONE FARM $$ • 9940 Sir Francis Drake Blvd. • 415-663-1020
• roundstonefarm.com

BEAR VALLEY COTTAGE $$$$ • 88 Bear Valley Road • 415-663-1777
• bearvalleycottage.com • 15% discount for those hiking in.

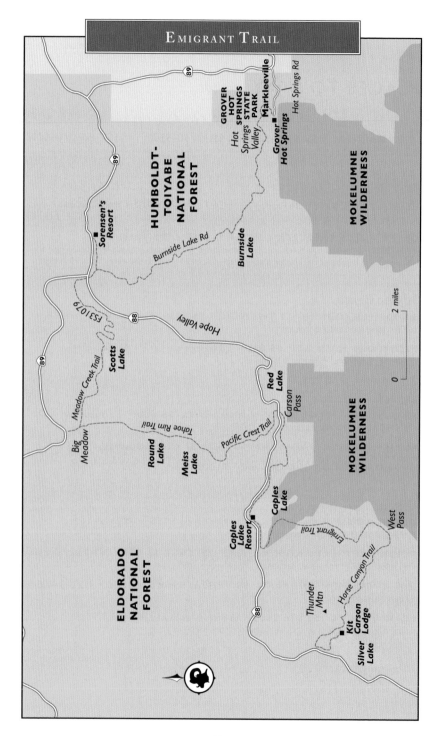

EMIGRANT TRAIL

Markleeville

89

GROVER HOT SPRINGS STATE PARK

Hot Springs Valley

Hot Springs Rd

Grover Hot Springs

89

HUMBOLDT-TOIYABE NATIONAL FOREST

MOKELUMNE WILDERNESS

Sorensen's Resort

Burnside Lake Rd

Burnside Lake

88

FS31079

Hope Valley

89

Scotts Lake

Red Lake

Big Meadow Creek Trail

Tahoe Rim Trail

Carson Pass

Pacific Crest Trail

0   2 miles

Big Meadow

Round Lake

Meiss Lake

Caples Lake

MOKELUMNE WILDERNESS

ELDORADO NATIONAL FOREST

Caples Lake Resort

Emigrant Trail

West Pass

88

Thunder Mtn

Horse Canyon Trail

Kit Carson Lodge

Silver Lake

Crossing the Sierra on the Emigrant Trail

> No wealth can buy the requisite leisure, freedom, and indepen-
> dence which are the capital in this profession. It comes only by
> the grace of God. It requires a direct dispensation from Heaven
> to become a walker."
>
> —HENRY DAVID THOREAU, "Walking"

Caples Lake

You can't see anything from a car, you have got to get out of the god-damned contraption and walk.

—EDWARD ABBEY,
Solitaire: A Season in the Wilderness

THIS CHALLENGING TWO- OR THREE-DAY HIKE crosses the Sierra Nevada from east to west. It passes through some of the most breathtaking parts of these majestic mountains, traveling along the trail of the Pony Express and in the footsteps of adventurers who once sought fortune in the gold rush of the mid-1800s. Each day ends at a beautiful mountain resort. Take an extra rest day or two, and enjoy good food, peaceful settings, and a relaxing sauna. The hike crosses Carson Pass and West Pass. The longest day is 19 miles. The first two days will make a lovely walkabout. Day 3 is especially challenging and should be attempted only by experienced hikers. The mountain trail is poorly maintained and may require some cross-country hiking. The trek is perhaps made easier knowing that earlier travelers on this route were hauling all their worldly possessions over the passes by wagon. Walk back into history and across the Sierra Nevada Mountains.

ITINERARY

DAY 1:	Grover Hot Springs to Hope Valley	**10.5**
DAY 2:	Hope Valley to Caples Lake	**19.1**
DAY 3:	Caples Lake to Silver Lake	**12.0**
TOTAL MILEAGE		**41.6**

GOLD WAS DISCOVERED IN CALIFORNIA in January 1848, and word of unbelievable riches spread around the world. Sam Brannan, who ran a general store at Sutter's Fort, was one of the first to learn of the discovery. Thinking that selling supplies to prospectors would be easier and more profitable than mining, he traveled to San Francisco and paraded through the streets waving his hat and shouting, "Gold! Gold! Gold from the American River." San Francisco emptied overnight, and the word spread.

Treasure seekers from South America, Australia, and China poured in by sea. Entire crews abandoned ship after passing through the Golden Gate, and San Francisco's harbor filled with empty ships, creating what looked like a "forest of masts." Word of the discovery reached Washington, D.C., in November 1848, and President James Polk, wishing to solidify America's new claim on California, announced the discovery to the nation. The American gold rush was on.

Thousands came by sea, calling themselves Argonauts after Jason and his crew, who sought the Golden Fleece in Greek mythology. Sailing around South America required five to six months, and many perished in the treacherous storms off Cape Horn. Others sailed to the Central American Isthmus, crossed it by land, and picked up another ship on the Pacific shore. Scores succumbed to yellow fever, cholera, and typhoid while slogging over swampy jungle trails.

However, because traveling by sea cost a princely sum—between $200 and $500 (about $6,500–$16,300 in today's dollars)—most chose the overland route. *The Emigrants' Guide to Oregon and California,* published in 1845, set the price of the latter at $50–$60.

Seeking fortune and adventure, they came to St. Louis and traveled for six months by horse, by oxcart, and on foot on the Oregon Trail over the plains along the Platte River before reaching Fort Laramie and the breathtaking scenery of the Rockies. Most left the Oregon Trail north of the Great Salt Lake at Sublette's Cutoff and made their way to the headwaters of the Humboldt River, to follow its meandering and heartbreaking course through Nevada and the Great Basin.

The Humboldt starts out with freshwater and rich pastures, but unlike most rivers that grow as they travel downstream, it disappears into the desert sands,

Carson River in Hope Valley

turning into stagnant pools and alkaline plains before finally expiring in the Humboldt Sink. The last 150 miles of the river trail were littered with carcasses of cattle and oxen, discarded furniture, and abandoned wagons. Finally the pioneers crossed the Carson Desert and followed the Carson River into the Sierra Nevada. This route became known as the Emigrant Trail.

Despite higher passes and deeper snow than anything encountered in the Rockies, 20,000 adventurers crossed this route in 1849. Up to 50,000 a year followed from 1850 to 1852 before other routes drew travelers away.

On a crisp autumn day, my friend Scott and I set out to cross the Sierra on the trail of these early pioneers. A 41-mile ramble, this hike starts at Grover Hot Springs in the eastern Sierra, climbs out of Hot Springs Valley, and descends into Hope Valley. Then after crossing Carson Pass, it drops to Caples Lake, climbs over West Pass, and ends deep in the western Sierra at Silver Lake. The route crisscrosses the Emigrant Trail and for stretches follows the footsteps of the pioneers. Along the way, you'll visit some of the most charming resorts and beautiful country in the Sierra.

Day I: Grover Hot Springs to Hope Valley

GROVER HOT SPRINGS STATE PARK is just west of Markleeville. You can start the journey with a hot soak and a cold plunge in the pools. Our trail begins at the northwest corner of the park's campground, skirting the broad, lush meadows of Hot Springs Valley (5,900'). Ascending the north face of the valley, the trail passes through forests of white fir, sweet fragrant Jeffrey pine, and red cedar. After the trail climbs gradually for 2 miles, the last mile of the 1,500-foot ascent is steep. Ancient, stately junipers with deep-red bark and dense, blue berries cling to granite cliffs.

From the crest, the view opens to the east, following the pastoral meadows of Hot Springs Valley down to the deep cut of the Carson River. Forested mountains tower above the valley. Farther east the forests thin, replaced by the desert sagebrush mountains of Nevada and the Great Basin.

We made this trek in mid-September, after the summer crowds, and, we hoped, before the winter snows. The 0.5-mile walk from the crest down to Burnside Lake (8,143') passed through meadows of grasses fading to brown, and skunk cabbage already saffron yellow and bent over, waiting to be blanketed in snow. The aspens at this elevation, higher than 8,000 feet, were starting to turn gold.

Burnside Lake rests in a high Sierra basin. Tall grasses grace most of its shoreline, but there are spots for a picnic and a swim in the clear waters. A dirt road descends a rolling 6 miles to Hope Valley. Sensible travelers will take this route and enjoy a 10.5-mile day of hiking. But not us. We spotted an interesting-looking

The view as you hike out of Hot Springs Valley

trail on the map that wound through the mountains above the valley and promised to take us right to our destination, Sorensen's Resort. After wandering for 4 miles, our trail sputtered out in the forest, and we had to turn back. Our 7:30 dinner reservation slipped by, and we walked the final miles with the glow of the Milky Way lighting our path.

As we staggered into Sorensen's at 9 p.m., the restaurant had just closed. Our host, after hearing of our 18-mile adventure, offered only sympathy, so we dined on crackers, Brie, and salami. Scott took a long draw on his Lagunitas IPA and said, "This is the best beer I have ever had." I could not argue.

Sorensen's Resort (7,000') lies at the east end of Hope Valley. Sitting right on top of the Emigrant Trail, it nestles in an aspen grove across the highway from the West Fork of the Carson River. Cabins with fireplaces, kitchens, and comfortable beds, plus a sauna and a fine restaurant, mean a sojourner can rest in comfort.

The Emigrant Trail was blazed and the valley named not by gold seekers traveling west but by a Mormon party heading east to the Salt Lake basin. In 1846 the Mormons traveled west to flee the persecution that plagued them in Illinois and Missouri. Brigham Young accepted a request from President James Polk to form a battalion that would travel to California to fight in the war with Mexico, and 500 men and 90 women set out on the Santa Fe Trail to San Diego.

They arrived a month after the war ended and were discharged in July 1847 at the sleepy pueblo of Los Angeles. Some headed to Yerba Buena (San Francisco's earlier name), and others traveled north through the Central Valley. Eighty of these men found work with Sutter's Fort at the confluence of the Sacramento and American Rivers. Six joined James Marshall and traveled 45 miles up Rio de los Americanos to build a sawmill in a beautiful valley that local Indians called *Coloma*. Marshall discovered gold in January 1848, and the history of California and America changed forever.

Orders came from Brigham Young for the Mormons in California to join the other saints in Salt Lake Valley, and on July 3, 1848, 1 woman, 45 men, 150 oxen, 150 horses and mules, and 17 wagons set out. Following trails that Indian traders used for perhaps 10,000 years, they forged a new wagon route across the Sierra. Crossing two great passes, West Pass at 9,550 feet and Carson Pass at 8,576 feet, they arrived in a serene valley. Henry William Bigler, a member of the first Mormon party, wrote in his journal: "July 29, Moved across about one mile and half and camped at what we called Hope Valley, as we now began to have hope."

Continuing east down the Carson River and turning northwest, they found the Truckee River. Meeting a group of 18 wagons heading for the gold country, the Mormons drew a map of the new route. Others followed: first a trickle of fortune hunters, then a flood. In *California: A Trip Across the Plains, in the Spring of 1850*, James Abby wrote of the exhilaration his party felt when they reached Hope Valley after the long journey across the country:

> *Here for the first time on our route the picture of the mountain scenery is fully realized; the mountains close in upon us on every side, and raise their lofty peaks high toward heaven.*

Day 2: Hope Valley to Caples Lake

LEAVING SORENSEN'S RESORT, cross the Carson River on the CA 89 bridge, and walk along the western edge of the valley. Hope Valley is a transition zone from the eastern to the western Sierra. Small streams and marshes fill the low spots, with sagebrush growing on higher ground. In the early 1850s, the valley, a spot to gather strength before ascending Carson Pass, filled with hundreds of wagons and grazing livestock.

After 2 miles, a dirt road (marked 31079) climbs the valley's western slope to Scotts Lake (8,050'). Then a lovely trail gradually descends along Meadow Creek through forests of juniper, giant aspen, lodgepole pines, and white fir. It feels lush compared to the drier eastern side. Join the Tahoe Rim Trail, and take it south from Big Meadow. The rolling trail climbs gently 3 miles to Round Lake. After 2 more miles, join the Pacific Crest Trail in verdant Meiss Meadow.

The headwaters of the upper Truckee River start here and flow north to Lake Tahoe. In 1878 Louis Meiss bought 1,000 acres of wilderness that included this meadow. Every summer he drove his cattle to the high country to graze on tall grass. He and his wife, Elizabeth, built a log barn and a two-story cabin where they raised 10 children.

Weather can change quickly in the Sierra. So far we had hiked under sunny skies, but the clouds moved in and a gentle rain fell, settling the trail dust and sweetening the mountain air. As you climb out of the meadow, the view north is breathtaking. Mountains frame the broad, lush valley, and in the distance the deep blue waters of Lake Tahoe sparkle, surrounded by towering peaks.

A fierce wind blew from the west as we approached Carson Pass. The trail passes through a vast aspen forest where, bracing against the howling gales that blow through the pass, the trees bow to the east and none stands more than a dozen feet high. The trail meets CA 88 just west of Carson Pass. Head west, paralleling the highway, descending 1,600 feet in 3 miles to Caples Lake Resort (7,800').

Our housing karma was not really clicking on this trip, and the reservations we'd made for two nights in a cabin were misfiled. A cabin and its kitchen would

Meiss Ranch

open up for the second night, but only a small room in the lodge was available for the first night. The resort has no restaurant. We had deposited a cache of gourmet delights in advance, but the lodge had only a small microwave. Scott's East Indian *sag paneer* and *aloo gobi* should have simmered on the stove. Instead they were microwaved and eaten out of plastic yogurt containers with crackers as utensils. They had the consistency and taste of mud.

After a few bites he asked, "What do ya think?"

I contemplated the glop. "Up until now I thought the worst meal I ever had was in a village in central India—a disgusting lentil gruel with stale chapaties. After dinner the waiter set the dishes on the ground for the dog to clean. If it weren't for this beer, *this* would be the worst meal of my life."

Scott put his yogurt container and cracker down beside his bed. "No argument," he said. After pausing for a moment, he added, "I once ate undercooked pig in a fishing village in the Philippines. I was sick for days. That meal was worse than this."

And so it went, recalling our worst and then our best meals.

"A dim sum feast in Singapore."

"An inedible vegan nut loaf at a Berkeley meditation retreat—I have felt sorry for vegans ever since."

Scott studied his Anchor Steam, drank, and said, "This is the best beer I have ever had in my life."

How many occasions in one lifetime can a person make this claim? Perhaps countless. All we need is a good day of hiking in the Sierra, a comfortable bed in a beautiful spot—even without the best cuisine—and we become more alive. Our endorphins are singing, and simple pleasures bring us joy.

The next morning we moved into a rustic cabin with a fireplace and full kitchen where we cooked and feasted. A snow and rain storm raged outside. When it let up, we walked to the shoreline and watched storm clouds battle above Caples Lake and the surrounding rugged Sierra peaks.

Day 3: Caples Lake to Silver Lake

THE FIRST TWO LEGS OF THIS JOURNEY crisscross the Emigrant Trail, but the last leg follows it for half a day. Crossing 8,576-foot Carson Pass with horses, mules, oxen, and wagons proved an arduous task for the pioneers, but climbing 9,550-foot West Pass was the most difficult trial they faced; they called it "Conquering the Elephant." After that, the trail to Old Hangtown (Placerville), with the promise of fortunes, was comparatively easy. For the modern trekker, with only a light day pack, this leg is a 12-mile hike that plunges deep into the Sierra wilderness.

Silver Lake

Day 3 of this walkabout can be challenging because the trail from Caples Lake to West Pass is poorly marked and maintained. You may lose the trail at times and need to hike cross-country. Frank Tortorich Jr. has written an excellent guide for this trail: "Hiking the Gold Rush Trail: A Hiking Guide over West Pass." Please see The Route, page 40, for more information.

Leaving Caples Lake Resort, hike along the highway to the dam at the western end of the lake. Then follow the trail along the southwestern shore to a marker for the Historic Emigrant Trail. Before the dam was built in 1922, the basin held two small lakes. The Emigrant Trail passed right through the middle of what is now Caples Lake. Wagons fanned out across the basin, livestock grazed, and travelers rested for the hard push over the final pass. The pioneer wagons, with no brakes or springs, provided a bone-jarring ride, so most forty-niners walked the 2,000-mile journey. They averaged 14 miles a day across the prairie and 6–10 miles in the mountains.

Heading south, the trail gradually ascends through pinewoods. You may spot rust stains on boulders and granite worn smooth from wagon wheels, but it is amazing how little trace there is of the thousands of wagons, cattle, horses, oxen, and pioneers who traveled this same trail. Imagine the fear and excitement those adventurers felt as they climbed to West Pass. They had come so far, and now they were crossing the last great barrier before reaching their dreams. Perhaps some thought they could fill their pockets with gold nuggets lying in streambeds, but most knew they faced hardship in the Sierra foothills and a strong chance of losing everything in the search for riches.

An hour from Caples Lake, the trail passes through wildflower meadows on the back side of Kirkwood Ski Resort. We had the trail to ourselves in September, but in the winter hundreds of skiers and snowboarders fly over the tracks first laid by oxen-drawn wagons little more than a century and a half ago.

Emerging above treeline, the worn trail is still fairly easy to spot; it cuts right to left under a snowfield and up a rock-strewn mountainside to the pass. Imagine pushing a wagon filled with all your worldly goods while oxen strained to pull it over the ridge. Archer Butler's party scaled West Pass on August 14, 1849, an experience he recounted in *Forty-niners:*

> . . . *leaving the lake at its southwestern extremity, [we] soon commenced the assent of the western ridge, the loftiest chain in all these ranges of mountains. The last ascent is six miles . . . The last two miles of the ascent are terrific, being excessively steep, and a part of the way so sideling that it is necessary for several men to brace themselves against the wagon to prevent its upsetting and rolling down the side of the mountain. By doubling teams, and assisting with manual strength, we succeeded in gaining the top of this dreaded eminence by two o'clock in the afternoon . . . We now come to a break in the wall like a gateway; through this we pass, in and instant of New World of California burst at once upon our impatient sight.*

The summit provides a 360-degree view, with Caples Lake, Carson Pass, and mountain peaks stretching into Nevada in the east. Great mountainsides of exposed granite buffed smooth by ancient glaciers shine in the sunlight. To the west the mountains continue to the horizon before they drop to the foothills and Central Valley. Your destination, Silver Lake, sparkles like a jewel in a forested basin to the west.

Scott and I stopped for lunch, resting against a boulder overlooking hundreds of square miles of the Sierra. Horse Canyon Trail beckoned to us as it wandered above the treeline in the distance, but we were in no hurry to hike the last 5 miles of our journey. Neither of us wanted our adventure to end.

Scott said, "I think this hike is so relaxing because it narrows the choices of modern life. I'm always thinking about what I'm going to do next, where I'm going to go, what work needs to be done. I've felt free of that stress."

"We've reduced the distractions," I said.

"Right," he said. "I've felt more relaxed each day. Our first day I thought about all the things I need to do when I get home. Today my mind feels calm, and

I've really tuned into this beautiful wilderness. We haven't needed to make many choices, just pay attention to the trail and keep walking."

Horse Canyon Trail heads west through forests and then breaks through the treeline. A few western junipers cling to the rocks with thick gnarled trunks twisted and bent by fierce storms that rage along this open, western-facing slope below Thunder Mountain. In the Sierra, some of these junipers live 3,000 years. The trail gradually descends through fields of wildflowers. As winter approaches, most have turned shades of brown and red with hints of pale green, but a few orange paintbrushes and light-blue lupines survive to decorate the landscape.

The trail drops through dense forests of white fir and towering aspen and emerges on CA 88 just north of Silver Lake. Walk the highway shoulder a short distance, and turn on the road that runs along the north side of the lake. The Kit Carson Lodge sits on a peninsula with comfortable cabins, a store, and a good restaurant. Most of the cabins have porches overlooking the peaceful lake surrounded by thick pine forests and exposed granite. Ospreys soar gracefully above the waters and then abruptly dive, turning talons first to snare a fish for dinner. Put your feet up and savor the memories of crossing the Sierra in the footsteps of California's first inhabitants and those of the pioneers.

Thunder Mountain as seen from Horse Canyon Trail

THE ROUTE

All mileages listed for a given day are cumulative.

Day 1: Grover Hot Springs to Hope Valley

Drive 4 miles west from Markleeville on Hot Springs Road to the Grover Hot Springs State Park campground, and park at the end of the road that runs along west side of the campground ($8). The trail starts at the end of the road.

Walk from the Grover Hot Springs campground on the trail along the north side of the valley, following the signs to Burnside Lake. **3.8 miles**

Descend the gravel Burnside Lake Road to CA 88. **9.5 miles**

Hike east along the broad shoulder of CA 88 to Sorensen's Resort.

total miles 10.5

Day 2: Hope Valley to Caples Lake

Leaving Sorensen's Resort, hike west along CA 88 for 1 mile to CA 89, and cross the Carson River on the CA 89 bridge. Hike south on the west side of Hope Valley to the major Forest Service road (FS 31079) that climbs west out of the valley to Scotts Lake. FS 31079 can also be reached by continuing to walk along CA 88 for 1.4 miles beyond the CA 89 intersection. There is an open corridor paralleling CA 88 that is pleasant for walking. Turn right on a dirt road and right at the Y junction. After 0.3 mile, the road ascends to Scotts Lake. The rugged dirt road is marked with signs saying 31079 at both spots.

Leave Sorensen's Resort and hike to Scotts Lake. **6.0 miles**

Follow Meadow Creek Trail to the Tahoe Rim Trail at Big Meadow. **8.5 miles**

Turn south on the Tahoe Rim Trail to Round Lake. **10.6 miles**

Continue to Meiss Meadow and the Pacific Crest Trail. **13.0 miles**

Hike the Pacific Crest Trail south to CA 88 just west of Carson Pass. **15.4 miles**

Descend along CA 88 to Caples Lake Resort.

total miles 19.1

Day 3: Caples Lake to Silver Lake

The 3.6-mile section of the trail from Caples Lake to West Pass is poorly maintained and poorly marked. Keep an eye out for metal trail markers on trees and cairns left by other hikers. Frank Tortorich Jr.'s guide, *Hiking the Gold Rush Trail: A Hiking Guide over West Pass* ($14), is usually available at the Sorensen's Resort bookshop, at the Carson Pass Visitor Center.

Hike west along the shoulder of CA 88 to the dam at the west end of Caples Lake. Take the trail on the west side of Caples Lake to the trail marked HISTORIC EMIGRANT TRAIL. **1.9 miles**

Hike south on Emigrant Trail to West Pass. **5.5 miles**

Shortly past West Pass, take Horse Canyon Trail west to CA 88. **10.8 miles**

After a short walk south on CA 88 to Silver Lake, take the road on the north side of the lake. Follow the signs to Kit Carson Lodge.

total miles 12.0

A cabin at Kit Carson Lodge

TRANSPORTATION

Driving Directions with Two Cars

LEAVE ONE CAR AT YOUR FINAL DESTINATION, Caples Lake Resort or Kit Carson Lodge at Silver Lake, and drive the second car to Grover Hot Springs. Drive to Markleeville, turn right on Hot Springs Road, and continue another 4 miles. Park at the end of the road that runs along the west side of the campground ($8). Don't forget to stop at the Caples Lake Resort to drop off food for your stay. Caples Lake Resort has a very small store but no restaurant.

Driving Directions with One Car

WITH ONE CAR, THERE ARE THREE OPTIONS for returning to Grover Hot Springs from Caples Lake Resort or Kit Carson Lodge at Silver Lake. Ask your innkeeper if he or she can arrange for transportation. We have found that people go out of their way to assist inn-to-inn hikers. A ride-hailing service is possible, although not always available this far from cities. A third option is a taxi. These taxi services are centered in South Lake Tahoe. Quotes on fares from Silver Lake to Grover Hot Springs ranged from $60 to $100.

ELITE TAXI 530-580-8294
SUNSHINE YELLOW CABS 530-544-5555

Don't forget to drop off a supply of food at Caples Lake Resort. It has a very small store but no restaurant.

A Car-Free Option

THERE IS NO BUS SERVICE along this walkabout, but public transportation to South Lake Tahoe is available through Amtrak. Take the train to Sacramento and an Amtrak bus to South Lake Tahoe. The fare is $55 from Oakland and $73–$107 from Los Angeles. Go to amtrak.com for schedules and fares. For taxi services from South Lake Tahoe to Grover Hot Springs and returning from Silver Lake, please see previous section.

MAPS

NATIONAL GEOGRAPHIC'S *Lake Tahoe Basin* ($11.95) covers Days 1 and 2 of this walkabout. Their *Carson Iceberg, Emigrant and Mokelumne Wilderness Areas* covers Day 3. Go to shop.nationalgeographic.com.

PLACES TO STAY

LODGING COST

$ *less than $100* $$ *$100–$150* $$$ *$150–$200* $$$$ *more than $200*

Markleeville and Grover Hot Springs

Markleeville is 28 miles south of Lake Tahoe on CA 89. Grover Hot Springs State Park is 4 miles west of Markleeville at the end of Hot Springs Road.

CREEKSIDE LODGE $–$$ • 14820 CA 89 • Markleeville • 530-694-2511 • creekside-lodge.com • Adjacent to Wolf Creek Restaurant.

GROVER HOT SPRINGS STATE PARK $ • 530-694-2248 • parks.ca.gov • Beautiful campground a short walk from the hot springs.

Hope Valley

SORENSEN'S RESORT $$–$$$$ • 14255 CA 88 • East of the intersection of CA 88 and CA 89 • 800-423-9949 • 530-694-2203 • sorensensresort.com • Great restaurant serving breakfast, lunch, and dinner; cabins with fireplaces, kitchens, and comfortable beds, plus a sauna.

Caples Lake

CAPLES LAKE RESORT $–$$$$ • 1111 CA 88 • 1 mile east of Kirkwood on CA 88. • 209-258-8888 • capleslakeresort.com • Small lodge rooms, nine comfortable cabins with fireplaces and kitchens. Beautiful setting on Caples Lake. No restaurant, so drop off a cache of food to cook in your cabin. No kitchen in the lodge rooms. Small store.

Silver Lake

KIT CARSON LODGE $$$–$$$$ • 32161 Kit Carson Road • 5 miles west of Kirkwood • 209-258-8500 • kitcarsonlodge.com • Beautiful setting on Silver Lake. Hotel rooms and cabins with balconies overlooking the lake. Nice restaurant serving Continental breakfast and dinner. Small store.

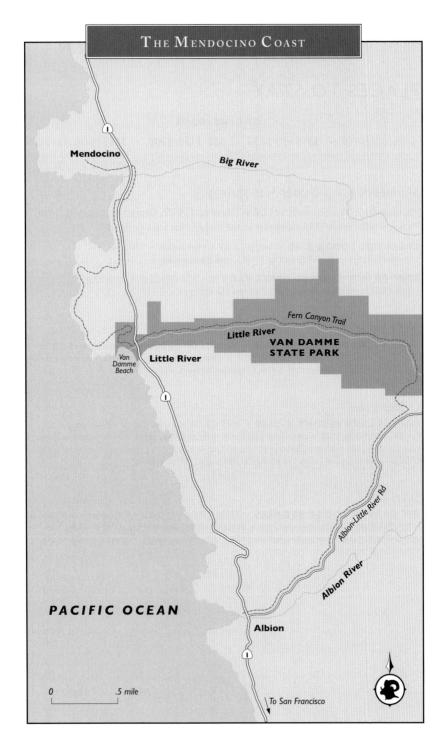

THE MENDOCINO COAST

Mendocino

Big River

Fern Canyon Trail

Little River

VAN DAMME
STATE PARK

Van
Damme
Beach

Little River

Albion-Little River Rd

Albion River

PACIFIC OCEAN

Albion

0   .5 mile

To San Francisco

The Mendocino Coast

The sight of the countryside, the succession of pleasant views, the open air, a sound appetite, and the good health I gain by walking, the easy atmosphere of an inn, the absence of everything that makes me feel my dependence, of everything that recalls me to my situation—all these serve to free my spirit, to lend a greater boldness to my thinking.

—JEAN-JACQUES ROUSSEAU, *The Confessions*

The Mendocino Coast

In my room, the world is beyond my understanding;
But when I walk I see that it consists of three or four hills and a cloud.

—WALLACE STEVENS, *Of the Surface of Things*

THIS EASY 14.1-MILE, TWO-DAY HIKE makes for a perfect romantic holiday traipsing along the rugged and beautiful Mendocino Coast. Along the way, you will stay in charming inns, dine on sumptuous cuisine, and explore the lush forests of the coastal range and the headlands along the edge of the wild Pacific. Take an extra day or two to wander the coast or to get a massage at the Little River Inn. Enjoy the many pleasures that the historic town of Mendocino has to offer—fine dining, taverns, inns, music, shops, and strolls along the headlands. Explore the wild beauty of the Mendocino Coast at 2 miles an hour.

ITINERARY
. . . .

DAY 1:	Albion to Little River	**8.3**
DAY 2:	Little River to Mendocino	**5.8**
TOTAL MILEAGE		**14.1**

Day 1: Albion to Little River

YOU CAN START THIS EXPLORATION of the wild Mendocino Coast at the Albion River Inn. It perches on a cliff overlooking a narrow bay framed by rocky bluffs, the mouth of the Albion River, and the vast Pacific stretching to the horizon. One of the loveliest inns on the California shore, it is a great place to start a romantic two-day, 14-mile hike on the Mendocino Coast. My wife, Heidi, and I took this hike in May after the winter rains and before the summer fog. Our room at the Albion was simple but elegant with a fireplace, overstuffed easy chairs, and complimentary wine and chocolate. The inn's restaurant overlooks lush coastal gardens and the bay. With more than 75 different offerings, the bar is a scotch drinker's paradise. The night of our arrival, we enjoyed a leisurely feast of roasted quail wrapped in honey-cured bacon and pan-roasted Alaskan halibut.

In the morning, as a relaxed pace took hold, we lingered over a hearty complimentary breakfast and lounged in Adirondack chairs on our porch until almost noon. The undulating bluffs across the bay were a dozen shades of green. The Pacific was calm, and the only sounds were the gentle waves caressing the cliffs

View from Albion River Inn

and the moan of a foghorn. Fishing boats entered the bay and slowly motored up the narrow river for home.

CA 1 hugs the steep coast between Albion and Little River to the north. There are no trails along the shore for the first section of this hike. Instead you head inland, hiking up Albion–Little River Road, a country lane with very little traffic that climbs out of the Albion River valley. The ascent is gradual, first through eucalyptus groves and then through forests of coastal redwoods and Douglas-fir. You pass occasional homesteads, some of which are only trailers tucked in the woods. Others are cottages on cleared topland with open fields and aging orchards surrounded by woodlands.

After 3 miles, the road levels to a broad plateau. Just past Little River Airport Road, you'll find the entrance to Van Damme State Park and the strange world of a Mendocino coastal pygmy forest.

Powerful planetary forces combined to shape this coastline and mountain range. Thin plates of the earth's crust float on a sea of semifluid mantle. The Pacific and North American Plates collide at California's western edge. The lighter, thinner Pacific Plate is forced under the North American Plate, grinding relentlessly and occasionally slipping to unleash jolting earthquakes. The edge of the North American Plate was forced up in folds and formed the coastal ranges 35–45 million years ago. Terraces created by the ocean's wave action were uplifted by the inexorable pressure of the Pacific Plate, creating an orderly stairstep of plateaus, each 100,000 years older and 100 feet higher than its neighbor to the west.

Stand on the grassland terrace that forms the bluffs and headlands on the Pacific shore. Look west at low tide and you can spot the flat, rocky bottom of a new terrace forming offshore. Turn east and see a terrace forested with towering redwoods, pines, Douglas-fir, Sitka spruce, and hemlock. Manzanita and tan oak grow on higher terraces. Still higher, the extraordinary pygmy forests struggle and endure, a phenomenon found nowhere else in the world.

For hundreds of thousands of years, the broad, flat surfaces of some higher terraces prevented runoff. Standing water filtered through the rock, leaching nutrients and leaving a sandy, acidic soil on top of an iron-rich hardpan. An eerie forest of 100-year-old cypress trees stand only 2 feet tall with trunks an inch in diameter. Redwoods reach the height of only 5 or 10 feet. Some plants—such as Fort Bragg manzanita, Labrador tea, rhododendron, huckleberry, and the tiny insect-eating sundew—though stunted, thrive in this environment.

Leaving the pygmy forest, Fern Canyon Trail descends from the plateau and winds through a lush redwood forest to Little River. Signs of spring were everywhere on the warm afternoon of our hike. Eight-foot-high California rosebays, a native rhododendron, were heavy with dense clusters of fragrant violet flowers. Pink bleeding heart, yellow violets, red-orange paintbrushes, pale-blue forget-me-nots, and yellow lupines decorated the woodlands. On the canyon's floor, ferns line the banks of Little River. They sprout from massive redwood stumps, reminders of

A redwood forest in Van Damme State Park

an ancient forest clear-cut in the last half of the 1800s for the houses of booming San Francisco. Second-growth giants now soar to the sky, forming a dense canopy.

Fern Canyon Trail ends in a campground across CA 1 from Van Damme Beach. The Little River Inn immediately south of the beach welcomes you after the first day's hike of 8.3 miles. Originally a Victorian home built in 1870, it has expanded into a complex of whitewashed cottages and rooms overlooking the Van Damme Beach cove and the Pacific. Sit back on your porch's rocking chair and watch ospreys circle patiently and then abruptly dive for dinner. Stay an extra day and treat yourself to a massage at the spa. The inn's restaurant looks out on beautiful gardens that are lit at night. We dined on pine nut–crusted salmon and cioppino rich with fresh fish, mussels, and clams.

Day 2: Little River to Mendocino

THE SECOND DAY'S HIKE is an easy 5.8-mile stroll along the bluffs above the rugged shoreline. Leaving Little River, hike down to Van Damme Beach, and take the path at its north end, up a gully dense with wildflowers and escaped roses, calla lilies, and red and purple fuchsia. Turn right at the road, take a short walk north on the highway, and pass through a break in the fence across from the Glendeven Inn to enter the northern section of Van Damme State Park. Follow the forest path through pines to open grasslands and the rugged coast.

The coast, both north and south of Mendocino, is one of the most spectacularly beautiful in California, but this southern section is far from roads and little used. The trail hugs the coast on the edge of rocky cliffs. Waves crash on the rock shelves and outcroppings scattered just offshore. Two-foot-high sea palms stubbornly cling to the rocks as endless waves crash, bending them over until they look as if they will surely be torn from their moorings. Then they spring back on flexible stalks to wait for the next assault. Lush grassy promontories jut into the sea, but as the trail approaches, a delicate patchwork garden unfolds. Wild strawberries, blue-eyed grass, purple and yellow Douglas irises, California poppies, buttercups, and masses of tiny yellow daisies hug the ground for protection against stormy winds off the Pacific. Only stands of yellow lupine bushes stretch to more than 4 inches high.

Gray whales migrate south in late fall. Bring binoculars, and you can spot them spouting far out to sea. In late winter and early spring they head back north with their calves, much closer to shore. In summer you may see humpbacks, orcas, or dolphins. Heidi and I stopped to watch a mother harbor seal swim with her newborn pup among the rocks in what seemed to be an early lesson in the art of living in the sea. They swam together, almost always touching. She nuzzled her pup, and they dove in turquoise water so clear we could watch their shimmering bodies deep below the surface. They emerged with the baby clinging to her back. Mom floated on her back while her baby glided in a circle around her head. Then she nuzzled him again, and they dove.

Hiking along this magnificent coast, you may feel you are walking in the footsteps of the Pomo Indians. They dwelled for thousands of years in what is now Sonoma, Lake, and Mendocino Counties. On the Mendocino Coast, game, sea life, nuts, grains, roots, acorns, and wild vegetables were bountiful. A small band might occupy a territory of only 20 square miles with two river drainages and enjoy great abundance. Warfare was rare, and the Pomo developed a rich culture of secret societies, extravagantly dressed spirit impersonators, a world creator, and beautifully refined baskets. They lived mostly inland in valleys beyond the redwood belt, but every summer they moved to the coast to inhabit villages of redwood-bark houses and to fish the rivers and ocean.

As we strolled along the coast, dozens of harbor seals sunbathed on offshore rock shelves. Most did not even open a sleepy eye to notice us, but the new mothers, resting with their pups, although separated from us by deep channels, swayed and paced while anxiously watching. A northern harrier, a raptor with a unique style of hunting, slowly soared and floated only a few feet above the grassy hillside that climbed to the next terrace, ready to dive for an unsuspecting field mouse.

The trail passes by three decaying fences. Follow the path on the south side of the last fence up the hill to a parking area along the highway. After a brief walk on the grassy shoulder, take Brewery Gulch Drive, a section of the old coastal highway that winds along the bluffs. Soon the town of Mendocino, perched on the headlands at the mouth of Big River and the rim of Mendocino Bay, comes into view. It is difficult to imagine a prettier setting or a more picturesque village.

Europeans first visited this coast when Juan Rodríguez Cabrillo explored Cape Mendocino in 1542. Only a few Spanish and English ships sailed these waters until 1812, when Russians established their southernmost North American outpost, a sea otter hunting camp, Fort Ross. They were the first Europeans to explore the Mendocino Coast on foot. Fearing attack from Spanish warships, they allied with the local Pomo, trading, employing them as laborers, and marrying Pomo women. Relations eventually deteriorated when settlers kidnapped Pomo children and shipped them back to Russia. By 1841 the sea otters were depleted, and the Russians sold Fort Ross to John Sutter, a Swiss American pioneer who used the lumber to build a settlement near what would become Sacramento. They left California, and the Pomo lived as before until the rush for California's gold changed everything.

In the early 1850s, San Francisco was a boomtown with an insatiable hunger for lumber. J. B. Ford, a lumberman, explored Big River in 1851 and found his own mother lode, *Sequoia sempervirens*, the coast redwoods. The tallest trees on earth, they grow for more than 2,000 years to heights of 360 feet, with diameters of 20 feet. With a range extending from Monterey to southern Oregon, these mighty giants thrive on the Mendocino Coast. During California's long, dry summer season, fog flows up the steep canyons of the coastal range. The dense redwood foliage harvests water droplets from the fog and drops up to 55 additional inches of precipitation each year. With a beautiful reddish-brown grain, redwood lumber is resistant to insects and decay. It was ideal for California's booming building market. A single tree could produce 15,000 shingles. Ford soon established a sawmill and floated redwood logs down Big River. Working upstream, his crews clear-cut the trees, burning the slash and leaving devastation where there had once been magnificent virgin forests.

The concept of private property was new to the Pomo Indians. Using the land and its bounty, including the crops of settlers, was the natural way for the Pomo, but this was considered thievery by the Euro-Americans. By 1857 thousands of Indians were rounded up and forced to settle on a 25,000-acre reservation with Fort Bragg as its headquarters. Because of the white settlers' lust for land,

Approaching the town of Mendocino

the reservation was surveyed and sold off in the late 1860s. In those few short years, poor crops, disease, starvation, and outright genocide virtually destroyed the Pomo people of Mendocino County. Around 5,000 Pomo Indians still live in their ancestral territory today. Many carry on the tribe's traditions and still make some of the finest examples of Native American baskets.

Unlike the Pomo, the town of Mendocino thrived, and in the 1870s and '80s, the residents built lovely Victorian houses with large porches, bay windows, elaborate trim, and steep gabled roofs. Most homes had their own wells, windmills, and often ornate water towers. Many of those houses and water towers survive today, and the architectural style continues.

The lumber played out in the early 1900s, and Mendocino was forgotten by all but a few stubborn souls. The back-to-the-land movement of the 1960s and '70s brought an influx of new settlers, some of whom are pillars of the community today. Mendocino became an artists' colony and now a tourist destination with a strong, vibrant community.

Continue walking on Brewery Gulch Drive as it arcs along the coastal cliffs for a mile before returning to the highway just south of town. Stroll into Mendocino by walking the bridge over Big River, home to abundant wildlife. If you rent kayaks or canoes at Catch-a-Canoe (707-937-0273), you'll paddle with harbor seals, river otters, and dozens of bird species. Enjoy the many pleasures that Mendocino has to offer—fine dining, taverns, inns, and beautiful hikes along the headlands—and savor the memories of a stroll along the magnificent Mendocino Coast, hiking inn to inn.

THE ROUTE

All mileages listed for a given day are cumulative.

Day 1: Albion to Little River

Ascend Albion–Little River Road, a quiet country lane that climbs out of the Albion River valley. It starts at CA 1 between Albion River Inn and the turnoff to Albion River Campground and Marina. Follow Albion Road to Van Damme State Park pygmy forest. The park entrance is just beyond the intersection with Little River Airport Road.   **3.5 miles**

Take the dirt path adjacent to the pygmy forest, and hike to Van Damme Beach on Fern Canyon Trail.

total miles 8.3

See Places to Stay, page 55, for distances and directions to the inns of Little River.

Day 2: Little River to Mendocino

Return to Van Damme State Park. Cross the highway, and walk north on the beach 0.2 mile. On the right you will see a gully. Take the unmarked path at the far end of the gully up to the road (Peterson and Headlands Lane). Walk right on the road and left on the highway for a few hundred yards. Across from Glendeven Inn, pass through a break in the fence, and take the trail to and along the coast. Pass by two decaying fences. Before you reach the third, you will come to a gulch leading down to a cove. Two paths climb from the gulch. Take the one on the left back to CA 1 and the Chapman Point Trailhead parking area. **2.3 miles**

Walk 0.3 mile on the grassy shoulder of CA 1, and take Brewery Gulch Drive until it arcs back to the highway. **3.3 miles**

Cross the bridge over Big River into Mendocino.

total miles 5.8

TRANSPORTATION

Driving Directions

ALBION IS 150 MILES NORTH of San Francisco, and the drive takes approximately 3 hours. Head north on US 101 to Cloverdale. Turn west on CA 128. The drive from Cloverdale to the Pacific Ocean and CA 1 takes approximately 90 minutes. Turn north (right) on CA 1 and drive another 4 miles to Albion.

If you are coming from the north, take US 101 to Willits, and turn west on CA 20. The drive from Willits to Fort Bragg and CA 1 takes approximately an hour. Turn left on CA 1. Mendocino is 10 miles south of Fort Bragg. Albion is 7 miles south of Mendocino.

Returning to Albion from Mendocino

THE MENDOCINO TRANSIT AUTHORITY (MTA) runs two buses from Mendocino to Albion each weekday at 8:05 a.m. and 4:20 p.m.; visit mendocinotransit.org. Hey Taxi (707-962-0800) and O Bar 11 Door to Door (707-321-6655) provide taxi service from Mendocino to Albion.

Little River Inn

Public Transportation

BUSES ARE AVAILABLE from San Francisco to Mendocino. Take BART to the San Francisco Powell St. Station, and walk a few blocks to Seventh and Market Streets. Take Golden Gate Transit Bus 101 to the Second St. Transit Mall in Santa Rosa. The trip takes 2.5–3 hours; go to 511.org to plan this leg of the trip.

Buses leave the Second Street Transit Mall in Santa Rosa for Mendocino every day at 1:45 p.m. and 3:55 p.m., arriving at 5:30 p.m. and 7:26 p.m.; go to mendocinotransit.org for details.

The Mendocino Transit Authority (MTA) runs two buses each weekday from Mendocino to Albion at 8:05 a.m. and 4:20 p.m.; contact the MTA at mendocinotransit.org. Hey Taxi (707-962-0800) and O Bar 11 Door to Door (707-321-6655) provide taxi service from Mendocino to Albion.

Flying into the Bay Area

FROM SFO TAKE BART to the Powell St. Station ($8.95), and follow the public transportation directions above. From Oakland International Airport take the BART Shuttle to the Oakland Coliseum BART Station. Take BART to the San Francisco Powell St. Station, and follow the public transportation directions above. The trip takes approximately 40 minutes and costs $10.20.

MAPS

THE CALIFORNIA STATE PARKS WEBSITE provides a free map you can download that covers most of this walkabout. Visit parks.ca.gov, search for "Van Damme" and click on the park brochure.

PLACES TO STAY

LODGING COST

$ *less than $100* $$ *$100–$150* $$$ *$150–$200* $$$$ *more than $200*

Albion

ALBION RIVER INN $$$–$$$$ • 3790 N. CA 1 • 800-479-7944
• albionriverinn.com • Full breakfast included. Great dining and nice bar.

ALBION RIVER CAMPGROUND AND MARINA $$$ • 33800 Albion River North
Side Road • 707-937-0606 • albionrivercampground.com • 3 RVs available for lodging.

Little River

LITTLE RIVER INN $$$$ • 7751 N. CA 1 • 0.2 mile south of Van Damme State
Park entrance. Take the history trail just east of the entrance kiosk. • 707-937-5942
• littleriverinn.com • Good restaurant and bar.

COTTAGES AT LITTLE RIVER COVE $$$–$$$$ • 7533 N. CA 1 • 0.3 mile south
of Van Damme State Park entrance • 707-937-5339 • cottagesatlittlerivercove.com

GLENDEVEN INN $$$$ • 8205 N. CA 1 • 0.4 mile north of Van Damme State Park
entrance • 707-937-0083 • glendeven.com • Full breakfast included.

Mendocino

These are a few of the many places to stay.

THE MENDOCINO HOTEL AND GARDEN SUITES $–$$$$ • 45080 Main St.
• 800-548-0513 • 707-937-0511 • mendocinohotel.com

THE STANFORD INN $$$$ • 44850 Comptche-Ukiah Road • Directly across CA 1 at
the end of Brewery Gulch Road on the south side of Big River • 707-937-5615 • stanfordinn
.com • Beautiful gardens and a gourmet vegetarian restaurant serving fresh homegrown produce.

MACCALLUM HOUSE INN & RESTAURANT $$$–$$$$ • 45020 Albion St.
• 800-609-0492 • 707-937-0289 • maccallumhouse.com • Full breakfast included.

ALEGRIA OCEANFRONT INN & COTTAGES $–$$$$ • 44781 Main St.
• 707-937-5150 • oceanfrontmagic.com • Breakfast included.

SEAGULL INN $$–$$$ • 44960 Albion St. • 707-937-5204 • 888-937-5204
• seagullbb.com • Breakfast included.

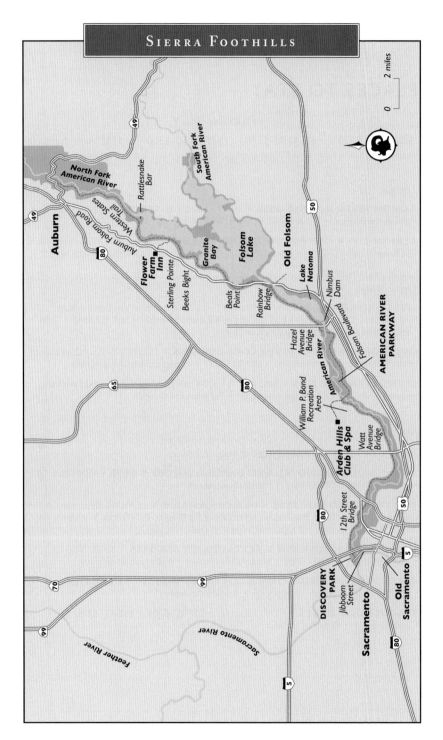

SIERRA FOOTHILLS

0   2 miles

North Fork
American River

Rattlesnake
Bar

South Fork
American River

Auburn

Auburn Folsom Road

Western States Trail

Flower
Farm
Inn

Sterling Pointe

Beeks Bight

Granite
Bay

Folsom
Lake

Old Folsom

Lake
Natoma

Nimbus
Dam

Beals
Point

Rainbow
Bridge

Folsom Boulevard

AMERICAN RIVER
PARKWAY

Hazel
Avenue
Bridge

American River

William P. Bond
Recreation
Area

Arden Hills
Club & Spa

Watt
Avenue
Bridge

12th Street
Bridge

DISCOVERY
PARK

Jibboom
Street

Sacramento

Old
Sacramento

Sacramento River

Feather River

SIERRA NEVADA FOOTHILLS ALONG THE AMERICAN RIVER

Auburn to Sacramento

We are rapidly descending into the spring and we are leaving our snowy region far behind; everything is getting green; butterflies are swarming; numerous bugs are creeping out, wakened from their winter's sleep, and the forest flowers are coming into bloom.

—JOHN C. FREMONT, *March 1, 1844,*
journal entry along the American River

American River

One's destination is never a place, but rather a new way of looking at things.

—HENRY MILLER, *Big Sur and the Oranges of Hieronymus Bosch*

THE AMERICAN RIVER STARTS HIGH IN THE PEAKS of the Sierra Nevada. It winds and crashes through deep canyons down to the foothills, where it is eventually tamed to form Folsom Lake. Released again, it flows wide and powerful to meet the Sacramento River. The discovery of gold on the American in 1848 brought a stampede of thousands to mine its banks and create a new California.

This 66-mile, four-day walkabout starts in the foothills town of Auburn and descends downstream, along the river. Spring is the perfect season for this hike, when the willows and cottonwoods are leafing out, wildflowers grace lush meadows, and the river is raging. Along the way you will visit a country B&B, inns on the river bank, and a luxurious resort and spa. Hike back in time through the old towns of Auburn, Folsom, and Sacramento, and enjoy saloons, a brewpub, live music, and excellent restaurants. Walk in the footsteps of the pioneers, hiking from inn to inn through the Sierra foothills along the American River.

Looking for a fun weekend inn-to-inn hike? Try the first two days of this walkabout. See page 70 for details.

ITINERARY

DAY 1: Auburn to Flower Farm Inn	**16.9**
DAY 2: Flower Farm Inn to Old Town Folsom	**16.2**
DAY 3: Old Town Folsom to Arden Hills Resort, Club & Spa	**16.3**
DAY 4: Arden Hills Resort, Club & Spa to Old Sacramento	**16.8**
TOTAL MILEAGE	**66.2**

Day 1: Auburn to Flower Farm Inn

IT WAS A CHILLY MORNING in late January 1848 when James Marshall walked the millrace below the sawmill that he and his Mormon crew were constructing to supply lumber for Captain John Sutter's ambitious building plans. They had diverted Rio de los Americanos into a narrow channel as it flowed through the valley named Coloma. The river now passed below the mill at a velocity that would drive the waterwheel that powered his saw. He stooped to pick up two gleaming pebbles and examined their luster in the morning sunlight. Pounding one between two rocks, he "found it could be beaten into different shape, but not broken. I then collected four or five more pieces." His discovery would change the course of history for the United States, for California, and for the American River.

On May 16, 1848, just a few months after Marshall's discovery, Claude Chana, a French prospector, camped on the banks of a small foothills creek, Auburn Ravine. He panned for gold in the frigid water and was rewarded with three heavy nuggets. A rush of treasure hunters followed, and the village of Auburn—the oldest gold rush town in California—was born. First a hamlet of tents sprang up, but fires laid it to waste. Still the town prospered, becoming the commercial center for the surrounding mining towns and a major stop on the road to Sacramento and San Francisco. Brick replaced wood and canvas, and many buildings from the 1890s have been restored to house the commercial enterprises of modern Old Town Auburn.

Our journey starts here. There are a few inns within a mile of Old Town. Others are farther away, along the interstate, but Old Town is worth a visit. The Auburn Ale House brewery has a nice selection of pub food and drafts. Across the street, the Edelweiss Restaurant, a good breakfast spot with a wide selection of omelets, is a local hangout where Auburnians meet to discuss the news of the day.

Flower Farm Inn

Looking down on the American River from Cardiac Hill

Leaving Old Town Auburn, walk up Sacramento Street through what was once the center of Chinese businesses and the red-light district. There were few women in the gold country during the 1850s. Here was a neighborhood where a miner with gold dust in his pocket could find gambling, opium, and other diversions. He might depart with his pockets empty.

A mile from Old Town, you will join Western States Trail. See The Route (page 70) for directions to the trailhead. Best known as a horse path, the trail winds behind the easternmost houses of Auburn through an oak forest and along a pretty irrigation canal until it reaches Maidu Avenue (2.5 miles). The famous Tevis Cup Ride, a one-day, 100-mile horse race from Squaw Valley to Auburn, follows this route. Western States Trail continues down the American River with "staging areas" for parking horse trailers.

This is also the route of the Western States 100, a footrace that starts in Squaw Valley and ends at Placer High School in Auburn. Starting with a 2,200-foot ascent out of Squaw, runners navigate 100 miles of mountain trails with more than 18,000 feet of cumulative elevation gain. Timothy Olson set a race record in 2012 with the extraordinary time of 14:46:44.

Auburn sits atop the western slope of the American River Canyon, just downstream from the confluence of the North and Middle Forks of the river. The whitewater churns and winds far below. Our hike starts at an elevation of 1,359 feet and drops to 50 feet in Sacramento, but 900 feet of that descent happens within a few miles of Maidu Avenue. You can either continue along the irrigation canal 0.7 mile and then make a steep descent on trails to the river or follow the road from the entrance to the China Bar Area for a more gradual, paved descent. Please see The Route (page 70) for more details.

The American was raging on the April morning when my friend Scott and I set out on this walkabout. It was early spring after the wettest rainy season in more than a decade, but on this day the skies were clear and sunny. Racing through the narrow canyon, conforming to and sculpting its contours, the river roiled, whitewater crashing into boulders and bounding off canyon walls.

The three forks of the American have their sources high in the Sierra. On the western slopes of Granite Chief, above Squaw Valley, the North and Middle Forks are born at around 8,000 feet. They can each be crossed with a few steps while hiking the Pacific Crest Trail. Granted Wild and Scenic status in 1978, the North Fork surges through a canyon with sheer walls soaring 4,000 feet. Its raging Class IV–V rapids can be navigated only by the most expert rafters and kayakers. The two forks merge near Auburn. Originating at Echo Summit, above Lake Tahoe, the South Fork's more manageable Class II–III rapids make it the most popular river for rafting and kayaking west of the Rockies. The South Fork joins its two sisters at Folsom Lake.

Two trails follow the river downstream. The lower trail stays close to the water's edge and may be preferable in summer when the river is lower. In early spring it was mostly submerged in the high water. The upper trail ranges from 100 feet to 0.25 mile above the river. It passes through forests of oaks and gray pines. In early April, wildflowers were just starting to bloom: blue lupine, white and pale-blue Douglas iris, and buckbrush dense with clusters of sweet-smelling white flowers. Poison oak was also thriving after the winter rains. It was lush, blooming with small white flowers and stretching out to caress the unwary hiker.

After 4 miles of whitewater rapids, the canyon widens and the current slows, starting to back up and fill Folsom Lake. Its color turns from shades of glacial greens to browns as it decelerates and quiets. Our route passes old mining towns that have been swallowed by the lake and have left few traces. Rattlesnake Bar was a thriving hamlet of 1,000 miners in 1865. A Mormon community mined Horseshoe Bar in 1848. There were more than 35 gold mining settlements along both sides of the American.

Now you are hiking along Folsom Lake, a vast reservoir formed by the Folsom Dam, which was built in 1955 for flood control, Central Valley irrigation, hydroelectric power, and recreation. The lake holds 1 million acre-feet of water. It was rapidly filling with spring snowmelt, and the gates of the dam were thrown open to leave room for when the weather in the Sierra turns warm and the snowpack melts in earnest. The trail is lovely, passing through forests and meadows. It was muddy at times but always passable and always feeling like a gradual descent.

You will reach the sign for Sterling Pointe Trail at 14.3 miles. Hike up to the staging area, and follow The Route (page 70) along Lomida Lane to Auburn-Folsom Road. Turn right and proceed 0.2 mile to Flower Farm Inn. The only inn along this section of the river, it is a delightful oasis with cottages, a café, a nursery, and beautiful gardens. Chinese Silkie chickens, white and gray with fluffy plumage reaching all the way to their feet, have the run of the grounds. Fran, our host, learning that we had arrived on foot, disappeared into the back room. He emerged with a complimentary bottle of cabernet and the number for the Loomis pizza parlor. That evening we sat on the porch of our cottage in the last warm rays of the setting sun dining on pizza and sipping wine, content after a very pleasant day of hiking. The café is open Wednesday–Monday, 7:30 a.m.–4 p.m., with a great selection of sandwiches for the trail or for dinner.

Day 2: Flower Farm Inn to Old Town Folsom

JOHN BOWLER, THE FLOWER FARM INN'S PROPRIETOR, served us a delicious breakfast of sausages and farm-fresh eggs in the dining room of the main farmhouse. Affable and friendly, John is a former high school art teacher and now a very happy innkeeper. The B&B is a popular venue for weddings and a welcome refuge for an inn-to-inn hiker.

Retrace your steps back to the Sterling Pointe staging area and Western States Trail. Continue downriver. After hiking through the forest for a mile, we spotted the lower trail along the shoreline and decided to hike it until it disappeared into the rising lake. We had to periodically scramble to higher ground when the trail dipped beneath the surface or into a tributary. Views of Folsom Lake and the surrounding countryside opened up when we left the wooded upper trail. This is a hot and arid land in the summer, dominated by oaks and massive granite outcroppings, but in early spring it is verdant—long gray-green needles of stately gray pines, yellow-greens of freshly emerging willow and blue oak leaves, and deep-green grasses of every shade gracing the shoreline. Rounding a bend, the trail passed through broad fields of deep-blue lupine. Buckeyes became more prevalent as the trail descended, their tender spring leaf bundles unfolding. Turkey vultures and red-tailed hawks circled slowly on warm updrafts. Wild turkeys scampered across the trail and chortled in the woods. A small herd of mule deer grazed on the tall shoreline grass. Across the lake, to the east, the snowcapped peaks of the Sierra towered in the distance.

The trail follows a long ditch that winds along the contours of the lake. It is overgrown, and trees now grow out of its base. This crumbling artifact is a remnant of advanced gold mining techniques.

The gold that miners worked so hard to harvest started its journey 200 million years ago in a fiery sea of molten rock deep beneath the surface of the earth. Occasionally, the liquid rock would find a fault in the earth's crust and erupt as a volcano. One massive molten bubble ascended to near the surface and cooled, creating the Sierra Nevada Batholith, a mass of granite beneath California and Nevada. As the bubble cooled, individual minerals froze into solid rock at different rates, forming veins. The Sierra Nevada Batholith was rich with veins of gold-bearing quartz.

Ten million years ago the immense pressure of the North American Continental Plate grinding over the Pacific Ocean Plate caused uplifts and folds, forming the Sierra Nevada Mountains. The earth's thin mantle crumbled and eroded, exposing the granite. During ice ages, glaciers ground, polished, and carved Sierra valleys and peaks. In warmer periods, water and ice filled cracks in the rock surface, breaking off pieces that tumbled into rivers to be pummeled by racing currents. The grinding separated gold from quartz: the lighter quartz washed downstream, while the heavy gold sank, accumulating beneath boulders and in eddies.

The first miners employed a shovel and knife to search for gold nuggets, but it soon became clear that most of the gold was in the form of very small flecks

Fields of springtime lupine

Approaching Folsom, pass through an aged olive grove.

and grains. A new technology was adopted: panning. A miner scooped a slurry of gravel and water into his broad, flat pan and swirled it, washing the lighter pebbles over the edge and leaving behind the heavier gold dust.

Soon the individual entrepreneur gave way to collectives using an advanced technology, the "California cradle." One man shoveled ore into a sieve about the size and shape of a cradle, and another poured in buckets of water, washing the mixture down the floor of the cradle over strips of wood. The heavy gold sank and settled behind the strips. A third man rocked the cradle, moving the lighter minerals out the bottom. They stopped frequently to remove the gold dust and nuggets.

The cradle gave way to the more efficient "long-tom," three planks, 9–12 feet long, nailed together. The team shoveled ore into one end, and water was supplied by buckets, a hose, or a small canal. The long-tom needed to be emptied only twice a day, saving much of the cradle's drudgery.

There was serious money to be made. Individual entrepreneurial miners were replaced by corporations, and the miner became a wage slave. Rivers were dammed, partially or entirely, diverting the flow from their beds and exposing new territory for surface mining. Water was redirected into ditches and flumes. The long ditch running along the banks of Folsom Lake and Western States Trail is part of North Fork Ditch, built by the Natoma Company between 1852 and 1854.

The land becomes less wild, and there are more signs of civilization as you pass Granite Bay, 6.9 miles from the start of the second day's hike. We had seen only a few other hikers and no houses from the trail since we'd left Auburn, but as the massive Folsom Dam comes into view, fishing boats are more common, teenagers gather on the shoreline, and the trail follows the crest of tall levees. The South Fork of the American River, the branch where James Marshall made his discovery, flows into Folsom Lake across from Granite Bay. The three forks have joined into one river.

The American River Parkway, a paved bike trail, starts its 31-mile journey to Old Sacramento at Beals Point (11.7 miles), just above Folsom Dam. It was a bit of a shock to leave the soft, convoluted woodland and shoreline trails to feel unyielding asphalt under our feet. Fortunately Western States Trail separates from the paved trail just below Folsom Dam.

This spring the Sierra was blanketed with its deepest snowpack in 60 years, and the river surged through the dam's open gates. Below the dam, Folsom State Prison, built in 1880, stands ominously across the river like an ancient massive medieval citadel. Johnny Cash's mournful "Folsom Prison Blues" ran through my mind. "I'm stuck in Folsom Prison, and time keeps draggin' on."

The trail passes through an aged olive grove and then returns to the river as it approaches the town of Folsom. Cross the river on Rainbow Bridge, and walk a short distance into Old Folsom.

Restaurants, taverns, and shops line recently renovated Old Town. We dined on delicious Mexican cuisine at Qbole and then capped the night at the Folsom Hotel and Saloon, where a local rock band played for a raucous and appreciative crowd.

The first two days of this walkabout would make a great weekend inn-to-inn hike. A light-rail train provides an easy ride into Sacramento. If you are hiking all the way to Old Sacramento, Folsom is a nice place to stop over for a rest day.

Day 3: Old Town Folsom to Arden Hills Resort, Club & Spa

ALTHOUGH JAMES MARSHALL had intended to stay in Coloma until construction of the sawmill was completed, his discovery of gold compelled him to return on the muddy trail to Sutter's Fort. He and Sutter ran more tests, submerging a nugget in nitric acid. It came out untarnished. Sutter concluded, "I declare this to be gold."

Sutter tried to keep the discovery a secret, but rumors slowly started to spread. Still, there was no great rush until Sam Brannan took action. Brannan had recently opened a general store at Sutter's Fort and thought that selling supplies to prospectors would be easier and more profitable than doing the backbreaking work of mining. Quietly he bought up all the gear and mining supplies a gold miner might need. On May 12, taking a small quinine bottle of gold dust to San Francisco, he marched through the streets waving his hat crying, "Gold! Gold! Gold from the American River!"

Almost overnight, San Francisco nearly emptied, its inhabitants heading for Sutter's Fort and the American River. The citizens of Monterey and Los Angeles soon heard of the riches and also headed for the hills. The military governor of California, Colonel Richard Mason, noted in August 1848:

> *The discovery of these deposits of gold has entirely changed the character of Upper California. Its people, before engaged in cultivating their small patches of ground and guarding their herds of cattle and horses, have all gone to the mines, or are on their way thither; laborers of every trade have left their work, and tradesmen their shops; sailors desert their ships as fast as they arrive on the coast, and several vessels have gone to sea with hardly enough hands to spread a sail."*

The news spread by ship, and treasure seekers from South America, China, and Australia poured in by sea. It took until November 1848 for word to reach Washington, D.C. President James Polk, wishing to solidify America's new claim on California, announced the discovery to the nation, and the American gold rush was on.

Leaving Folsom, return to Rainbow Bridge, cross the river, and turn left on the bike trail. As you depart Folsom, you are walking through what once was the African American gold mining settlement of Negro Bar, founded in 1849. By 1850–51 there were 700 inhabitants, a store, and two hotels. In 1855 the town of Folsom was created, swallowing the small hamlet of Negro Bar.

The river moves briskly through Folsom, but it soon slows as it flows into Lake Natoma, a narrow reservoir that our trail follows for the next 5 miles until the Nimbus Dam. The hiking/biking trail winds along the northern shoreline on a narrow corridor between the lake and steep bluffs. The cliffs reveal layers of sandstone, lava flows, and the remnants of an ancient riverbed.

Mining technology continued to advance, and hydraulic mining was applied to these bluffs in the 1880s to profitable and devastating effect. Ditches were dug and pipes laid from an upstream dam. Swivel-mounted cannons concentrated the pressure of gravity-fed water with incredible force. The blast of water tore into the hillside, washing away tons of rock and soil. A Sacramento paper reported on one hydraulic operation:

Redbuds, some standing 20 feet high and wide, bloom in the spring.

With a perpendicular column of water 120 feet high, in a strong hose, of which they work two, ten men who own the claim are enabled to run off hundreds of tons of dirt daily. So great is the force employed that two men with the pipes, by directing streams of water against the base of the high bank, will cut it away to such an extent as to cause immense slides of earth, which often bring with them large trees and heavy boulders. . . . After these immense masses of earth are undermined and brought down by the streams forced from the pipes, those same streams are turned upon the tons of fallen earth, and it melts away before them, and is carried through the sluices with almost as much rapidity as if it were a bank of snow.

After a few miles, the bluffs recede, the land on the north side of the lake widens, and the paved bike trail strays away from the shoreline. A horse and hiking trail leaves the paved bike trail and heads off along the river through a shady oak forest. The hiking and horse trail is often marked as Western States Trail, as Pioneer Express Trail, or with the symbol of a horse and rider. It usually runs close to the river and through the forests. We tried to stay off the paved path whenever possible, and we managed to hike trails for probably 22 of the 28 miles between Folsom and Old Sacramento, the final two days of this walkabout. The feet somehow relax when they walk on soft, uneven earth and tire more quickly when walking on unforgiving asphalt.

American River Parkway is the longest continuous linear park in the United States. It appears as a narrow strip of green on the maps, but it feels expansive on the trail. The hiker knows that civilization is only a mile or two away, but the forests are deep and tranquil. We could not hear the sounds of traffic, lawn mowers, or even the conversations of bikers, only spring songbirds, the breeze through the trees, the river, and the chortle of wild turkeys in the woods.

The trail crosses the river 5.2 miles from Folsom on Hazel Avenue, just below Nimbus Dam. Now the river flows wild and powerful to its final destination, the confluence with the Sacramento River. It is controlled by the Folsom and Nimbus Dams, but the dam gates were opened wide this April morning. Islands were submerged, their willows and cottonwoods standing strong in the mighty current.

The trail winds through dense woods; open grasslands; and riparian forests of willows, cottonwoods, and box elders. Black walnuts and buckeyes join the forests of valley and live oaks. Redbuds, some standing 20 feet high and wide, were just coming into full bloom with brilliant lavender flowers. Canada geese and pairs of mallards rested from their long migrations in quiet eddies. Western pond turtles took sunbaths on logs. Fallen trees reveal the work of beaver. Rainbow trout, salmon, steelhead, and bass call the river home. We paused to watch three graceful river otters fishing and gamboling in a backwater, chasing each other, tumbling in an embrace, and then diving and streaking off. Butterflies grazed on wildflower blossoms.

Cross the river one more time at 14.1 miles, and enter William B. Pond Recreation Area. Turn inland shortly after the bridge to the park entrance and Arden Way. Follow The Route (page 70) to the Arden Hills Resort, Club & Spa. There is other lodging off Sunset Boulevard. See Places to Stay (page 74) for hotels and directions.

The Arden Hills Resort, Club & Spa is a fun place and a good value. The rooms are spacious and elegant, and a deep, soothing bathtub with jets massages the hiker's weary muscles. You become a member for the days you stay, and you can use the Jacuzzi, pools, tennis and basketball courts, and spa. This is a great place for a rest day before the final leg of the hike. Enjoy a massage and even a pedicure. The restaurant is excellent: Scott dined on vegetarian pasta, and I feasted on melt-in-your-mouth prime rib. They will send you off in the morning with a full complimentary breakfast prepared to order by the chef.

Day 4: Arden Hills Resort, Club & Spa
to Old Sacramento

RETRACE YOUR STEPS back to William B. Pond Recreation Area, and head downstream for the final 16.8-mile leg of the journey. Hiking along the north bank, you pass a series of man-made ponds and backwaters, the product of gold- and gravel-dredging operations in the early 1900s.

The discovery of gold on the American River sparked a rush bent on extracting wealth at any cost to the river—redirecting its flow, blasting its escarpments with hydraulic cannons, dredging its bed and banks, damming for power and flood control. Still, the mighty American is far from tamed or subdued. It is powerful, wild, and beautiful. Fish and aquatic life thrive in backwaters carved by dredges. Herons and egrets fish in the still waters.

The river swings northeast 2 miles just past the Home Avenue Bridge and then turns northwest for its final 6 miles. We had planned to stay on the river's north bank through Discovery Park and to cross into Old Sacramento on Jibboom Street, just before the confluence, but the river swelled, and parts of the trail and bike path were flooded. A couple pushing their possessions in a shopping cart told us Discovery Park was completely flooded and that it would

Flooding on the lower American River

be impossible to get to Old Sacramento on foot from the north bank. Try as humans might, the American will not be controlled. They directed us to cross the river on the pedestrian bridge just before 12th Street and to stroll into town on the Two Rivers Trail along the river's south shore. As we hiked, we could see that Discovery Park was completely submerged.

We strolled along the wooden sidewalks of Old Sacramento to the Hostelling International hostel, a beautiful old mansion with a friendly staff, and stayed in a very inexpensive private room. That evening we crossed the Sacramento River on Tower Bridge to Raley Field and cheered the Rivercats to victory over the Tacoma Rainiers. Walking back, we stopped on the bridge to watch the river run wide and swift. The great rivers of Northern California, including the American, pour out of the mountains to join the Sacramento on its journey to San Francisco Bay. Great branches and massive trees passed below us in the powerful current.

This ends a 66-mile journey along the American River, a hike that descends from the foothills of the Sierra to the Sacramento Valley. It is a walkabout through extraordinary country and through history. Along the way, the hiker visits wonderful inns and interesting towns. This is a great springtime adventure, hiking inn to inn along the American River.

A Weekend Inn-to-Inn Hiking Adventure on the American River

THE FIRST TWO DAYS OF THIS WALKABOUT, from Auburn to Old Town Folsom, make a spectacular springtime weekend adventure. You can return to Auburn by taxi. Try Folsom Taxi (916-550-7730) or Express Cab (916-220-9000). If you are going to Sacramento, take the light rail. Check for schedules at sacrt.com and click on the online trip planner icon. For travel by train, see the Transportation section.

The idea for this walkabout was inspired by Steve McGinty. Thank you, Steve!

THE ROUTE

All mileages listed for a given day are cumulative.

Day 1: Auburn to Flower Farm Inn

From the center of Old Town Auburn, walk up Sacramento St. to Auburn-Folsom Road. **0.2 mile**

Turn right on Auburn-Folsom Road to Pacific Ave. **0.7 mile**

Turn left to Portland Ave. **1.0 mile**

Turn right on Western States Trail along the irrigation canal until it crosses a paved street. **2.0 miles**

Continue along the irrigation canal to Maidu Ave. **2.5 miles**

There are two routes from Maidu Ave. to the river. You can continue along the irrigation canal trail another 0.7 mile until you reach a very steep trail to the left. A clear view of the river opens up at this point. Descend steep Cardiac Hill to the gravel parking area. There are many side trails, but stay on the main trail, and keep heading down. Or you can hike the paved road from the entrance to China Bar Area (100 yards downhill on Maidu Ave.) and descend to the gravel parking area. Pass through the metal gate and walk the road. You will reach a paved parking area after 0.8 mile. Follow the sign toward OREGON BAR RIVER ACCESS. Take Western States Trail heading downstream. **5.3 miles**

To Rattlesnake Bar   **11.3 miles**

To Sterling Pointe Trail   **14.3 miles**

Turn right on Sterling Pointe Trail to the parking lot and staging area.   **14.6 miles**

Take the road out of the parking lot. Turn right on Lake Forest Dr., which becomes Lomida Lane, to Auburn-Folsom Road   **16.7 miles**

Turn right to Flower Farm Inn.

total miles 16.9

Day 2: Flower Farm Inn to Old Town Folsom

Return to Western States Trail.   **1.4 miles**

Turn right to Beeks Bight.   **4.5 miles**

To Granite Bay   **6.9 miles**

To Beals Point   **11.7 miles**

Join the American River Bikeway. Follow it around the Folsom Dam to Rainbow Bridge.   **16.0 miles**

Cross Rainbow Bridge into Old Town Folsom.

total miles 16.2

Day 3: Old Town Folsom to Arden Hills Resort, Club & Spa

Return to Rainbow Bridge, cross the river, and turn downstream.   **0.2 mile**

Follow the paved bike trail or hiking paths to Nimbus Dam.   **4.9 miles**

Cross the river on Hazel Ave. Bridge.   **5.2 miles**

Continue along the south side of the river until the bike trail crosses the river, and enter William B. Pond Recreation Area.   **14.1 miles**

If you are staying at the Arden Hills Resort, Club & Spa, walk to the park entrance and on Arden Way to Fair Oaks Blvd.   **15.6 miles**

Turn left on Fair Oaks Blvd. Stay on the south side of the street, on the sidewalk. Cross at Jacob Lane. Arden Hills Resort, Club & Spa is on the north side of Fair Oaks, 200 yards beyond Mission Ave. and the Fair Oaks Boulevard Nursery.

total miles 16.3

If you are staying at one of the other hotels listed in Places to Stay (page 74), leave the river 9.4 miles downstream from Folsom at the Sunrise Blvd. Bridge. Hike south 1.9 miles on the bike path that parallels Sunrise Blvd. to Folsom Blvd.

Day 4: Arden Hills Resort, Club & Spa to Old Sacramento

Return to William B. Pond Recreation Area and the American River Parkway along Fair Oaks Blvd. and Arden Way.   **2.2 miles**

Hike downstream on the north side of the river to the Watt Ave. Bridge.   **5.1 miles**

A sitting room at Flower Farm Inn

To the 12th St. Bridge   **12.5 miles**

To Discovery Park and Jibboom St.   **15.1 miles**

Cross the American River just before it joins the Sacramento River on Jibboom St., and walk into Old Sacramento.

total miles 16.8

TRANSPORTATION

Driving Directions

AUBURN IS ABOUT 200 MILES EAST of the San Francisco Bay Area, 100 miles southwest of Reno and 35 miles from Sacramento. Take I-80, exit at Maple St. (#119A), and drive a few blocks into Old Town Auburn. At the end of the walk-about, you can return to Auburn from Sacramento by train on Amtrak (amtrak .com) for $16. Checker Cab Taxi (916-532-2984) can pick you up at the Auburn train depot and return you to your car.

By Train

TAKE A BEAUTIFUL AND RELAXING TRAIN TRIP to Auburn from the Bay Area ($35), Los Angeles ($62), or Reno ($63) on Amtrak (amtrak.com). The trip may include a ride from Sacramento on an Amtrak bus.

Flying into the Bay Area

FOR TRIP PLANNING from the airport to Amtrak, visit 511.org. From SFO take BART to the Oakland Coliseum Station ($9.70), and walk a few minutes to the Amtrak Station. From the Oakland International Airport, take the BART Shuttle to Oakland Coliseum BART Station ($1.95) and walk a few minutes to the Amtrak Station. Then follow the "By Train" directions above.

MAPS

THE FOLSOM LAKE STATE RECREATION AREA offers a free map and brochure covering the first two days of this walkabout from Auburn to Folsom. You can download a copy at parks.ca.gov and search for "Folsom Lake." For a better hard copy, call 916-988-0205, and they will mail you a free map.

The American River Parkway Foundation provides an excellent map of the river and trails from Beals Point on Folsom Lake to the Sacramento River, Days 3 and 4, for $5 at arpf.org.

PLACES TO STAY

LODGING COST

$ less than $100	$$ $100–$150	$$$ $150–$200	$$$$ more than $200

Auburn

AUBURN HOLIDAY INN $$–$$$ • 120 Grass Valley Hwy. • 530-887-8787 • 800-814-8787 • auburnhi.com • 0.6 mile from Old Town.

POWER'S MANSION INN $$–$$$$ • 195 Harrison Ave. • 916-425-9360 • powersmansion.com • 0.9 mile from Old Town.

Loomis

FLOWER FARM INN $–$$$$ • 4150 Auburn Folsom Road • 916-652-4200 • flowerfarminn.com • Breakfast included. • See The Route (page 70) for directions from the trail.

Folsom

LAKE NATOMA INN $$–$$$$ • 702 Gold Lake Dr. • 916-351-1500 • 800-808-5253 • lakenatomainn.com

BRADLEY HOUSE $$–$$$ • 606 Figueroa St. • 916-355-1962 • bradleyhousefolsom.com

Between Folsom and Sacramento

ARDEN HILLS RESORT, CLUB & SPA $$$–$$$$ • 1220 Arden Hills Lane • Sacramento • 916-482-6111 • ardenhills.club • Breakfast included. • See The Route (page 70) for directions from the trail.

LA QUINTA $–$$ • 11131 Folsom Blvd. • Rancho Cordova • 800-753-3757 • laquintasacramentoranchocordova.com • Continental breakfast included. • Leave the river 9.4 miles downstream from Folsom at the Sunrise Blvd. Bridge. Hike south 1.9 miles on the bike path that parallels Sunrise Blvd. to Folsom Blvd.

MARRIOTT $$$–$$$$ • 11211 Point East Dr. • Rancho Cordova • 888-236-2427 • marriott.com • Leave the river 9.4 miles downstream from Folsom at the Sunrise Blvd. Bridge. Hike south 1.9 miles on the bike path that parallels Sunrise Blvd. to Folsom Blvd.

Upper American River

Old Sacramento

These are a few of many places to stay.

DELTA KING HOTEL $$–$$$$ • 1000 Front St. • 916-444-5464
• deltaking.com • Riverboat hotel. Breakfast included.

**EMBASSY SUITES BY HILTON SACRAMENTO RIVERFRONT
PROMENADE $$$$** • 100 Capitol Mall • 916-326-5000 • embassysuites3
.hilton.com • Breakfast included.

VAGABOND INN $–$$ • 909 Third St. • 916-446-1481 • vagabondinn.com
• Continental breakfast included.

HI SACRAMENTO HOSTEL $–$$ • 925 H St. • Seven blocks from Old Sacramento
• 916-668-6631 • hiusa.org

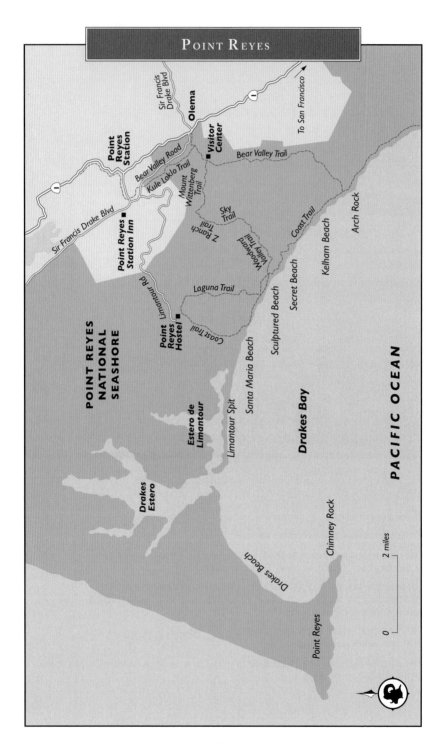

POINT REYES

Sir Francis Drake Blvd

Olema

To San Francisco

Point Reyes Station

Visitor Center

Bear Valley Road

Bear Valley Trail

Kule Loklo Trail

Mount Wittenberg Trail

Sky Trail

Arch Rock

Point Reyes Station Inn

Coast Trail

Z Ranch Trail

Woodward Valley Trail

Kelham Beach

Secret Beach

Sir Francis Drake Blvd

Limantour Rd

Laguna Trail

Sculptured Beach

POINT REYES NATIONAL SEASHORE

Point Reyes Hostel

Coast Trail

Santa Maria Beach

Estero de Limantour

Limantour Spit

Drakes Bay

Drakes Estero

PACIFIC OCEAN

Chimney Rock

Drakes Beach

Point Reyes

2 miles

0

Exploring Point Reyes National Seashore

travel weary
just as I finally find lodging—
wisteria blossoms

— MATSUO BASHO, *Knapsack Journey*

View from the Coast Trail

Find joy in the sky, in the trees, in the flowers,
There are flowers everywhere
For those who want to see them.

—HENRI MATISSE, *Matisse on Art*

WITH 71,000 ACRES OF COASTAL HILLS, dense forests, pristine beaches, and 150 miles of hiking trails, Point Reyes National Seashore is a walkabout paradise only an hour and a half north of San Francisco by car or bus. This easy 27-mile walkabout over three days explores the central portion of the park. You'll stay at lovely inns in Olema and Point Reyes Station and a hostel set deep in the park where you can commune with deer, bobcats, elk, and other residents of this enchanted wilderness. Stay an extra day or two and explore the esteros and miles of beautiful beaches.

ITINERARY

DAY 1:	Point Reyes Station to Point Reyes Hostel	**10.8**
DAY 2:	Point Reyes Hostel to Olema	**12.1**
DAY 3:	Olema to Point Reyes Station	**4.1**
TOTAL MILEAGE		**27.0**

Day 1: Point Reyes Station to Point Reyes Hostel

START THIS WALKABOUT at Point Reyes Station, a quiet village on the edge of the park with shops, taverns, and eateries. The Station House Café offers organic, locally sourced cuisine, and local musicians play on Sunday nights. You can kick up your heels and dance at the Old Western Saloon across the street.

Leaving Point Reyes Station, hike quiet country lanes along marshlands at the southern tip of Tomales Bay, and enter the park. At 1.4 miles, you reach Kule Loklo, meaning "Bear Valley," a re-created Coast Miwok village. The lands of the Coast Miwok stretched from the Golden Gate north to Bodega Bay and east to Sonoma, what today is Marin and southern Sonoma Counties. Bands of the Olema tribe called Point Reyes home. At the center of Kule Loklo is the roundhouse, a communal and ceremonial structure 55 feet in diameter, built partially into the earth and supported by stout tree limbs. Acorn granaries, a sweat lodge, and conical houses made of redwood bark bring the village to life. A garden of native plants used by the Miwok for food, medicine, and basketry lies at the edge of the village.

The trail passes the park's visitor center. Stop to learn about the history, geology, and ecology of the park. Then take the Bear Valley Trail 0.2 mile, turn on the Mount Wittenberg Trail, and enter an enchanted wilderness. The trail climbs 1,100 feet through forests of Douglas-fir, bay, live oaks, ferns, poison oak, and forget-me-nots. When we hiked in early June, grassy fields were still green and decorated with dandelions and blue-eyed grass. Songbirds serenaded. Two black-tailed does and a fawn crossed the trail 50 feet ahead of us. We all stopped to stare at each other before they delicately stepped into the underbrush and disappeared.

After 1.8 miles on Mount Wittenberg Trail, it reaches the ridge and Z Ranch Trail, the end of the uphill hiking for the day unless you would like to ascend another 0.2 mile to the highest point in the park, the top of Mount Wittenberg (1,407'). Our route turns south (left) along the crest on Z Ranch Trail 0.4 mile and joins Sky Trail for another 0.8 mile. Views of the Pacific open periodically through the dense woods.

Take the Woodward Valley Trail, and descend 800 feet over the next 2 miles. Now the vast Pacific comes into full view. The great crescent shoreline of Drakes Bay arcs west all the way to Chimney Rock, a monolithic landmark at the tip of Point Reyes. The point was named by Spanish explorer Don Sebastian Vizcaíno on January 6, 1603. While sailing north from Monterey to explore the uncharted

Mount Wittenberg Trail

coastline, storms and heavy seas forced him to take shelter in Drakes Bay. Jutting south into the Pacific, the tall bluffs of the peninsula protected his ship from the westerly winds. It was the day of the Feast of the Three Kings, and out of gratitude, Vizcaíno named the point La Punta de Los Tres Reyes.

Turn right and follow the Coast Trail as it swings inland along Santa Maria Creek and back to the coastal bluffs above the Pacific. Inland, grassy hills climb sharply, and dense forests fill the creek canyons. The trail passes Coast Camp, one of four campgrounds in the park that can be reached on foot or by horse. The campgrounds fill up on summer weekends, but they are available on short notice most other days. Coast Camp lies in a sheltered meadow, protected from the ocean's winds by grassy dunes. Only 1.9 miles from the road, it is an easy way for Bay Area residents to get their wilderness camping fix. Make reservations at recreation.gov, or call 877-444-6777.

Just beyond the campground, you reach the sea, 8.5 miles from your starting point. Wide beaches—Santa Maria, Limantour, and Drakes—arc 11 miles west to Chimney Rock, interrupted only by the narrow entrance to Estero de Limantour and Drakes Estero. Santa Maria Beach is a beautiful spot to stop for lunch. Steep, sandy cliffs stretch to the southeast, bordering the broad beach. Lush gardens of pale blue lupine, lavender asters, bright yellow mustard, and orange paintbrush, nourished by seeps in the vertical walls, descend 100 feet to the beach.

From Santa Maria Beach, hike 2 miles up Laguna Trail to the Point Reyes Hostel. After hiking the mountains and coastline of Point Reyes National Seashore for 10.8 miles, you have arrived at a wonderful destination for a day or two of relaxation and exploration.

Staying at Point Reyes Hostel

Hostelling International USA provides travelers with inexpensive lodging in amazing settings throughout California and the United States. Tucked in a small valley, 1.5 miles from the coast and surrounded by wooded hills, the Point Reyes Hostel has four private rooms and 36 bunk beds in men's, women's, and coed dormitories. The private rooms are nice for a couple or a family. They are often reserved months in advance, especially for summer weekends, but a dorm bed can usually be booked on fairly short notice. The hostel has a full communal kitchen, a living room, a library, and an outdoor sitting area.

Most guests arrive by car, and we had dropped off a cache of food before we started hiking. After cooking dinner, along with a very exuberant troop of Girl Scouts, we sat down with Nancy, the hostel host. She knew about *Walkabout California* and described herself as "a distance walker." She had hiked 500 miles through Northern

Descending to the coast

Spain on El Camino de Santiago, the Way of St. James. For 1,000 years, since medieval times, pilgrims have walked this route, and they continue to hike all or part of this UNESCO World Heritage Site today. We spent a few hours sharing stories about great inn-to-inn hikes in California and about her pilgrimage.

"Distance walker." Doesn't that describe most people throughout history? Only in recent centuries did horses and carriages become the common mode of transport for the privileged. Throughout human history, all others who strayed from their home villages were distance walkers. Modern distance walkers include Nancy and her fellow pilgrims on El Camino de Santiago, other European inn-to-inn hikers, backpackers, and all of us who have taken a walkabout in California.

There is something primal about traveling long distances on foot, but modern life makes it easy to forget that this is part of our nature. Hiking multiple days in an extraordinarily beautiful setting like Point Reyes without setting foot in a car connects us to the land and to an essential part of ourselves. As each day passes, the connections deepen.

Stay an extra day or two at the hostel, and explore Estero de Limantour and Drakes Estero, estuaries that reach deep into the peninsula. The long, narrow finger of Limantour Spit separates the esteros from Drakes Bay. Small tidal coves and marshes branch from the main estuaries and cut into the rolling hills. Coyote brush and small pines grow on the grassy hillsides. Trails travel along the inlets, and although Estero de Limantour is only 2 miles from the road, few hikers and mountain bikers venture into this part of the park.

Hiking along Estero de Limantour, we rounded a curve and spotted a group of tule elk, females with a very young calf. They grazed and lounged by a small tarn while mallards swam in the shallows and an egret stalked along the shore. Tule elk once roamed California's hills and Central Valley, numbering half a million when

Europeans arrived. They were hunted relentlessly and were thought to be extinct by the 1860s. But in 1874, a group of less than 30 was discovered in the marshes of southern San Joaquin Valley. A rancher, Henry Miller, protected them, and they started to make a comeback.

In the fall of 1978, 17 tule elk were released into a reserve at the north end of Point Reyes National Seashore. The population grew, and today it is estimated at 450. In 1998, 28 were moved to the Limantour Beach area.

Rutting and breeding season, August–October, is an exciting time to hike the reserve. Female hormones are pumping, and massive bulls, 7 feet long and 4–5 feet tall at the shoulders, sport coats of beige, dark-brown manes, tan rumps, and impressive racks. The males bugle to attract females and chase off other males to form harems of up to 30–50.

Fighting and breeding is exhausting work, and it is rare that a bull can dominate a second season. After the rut, males form bachelor groups, and in the winter, they drop their antlers. Females remain in groups throughout the year, except between mid-May and mid-June when pregnant cows separate from the group to give birth. They return after about three weeks with their newborn calves.

Scholars believe Sir Francis Drake sailed the *Golden Hinde* into these waters on June 17, 1579, on his three-year voyage around the world. After rounding the tip of South America, he sacked Valparaiso and other Spanish coastal outposts.

The roundhouse at Kule Loklo, a re-created Miwok village

In March 1579 he captured the Spanish galleon *Calafuego* and stole enough gold, silver, and jewels to retire the debt of England. Sailing north as far as the Strait of Juan de Fuca, the entrance to the Puget Sound, he failed to find the Northwest Passage and returned south along the coast. His ship was leaking badly, and he feared discovery by Spanish ship captains who would have dearly loved to seek revenge for his plunder of their vessels. It is believed that he sailed into the shallow waters of Drakes Estero and stayed 36 days. His crew careened the ship, tipping the *Hinde* on her side, cleaning the hull, and repairing leaky seams.

Coast Miwok watched this amazing sight from the hills and then ventured down to greet the strangers. They met a party in exotic dress—sailors in cloth leggings and officers wearing stockings and shoes with buckles. The Miwok women wore deerskin skirts. The men, according to the ship's chaplain, Francis Fletcher, were naked, "as though proud of the suit nature gave them."

During the course of their five-week visit, the English ventured inland and found a land teeming with elk and deer. Black bears and grizzlies roamed the coastal mountains. The Miwok enjoyed a rich life. Archaeologists have found the remains of 139 Miwok villages in Point Reyes. Acorns were the main staple of the Miwok diet, but they also dined on harbor seals and sea lions; harvested oysters, clams, and mussels from the marshes along Tomales Bay; and netted salmon and steelhead seasonally from nearby streams.

Drake named the land Nova Albion because the cliffs along what is now Drakes Beach reminded him of his homeland. The Miwok must have stared in amusement and disbelief when he erected a sturdy post with a brass plate claiming this land for his queen, Elizabeth I.

Coast Miwok villagers gathered at night around a fire in the roundhouse while elders recited the tribe's sacred stories. The visit by the strange men in the sailing ship must have become part of the narrative. A few other explorers made contact briefly with the Miwok, but it would be almost two centuries before the next extended visit by Europeans. This time they came to stay.

The *San Carlos* sailed into San Francisco Bay on August 5, 1775, dropping anchor off Sausalito. It was followed the next year by soldiers and priests, who established a mission and presidio in a village they would call Yerba Buena. The San Rafael mission was founded in 1817, but by this time old-world diseases had devastated the Coast Miwok. It is estimated that they numbered 5,000 at the time of first contact with Europeans. Over the 65 years following the establishment of Mission Dolores in San Francisco, 90% perished. Soldiers rounded them up for slave labor on the ranches and missions, and many fled to the protection of the Russians at Colony Ross.

Day 2: Point Reyes Hostel to Olema

A LIGHT EARLY-MORNING FOG LIFTED as we departed from the hostel, and a bobcat crossed the trail 100 yards away. Brownish red with a white underbelly and not much bigger than a house cat, it stopped to study us with a relaxed, almost drowsy expression and then ambled into the underbrush.

You can shave a mile off this day's hike by returning to Santa Maria Beach on the Laguna Trail. If you take the slightly longer route on Coast Trail from the hostel, you can enjoy a long stroll along the beach. The tide was low when we walked the shore, and the sand was firm, perfect for hiking. We took off our boots and strolled barefoot. Two harbor seals surfaced just beyond the breaking waves and studied us. Ospreys soared overhead. One suddenly dove, snatched a fish in its talons, struggled to regain altitude, and flew inland with its catch. A line of California brown pelicans glided west just above the waves. Spotting a school of fish, they rose as a group and dove for lunch. Gulls flew in to pick up scraps in a chaotic feeding frenzy. We rested against a log. Although we had 12.1 miles to hike this day, with 16 hours of daylight there was no hurry.

The Coast Trail leaves the shore at Santa Maria Beach and follows the coastal bluffs 4.3 miles to Bear Valley Trail. It snakes in and out of creek drainages. Dense forests of 25-foot ceanothus with delicate lavender puffs of flowers at their tips descend the slopes to the creekbeds.

The long beaches and sand cliffs of the peninsula stretch to the west. Rocky bluffs and the rugged shoreline extend before you. To the south, the vast Pacific reaches the horizon, and on a clear day you can see the Farallon Islands jutting out of the ocean, 27 miles from shore. They were the peaks of the coastal range 10,000 years ago during the last ice age. When the glaciers receded, the coastline shifted 35 miles inland. Today the islands are home to an amazing abundance of sea life.

Francis Drake and his crew were the first Europeans to visit the Farallones, stopping to store seal meat for the voyage across the Pacific. Russian and American hunters, seeking precious pelts, wiped out the island's fur seals by 1838. Northern elephant seals, prized for their blubber, met the same fate by the 1880s. To satisfy the insatiable appetite of San Francisco's exploding population during and after the gold rush, hunters harvested eggs of the common murre, and their numbers plunged from a million to only a few thousand.

In 1909, President Teddy Roosevelt declared the Farallones a national wildlife refuge, and populations rebounded. The northern elephant seals returned in 1959, the northern fur seals in 1996. The islands now constitute the largest seabird rookery in the continental United States, with 350,000 birds, including a thriving population of common murres.

Hiking the Coast Trail

The islands perch on the edge of the continental shelf, where the ocean floor plunges 6,000 feet. The cold waters of the California current flow south from British Columbia, causing upwellings and enormous blooms of plant plankton in the spring. Krill eat the plankton, and birds, fish, and whales feast on the krill. Migrating dolphins and humpback, gray, and blue whales stop to feed in the nutrient-rich waters. From the Coast Trail you can spot gray whales migrating south in the fall, spouting far out to sea. They return in late winter and early spring for the journey north with their calves, this time much closer to shore.

The trail passes three small beaches that are fun to explore: Sculptured, Secret, and Kelham. It reaches the Bear Valley Trail at 7.1 miles from the hostel. A short hike to Arch Rock was a popular side trip from this junction until tragedy struck in March 2015. Seven hikers were atop the popular coast overlook when a 50-foot section of the cliff suddenly collapsed with a thunderous crash. Five scrambled and escaped unharmed, but two were hurled 75 feet to the beach, where one perished and one was seriously injured.

The Bear Valley Trail turns inland. It is a broad path that travels 4 miles through dense forest back to the visitor center, gradually ascending 2.4 miles to Divide Meadow, and then gradually descending to the trailhead.

Walk down the visitor center road to Bear Valley Road, turn right and hike a mile to Olema where there are several inns and B&Bs. Olema has two good restaurants, the Farm House and Sir and Star at the Olema, both near the intersection of CA 1 and Sir Francis Drake Boulevard. We spent a leisurely evening at the Farm House dining on fresh local oysters and succulent pan-seared seabass and horseradish-crusted cod, a nice way to end a beautiful day's hike.

Day 3: Olema to Point Reyes Station

THE FINAL LEG OF THIS WALKABOUT is only 4.1 miles. Return to the visitor center area along Bear Valley Road, and take the trail to Kule Loklo. Coast Miwok people continue to live in their historical land: the cities of Marin County, Bodega Bay, and around Tomales Bay. Betty Goerke, author of *Chief Marin*, writes of a gathering held here in 2001. Two hundred tribal members and supporters crowded into the roundhouse to celebrate the tribe's recent recognition by the federal government after years of struggle.

Your trail continues back to Point Reyes Station. You may want to stop for a while in the Coast Miwok village. It takes on a deeper meaning after you have immersed yourself in this land the native peoples called home.

Sitting in the Miwok village, I felt gratitude for their stewardship over thousands of years and now to all the recent citizens who worked to preserve and maintain this amazing wilderness that is only a short trip from the urban centers of the Bay Area. It is a land waiting to be explored. There is no better way than a long walkabout.

THE ROUTE

All mileages listed for a given day are cumulative.

Day 1: Point Reyes Station to Point Reyes Hostel

Walk south out of Point Reyes Station along CA 1. There is a broad shoulder, and traffic moves slowly on this stretch. Turn right on Sir Francis Drake Boulevard. Turn left on Bear Valley Road and go 0.3 mile. Turn right on the unmarked trail after the Limantour Road intersection. The Kule Loklo Trail takes you past a re-created Coast Miwok village and to the park's visitor center.   **2.8 miles**

Take the Bear Valley Trail 0.2 mile from the visitor center, and turn right on Mount Wittenberg Trail to Z Ranch Trail.   **4.8 miles**

Take Z Ranch Trail south (left) to Sky Trail to Woodward Valley Trail.   **6.0 miles**

Turn right on Woodward Valley Trail to the Coast Trail.   **8.0 miles**

Turn right on the Coast Trail to Laguna Trail.   **8.8 miles**

Turn right to Point Reyes Hostel.

total miles 10.8

Day 2: Point Reyes Hostel to Olema

You can cut a mile off this leg by returning to Santa Maria Beach on Laguna Trail, but you will miss a nice long hike on the shore.

Leaving the hostel, take the Coast Trail to the beach.   **1.6 miles**

Continue on the trail, or walk along the beach. The Coast Trail turns inland along the bluffs at Santa Maria Beach.   **2.8 miles**

Continue on the Coast Trail to Bear Valley Trail.   **7.1 miles**

Turn inland on Bear Valley Trail to the visitor center.   **11.1 miles**

Walk down from the visitor center to Bear Valley Road, and turn right to Olema.

total miles 12.1

Day 3: Olema to Point Reyes Station

Return to the visitor center area on Bear Valley Road.   **1.0 mile**

Take the Kule Loklo Trail back to Bear Valley Road.   **2.7 miles**

Turn left on Bear Valley Road to Sir Francis Drake Boulevard   **3.0 miles.**

Turn right on Sir Francis Drake Boulevard and left along the shoulder of CA 1 into Point Reyes Station.

total miles 4.1

TRANSPORTATION

Public Transportation from San Francisco

TRAVELING TO POINT REYES by public transit from almost anywhere in the Bay Area is efficient and inexpensive. Visit 511.org for easy trip planning.

From San Francisco, take BART to the Civic Center Station (see bart.gov). Walk a few blocks down Market Street to Seventh Street. Take Golden Gate Transit Bus 101 to the San Rafael Transit Center. The trip takes approximately 1 hour and costs $7. Schedules and other information are available at goldengatetransit.org. Take the West Marin Stagecoach 68 from the San Rafael Transit Center to Olema or downtown Point Reyes Station. This trip takes approximately 1 hour and costs $2. More information and schedules are available at marintransit.org.

Flying into the Bay Area

FROM SFO TAKE BART to the Civic Center Station ($8.95) and follow the public transportation directions on the previous page. From the Oakland International Airport take Oakland Airport BART to Oakland Coliseum Station. Take BART to the San Francisco Civic Center Station, and follow the public transportation directions on the previous page. The trip takes about 35 minutes and costs $10.20.

Coast Camp, one of four campgrounds at Point Reyes National Seashore

MAPS

THE POINT REYES NATIONAL SEASHORE WEBSITE (nps.gov/pore) provides a free downloadable map. This map is also available at the park's visitor center. Wilderness Press publishes an excellent map of the park, *Point Reyes National Seashore and West Marin Parklands,* for $7.46; visit wildernesspress.com to purchase. *Point Reyes National Seashore* for $10.95 by Tom Harrison Maps is also excellent; visit tomharrisonmaps.com.

PLACES TO STAY

LODGING COST			
$ *less than $100*	$$ *$100–$150*	$$$ *$150–$200*	$$$$ *more than $200*

Point Reyes Station

POINT REYES SCHOOLHOUSE $$$$ • 11559 CA 1 • 3 blocks north of the town center • 415-663-1166 • pointreyesschoolhouse.com

POINT REYES STATION INN $$–$$$$ • 11591 CA 1 • 3 blocks north of the town center • 415-663-9372 • pointreyesstationinn.com

Point Reyes National Seashore

POINT REYES HOSTEL $–$$ • 1390 Limantour Spit Road • 415-663-8811 • hiusa.org • Pack in your food or drop it off in advance.

Olema

OLEMA HOUSE (formerly The Lodge at Point Reyes) **$$$$** • 10021 CA 1 • 415-663-9000 • olemahouse.com

ROBIN'S RETREAT AND HONEYBEE COTTAGE $$–$$$ • 10210 Shoreline Hwy. • 415-663-1288 • robinsretreat.com

INN AT ROUNDSTONE FARM $$ • 9940 Sir Francis Drake Blvd. • 415-663-1020 • roundstonefarm.com

BEAR VALLEY COTTAGE $$$$ • 88 Bear Valley Road • 415-663-1777 • bearvalleycottage.com • 15% discount for those hiking in.

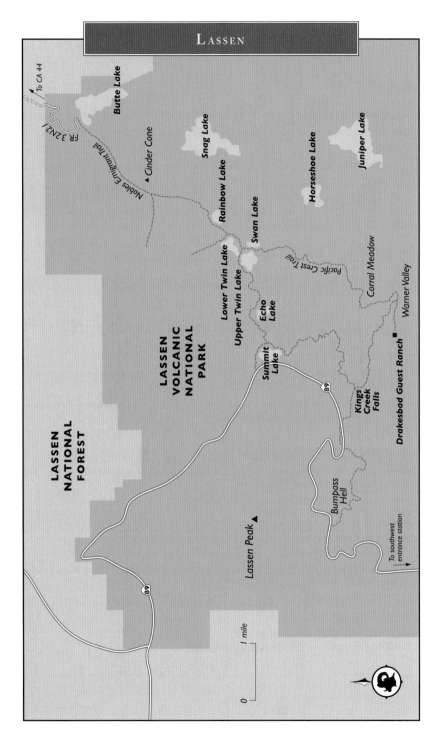

Exploring Lassen Volcanic National Park

Like gigantic geysers spouting molten rock instead of water,
volcanoes work and rest, and we have no sure means of knowing
whether they are dead when still, or only sleeping.

—JOHN MUIR, *The Mountains of California*

Lassen Peak from Upper Meadow

In everyday life, taking off your socks is an unnoticed chore;
peeling them off after a long day's walk is sheer delight.

—COLIN FLETCHER, *The Complete Walker IV*

ALONG THE PACIFIC RIM'S RING OF FIRE, the Cascade Mountains reach as far north as Mount Garibaldi in British Columbia. This range of massive volcanoes stretches south through Washington, Oregon, and Northern California. At its southern tip lies Lassen Peak, resting from its most recent eruption in 1917. Surrounding the mountain is Lassen Volcanic National Park, a wild and exotic Northern California treasure.

You can choose from two walkabouts through this enchanted land. The first, a two-day, 22.2-mile hike, requires two cars. It explores the park from its northeast to southwest corners. Starting in a land of lava beds and painted cinder dunes, you hike south to a lush hot-springs valley. The trail on the second hiking day explores mountain lakes and streams, deep glaciated canyons, and otherworldly hydrothermal landscapes.

The second walkabout is a 19.4-mile loop that starts high at Summit Lake and requires only one car. It explores the central park—a mountainous land of forests, lakes, and streams. Each trek offers a spectacular waterfall, mountain lakes for swimming, and windows into the earth's fiery interior.

The mountains of Lassen Volcanic National Park

Both walkabouts stop over at Drakesbad Guest Ranch, one of only two lodgings in the park. Stay a few days and enjoy soaking in the hot springs. Explore the verdant Warner Valley and surrounding landscape of boiling lakes and steaming fumaroles. Relax with fine dining and perhaps a therapeutic massage.

ITINERARIES

Butte Lake to Bumpass Hell

DAY 1:	Butte Lake to Warner Valley	**12.5**
DAY 2:	Warner Valley to Bumpass Hell parking area	**10.1**
TOTAL MILEAGE		**22.6**

Summit Lake Loop via Warner Valley

DAY 1:	Summit Lake to Warner Valley via Twin Lakes	**11.1**
DAY 2:	Warner Valley to Summit Lake via Kings Creek Falls	**8.6**
TOTAL MILEAGE		**19.7**

BUTTE LAKE TO BUMPASS HELL

Day 1: Butte Lake to Warner Valley

THE ONE ROAD THAT TRAVERSES THE PARK, CA 89, winds through its western half. My friend Scott drove up from Reno, and I came from the Bay Area. We met at the visitor center in the southwest corner of the park. A walkabout is a great way to reunite with distant friends and to spend long days together enjoying nature's beauty at 2 miles an hour.

Dropping a car at the Bumpass Hell parking lot, we drove north out of the park and then east on CA 44, reentering on Butte Lake Road in the park's northeast corner (see Transportation, page 106, for driving directions). Butte Lake has a campground and ranger station. At 6,053 feet, the lake's western shoreline was formed by ancient lava flows that partially filled its basin. Frozen rivers of black, ragged lava reach 100 feet high, shaping the convoluted shore of the lake. As we started our hike, a great blue heron stalked and a pod of mule deer grazed in the grassy shallows at the water's edge.

The trail heads south 1.2 miles through soft volcanic sand, cinders, until it reaches Cinder Cone. Eruptions in the 1600s formed the 750-foot-high cone and the Fantastic Lava Beds that flowed toward Butte Lake. The cone has an angle of repose of 30–35 degrees, the maximum angle that still prevents cinders from rolling down its side. It was formed by basaltic lava, which is rich in magnesium and iron. Lighter cinders were blasted for miles, and heavy volcanic bombs litter the base of the cone. A few stunted pines grow on its flanks, but the dense cinders discourage much vegetation. The ponderosa and Jeffrey pine forest surrounding the cone is thin, and other vegetation is sparse in the sandy soil.

It is difficult to distinguish Jeffrey pines from ponderosa pines. Both are mighty giants that can reach 200 feet in height. Each bears 8- to 10-inch needles in bundles of three. Their thick bark is an intricate and irregular patchwork. The Jeffrey flourishes at elevations between 6,000 and 9,000 feet in the Sierra, while ponderosas grow between 2,000 and 7,000 feet. In this zone they overlap. As we hiked around Cinder Cone, Scott approached one of the giants, put his nose into a deep furrow in the patchwork bark, and, smelling a light fragrance of vanilla, declared this one to be a Jeffrey. The scales on the cones of a ponderosa face outward and prickle when handled, but these cones had a smooth surface, confirming its identity.

If you are ambitious, you can climb the steep trail to the top of Cinder Cone over loose cinders. Two concentric paths circle the lip of the cone and the inside of the crater. The view from the top is worth the climb—the painted dunes, fantastic lava beds, Butte and Snag lakes, and, to the west, the 10,457-foot snowcapped Lassen Peak.

The great mountain and surrounding parkland lie at the southern end of the Cascade Range, but the mountain borders the Northern Sierra. John Muir referred to it as part of the Sierra when he visited Cinder Cone and wrote in *The Mountains of California*:

> *The Cinder Cone near marks the most recent volcanic eruption in the Sierra. It is a symmetrical truncated cone about 700 ft. high, covered with grey cinders and ashes, and has a regular unchanged crater on its summit, in which a few small two-leaved pines are growing. . . . Before the cone was built a flood of rough vesicular lava was poured into the lake, cutting it in two, and overflowing its banks, the fiery flood advanced into the pine-woods, overwhelming the trees in its way, the charred ends of some of which may still be seen projecting from beneath the snout of the lava-stream where it came to rest. Later still there was an eruption of ashes and loose obsidian cinders, probably from the same vent, which, besides forming the Cinder Cone, scattered a heavy shower over the surrounding woods for miles to a depth of from six inches to several feet.*

The history of this last Sierra eruption is also preserved in the traditions of the Pitt River Indians. They tell of a fearful time of darkness, when the sky was black with ashes and smoke that threatened every living thing with death, and recount that when at length the sun appeared once more, it was red like blood.

Muir died in December of 1914 at age 76, only six months after the next great eruption in the Cascades, Lassen Peak.

This section of the hike follows Nobles Emigrant Trail, forged by William Nobles in 1852 during the peak of the gold rush. Thousands of treasure seekers passed this way in the 1850s. It proved superior to the dangerous Lassen Trail that had opened in 1848 as a route from the Humboldt River in Nevada to the upper Sacramento Valley. The trail was used as a wagon route to California until 1869, when the Transcontinental Railroad was completed and the pioneer wagon roads fell into disuse.

Continue on the trail south of Cinder Cone toward Lower Twin Lake. After another 0.5 mile Nobles Emigrant Trail veers west. Stay left at this junction. Leaving the soft cinders behind, the trail becomes firm and easy. You pass three lovely jewel lakes—Rainbow, Lower Twin, and Swan. Wildflowers line the paths near the lakes until mid-July. When we hiked, late in the season, the second week of September, these small lakes were the perfect temperature for a leisurely swim.

Cinder Cone

The eastern half of the park has low mountains, meandering creeks, and dozens of lakes. This trail is an easy stroll for most of the first day's hike, rolling gradually between 6,300 and 6,800 feet through forests of white firs and Jeffrey, lodgepole, and western white pines. Lassen is one of the most lightly used national parks, averaging fewer than 500,000 visitors a year. Very few stray far from the Lassen Park Road (CA 89) in the park's western half. Only backpackers and a few day-trippers venture into the east side. We met only one other hiker until we reached Warner Valley.

Join the Pacific Crest Trail (PCT) at Lower Twin Lake, and head south, passing through several sections where fires have scarred the forest. Marked with bear scat and deer tracks, the trail turns southwest and descends through Grassy Swale along a meandering brook. The forest becomes lush, and boardwalks span marshy sections of the trail. Cross the brook and then Kings Creek at the Corral Meadow junction. Follow the signs south toward Warner Valley. The trail climbs 500 feet through a series of switchbacks until it reaches the crest overlooking Warner Valley and Drakesbad Guest Ranch. Descend the steep trail into Warner Valley Campground, turn right, and walk up the road a short distance to Drakesbad.

Warner Valley and Drakesbad Guest Ranch

Drakesbad Guest Ranch is a rustic hideaway at the south central end of the park. Hunters, trappers, and sheepherders visited the Warner Valley following the gold rush, but it was first settled by German immigrant E. R. Drake in the 1860s. Occasional visitors found him and camped for a few nights, enjoying soaks in his hot springs, but Drake valued his privacy more than profit and did little to develop a tourist business.

That changed in 1900, when Alex and Ida Sifford paid a visit and thought they had found paradise. They purchased the land from Drake for $6,000 and opened a rustic guest ranch, which the Sifford family operated until 1958, when they deeded it to the National Park Service. One of only two lodgings in the park, it is a gem that merits a stay of at least a few nights.

We arrived in time for the weekly barbecue feast. Guests gathered at picnic tables outside the lodge while Ed Fiebiger, who with his wife, Billie, hosted Drakesbad for 21 years, grilled steaks, chicken, and portobello mushrooms. There were buckets of beans, potato salad, and beer. As I savored a barbecued steak, I laughed at the thought that in spite of days of hiking, this adventure was one more walkabout where my caloric intake was going to exceed calories burned.

After all the guests were served, Ed joined us at our table. A jovial man with a thick shock of blond hair sprouting from his visor, he has a deep affection for

Barbecue night at Drakesbad Guest Ranch

Drakesbad. Pointing at Scott's bald head, he said, "Do you like my hair?" We agreed it looked good. He whipped off his visor, and the hair came off with it, exposing his shining scalp. Scott's face lit up, and he wrote down the website where he could purchase this marvelous invention. They even have visors with ponytails, according to Ed. Scott's eyes showed that his imagination was stirring with the possibilities. Ed and Billie have "retired" from hosting Drakesbad, though Billie still manages reservations and Ed relieves the current host, Nick, on his days off.

Hot Springs Creek meanders along the south side of the broad valley. Wildflowers grace the meadows and line the streams in the early season. Eagles and ospreys call Warner Valley home for part of the year. Mule deer gather in the meadows to graze at dusk. In the early morning, while enjoying a cup of coffee on our porch, we watched them retreat delicately and unafraid back into the woods. Deep in the night, listen for the nervous whinnying of Drakesbad's horses, signaling a nocturnal visit from the valley's black bears.

A generator provides electricity to the lodge, but kerosene lamps light the cabins. The absence of internet or cell phone coverage helps you unwind and tune into the beauty of Warner Valley. A hot spring heats the pool to between 95°F and 105°F. Even summer nights at this elevation (5,700') are cool, perfect for floating in the warm waters and gazing at the star-filled sky. Enjoy three hearty meals a day with plenty of fresh fruits and vegetables, along with a wide selection of wines and beer. Take short day hikes to the thermal hot spots in the south end of the park—Devils Kitchen, Boiling Springs Lake, and Thermal Geyser—or swim in lovely Dream Lake. Enjoy horseback riding or fly-fishing. The weary peregrinator might also want to be pampered with a therapeutic massage.

Before Euro-Americans first explored Warner Valley, it was part of the territory claimed by the Mountain Maidu, one of four tribes—including the Yahi, Yana, and Atsugewi—who spent summers in the park. They enjoyed a diverse diet of fish, game, seeds, nuts, and roots. Like rice in many Asian cultures, the acorn was the central and pervasive food for the Indians of Lassen. Living in small tribes, the village or group of small villages acted as a self-governing unit. Warfare was unusual, brief, and measured. Cool-headed chiefs would quickly negotiate the end of hostilities, and peace would return.

The Yana and Yahi's territory spread from Lassen Peak west to just above California's Central Valley. It is a rugged, mountainous land with dense forests and steep river canyons. The tribes probably lived in California for 3,000–4,000 years and settled in their Lassen-area home more than 1,000 years ago. Their population never exceeded 2,000–3,000. To get a sense of their territory, drive CA 32 between the park and Chico along Deer Creek. It is still almost impenetrable, a land of steep woods cut by raging rivers. The population of the Yana and Yahi territory may be no more dense today than it was in 1850.

They lived in small villages, each family with a conical lodge 10 feet high and 20 feet around. The exterior of each lodge was overlaid with slabs of pine or cedar bark, and the interior floors and walls were lined with mats made of tule reeds. At the center was a fire pit for cooking and warmth. They were cozy dwellings in a land where the climate can be harsh. In the hottest months of summer, the Yana and Yahi moved up the slopes of Lassen Peak. They called the mountain Wagaupa, or Little Shasta.

Unlike California's coastal Indians, who were decimated by the missions, the Indians of Lassen were relatively untouched by Spanish and Mexican rule. But after 1848, when gold was discovered and the Treaty of Guadalupe Hidalgo ceded California from Mexico to the United States, gold seekers flooded the state, and the Yana and Yahi people were plagued by Euro-American diseases for which they had no immunity—smallpox, tuberculosis, malaria, and dysentery. The concept of private property disrupted their way of life and livelihood, leading to conflicts with settlers. Wanting to protect their property and lives, the newcomers sent raiding parties to exterminate the Indians. They succeeded, and by 1865 the Yana were eliminated.

Between 1865 and 1867 armed raiding parties attacked Yahi villages along Mill Creek and murdered all but a handful, who then went into hiding. Rumors of a small band of Yahi living in the rugged forests along Deer Creek persisted for years. In 1908 a surveying party came across a hidden Yahi camp. The occupants melted back into the forest, and the surveyors took all their tools, blankets, and other implements as souvenirs. The next day, feeling remorseful, they returned to the camp to try to make some restitution, but the Indians had fled, now trying to live in a shrinking land without their means of subsistence.

In 1911 the last surviving Yahi, named Ishi, came out of the mountains to a slaughterhouse near Oroville. He was naked and starving. The sheriff, not knowing what to do with this man from another world, locked him in jail. To the sheriff's relief, Professor T. T. Waterman, an anthropologist from the University of California, visited Ishi and made a connection using words of the Yahi's closest relatives, the Nozi Indians. Waterman brought Ishi back to the university's museum, where he lived until his death from tuberculosis in 1916. The final member of the Yahi tribe had perished. Theodora Kroeber's wonderful book, *Ishi in Two Worlds*, recounts the life of the Yahi and of Ishi, a man of great dignity, curiosity, and wisdom.

Day 2: Warner Valley to Bumpass Hell

LEAVING DRAKESBAD GUEST RANCH, return to the Warner Valley Campground and the PCT. The trail climbs out of the valley, and in another mile, you reach a junction where you take the left fork leaving the PCT. The trail ascends gradually along the northern rim of Hot Springs Creek Canyon. Pass Bench Lake at 3.1 miles, a shallow basin that forms a 4-foot-deep pond in the spring. When we hiked by in September, the lake was completely dry, a dusty bowl adorned with balanced rock art, awaiting the winter snows.

After a short climb, the trail drops into the Kings Creek watershed. The forest becomes dense as you descend, and the roar of Kings Creek Falls (6,900') climbs to greet you. Cross the creek on a log bridge, and turn downstream a short distance to the overlook of the spectacular falls where Kings Creek drops 50 feet, crashing over a natural rocky staircase.

The trail follows the creek upstream 1.2 miles to Kings Creek meadows and the park road. When it forks with an equestrian trail to the right, take the left fork, which climbs a narrow gorge where the creek plunges, cascading over narrow stairsteps. At the top of the cascades, you stroll through an enchanting alpine plateau forested with red fir and lodgepole pines.

Cross the park road and enter Upper Meadow. Kings Creek meanders quietly through the grassy meadow, and to the northwest, massive Lassen Peak towers above.

Few people had visited what is now Lassen Volcanic National Park before May 30, 1914, when, after a 27,000-year slumber, the quiet volcano suddenly erupted, sending a cloud of smoke and steam high into the sky. Tourists, scientists, and reporters came to watch occasional volcanic bursts and to climb the mountain to the newly formed crater.

Ten more eruptions led up to the great blasts of May 1915. The mountain blew on May 19, and great rivers of lava poured down its west and northeast flanks, melting snow and creating a pyroclastic flow—a raging mile-wide flood of ash, water, and mud—that crashed into Lost and Hat Creeks. The muddy torrent picked up 20-ton boulders and swept them down the mountain.

The most powerful eruption occurred on May 22, sending a mushroom cloud soaring 30,000 feet into the sky and spewing ash as far as Winnemucca, Nevada, 200 miles away. A horizontal blast blew off the face of the mountain and sent a shock wave that uprooted forests and snapped trees as if they were matchsticks.

Benjamin F. Loomis photographed the eruption and its aftermath. His photos can be viewed in the Loomis Museum at Manzanita Lake. He described the May 22 blast:

The eruption came on gradually at first getting larger and larger until finally it broke out in a roar like thunder; the smoke cloud was hurled with tremendous velocity many miles high, and rocks thrown from the crater were seen to fly way below the timber line before they struck the ground.

Bumpass Hell—fumaroles, boiling springs, and bubbling mud pots

Eruptions then tapered off until they stopped in 1917. The next eruption in the Cascades, that of Mount St. Helens, wouldn't happen until more than 60 years later. Lassen's fiery blasts sparked the public's imagination, and in 1916 President Woodrow Wilson signed legislation declaring Lassen a national park.

There is no formal trail through Upper Meadow, but hike up the north side of the road until you see the entrance to the Kings Creek picnic area. Cross the road and hike through the picnic area to the trailhead to Bumpass Hell. The trail from Kings Creek picnic area to the Bumpass Hell parking lot provides some of the most spectacular vistas in the park. You pass through forests of lodgepole pine, mountain hemlock, and ponderosa pine. Fields of lupine and other wildflowers abound through mid-July. The trail swings by Cold Boiling Lake, a pretty mountain pond in a grassy knoll, where cold gasses bubble up through the earth. As it climbs, beautiful views open to the south. Crumbaugh Lake lies below, deep in a valley surrounded by lush meadows. In the distance stand Saddle Mountain, Mount Harkness, the north rim of Warner Valley, Lake Amador, and a succession of ridges stretching to the horizon.

After hiking 2.8 miles from the Kings Creek picnic area, you arrive at Bumpass Hell, a thermal wonderland of fumaroles, boiling springs, and bubbling mud pots. A boardwalk takes visitors through this eerie landscape, the largest hot spot in the park. The same magma that caused the eruptions of Lassen Peak in 1915 still superheats water reservoirs 3 miles deep in the earth. Steam works its way to the surface at Bumpass Hell as well as at Devils Kitchen, Boiling Springs Lake, and Thermal Geyser a dozen miles southeast. John Muir wrote in *The Mountains of California*:

> *Lassen's Butte is the highest, being nearly 11,000 ft. above sea-level. Miles of its flanks are reeking and bubbling with hot springs, many of them so boisterous and sulphurous they seem ever ready to become spouting geysers like those of the Yellowstone.*

Kendal Van Hook Bumpass, a cowboy, explored this area in 1864 and filed a claim for the mineral rights, also hoping to turn it into a tourist attraction. While venturing too close to a mud pot, his foot broke through the thin crust, and his leg plunged into boiling mud. He managed to recover, and a newspaper reporter talked him into returning to the site of the accident. Lightning struck twice—Bumpass made another false step, crashing through the eroded crust into 240°F boiling mud. This time the leg could not be saved and had to be amputated. Despite rumors to the contrary, there is no historical record that our hero was henceforth known as Stumpy Bumpass.

The final leg of the trail climbs to 8,400 feet, the highest point on this walkabout. While dropping down to the parking lot, you pass Lake Helen, with magnificent Lassen Peak in the background. Stop here for a moment before climbing into your car; breathe the crisp mountain air, and savor your exploration of one of America's most spectacular and least-visited national parks.

SUMMIT LAKE LOOP VIA WARNER VALLEY

Day 1: Summit Lake to Warner Valley

THE SECOND WALKABOUT is a 19.7-mile loop with two hiking days and requires only one car (see Transportation, page 106, for driving and parking directions). This walkabout starts and ends at lovely Summit Lake, perched at 7,000 feet in the shadow of massive Lassen Peak. The hike wanders through the park's central region past crystalline lakes and along mountain streams, with a stopover at Drakesbad Guest Ranch, where you can enjoy a soak in the hot springs and civilized comforts in a rustic setting.

Leave your car in the overnight parking area near the Summit Lake ranger station, and follow the trail to the northeast corner of the lake. Hiking along the eastern side of the lake, you reach a junction. Take the left trail toward Echo Lake. You'll return on the trail to the right.

On a calm day, stop to enjoy the view of 10,457-foot, snowcapped Lassen Peak reflected in the sparkling waters of Summit Lake. The massive volcano is resting since its last eruption a century ago. (See page 90 for more on Lassen Peak.)

The trail climbs for a mile until the turnoff to Bear Lakes. Don't forget to look behind you—inspiring views of the mountain open up on this stretch. A short distance beyond this junction, the trail descends to Echo Lake. Wildflowers flourish along its shoreline in the early season.

After climbing out of the Echo Lake basin, the trail continues to descend past tiny ponds to Upper Twin Lake. Follow the trail along the north shore of Upper Twin Lake. The trail divides as you approach Lower Twin Lake. Take the right fork along the south shore of Lower Twin Lake to the PCT.

Heading south on the PCT, you pass through several sections where fires have scarred the forest. The trail is marked with bear scat and deer tracks. Lassen is one of the most lightly used national parks, averaging fewer than 500,000 visitors a year. Very few stray far from Lassen Park Road (CA 89). Only backpackers and a few day-trippers hike this far east. You may have this section of the trail all to yourself.

The PCT turns southwest and descends through Grassy Swale along a meandering brook. The forest becomes lush, and boardwalks span marshy sections of the

Summit Lake and Lassen Peak

trail. Cross the brook and then Kings Creek at the Corral Meadow junction. Follow the signs south toward Warner Valley. The trail climbs 500 feet through a series of switchbacks until it reaches the crest overlooking Warner Valley and Drakesbad Guest Ranch. Descend the steep trail into Warner Valley Campground, turn right, and walk up the road a short distance to Drakesbad (see page 96 for a description of Drakesbad and the area's history).

Day 2: Warner Valley to Summit Lake

LEAVING DRAKESBAD GUEST RANCH, return to the Warner Valley Campground and the PCT. The trail climbs out of the valley, and in another mile you reach a junction where you take the left fork leaving the PCT. The trail ascends gradually along the northern rim of Hot Springs Creek Canyon. You pass Bench Lake at 2.8 miles, a shallow basin that forms a 4-foot-deep lake in the spring. When we hiked by in September, the lake was completely dry, a dusty bowl adorned with balanced rock art, awaiting the winter snows.

After a short climb, the trail drops into the Kings Creek watershed. The forest becomes dense as you descend, and the roar of Kings Creek Falls (6,900') climbs to greet you. Cross the creek on a log bridge, and turn downstream a short distance to the overlook of the spectacular falls where Kings Creek drops 50 feet, crashing over a rocky natural staircase.

At Kings Creek Falls, follow the signs toward Corral Meadow. The Kings Creek Trail follows the creek drainage on its north side, gradually descending over the course of 2 miles to the junction of the trail to Summit Lake near the confluence of Kings and Summit Creeks. The trail to Summit Lake ascends through verdant meadows and crosses several spring-fed streams that flow into Kings Creek. You emerge into Summit Lake's south campground. Walk to the lake and follow the trail around the east shore past the north campground to your car.

You may want to stop for one final rest on the eastern shore of Summit Lake to take in the awesome grandeur of Lassen Peak and its reflection in the crystal-clear waters. The giant rests while, deep in the earth's bowels, molten lava boils, straining to rise to the surface, erupt, and reshape the mountain once again. What better way to explore this ever-changing and enchanting land than a walkabout with a good friend?

THE ROUTES

All mileages listed for a given day are cumulative.

BUTTE LAKE TO BUMPASS HELL

The first trek explores the park from its northeast corner to its southwest corner and requires two cars, one parked at the Bumpass Hell parking lot and the other at Butte Lake. These directions describe the route starting at Butte Lake and ending at the Bumpass Hell parking lot, but you may want to hike it in reverse.

Day 1: Butte Lake to Warner Valley

See Transportation (page 106) for driving directions. Signage on the park's trails is generally excellent.

Hike Nobles Emigrant Trail from the western tip of Butte Lake to Cinder Cone. **1.2 miles**

Continue to Rainbow Lake. **4.4 miles**

Hike to Lower Twin Lake and the PCT. **5.2 miles**

Turn left and take the PCT to Swan Lake. **5.7 miles**

Hike to Corral Meadow Junction along Grassy Swale. **10.1 miles**

Continue on the PCT to Warner Valley and Drakesbad Guest Ranch. Leave the PCT at the Warner Valley Campground, turn right, and continue on the park road 0.5 mile until it ends at Drakesbad.

total miles 12.5

Day 2: Warner Valley to Bumpass Hell

Return to the Warner Valley Campground. Pick up the PCT next to site 7 and ascend out of Warner Valley to the junction of the trail to Kings Creek Falls.   **1.5 miles**

Take the left fork, leaving the PCT, to Bench Lake.   **3.1 miles**

Continue to Kings Creek Falls.   **4.1 miles**

Follow the trail upstream. The trail divides into an equestrian trail to the right and the hiking trail along the cascading creek to the left. Follow the trail to Upper Meadow.   **5.2 miles**

Ramble through the meadow on the north side of the road to Kings Creek picnic area.   **6.2 miles**

Find the trailhead to Bumpass Hell at the picnic area parking lot. Hike to Bumpass Hell.   **8.9 miles**

Continue to Bumpass Hell parking lot.

total miles 10.1

SUMMIT LAKE LOOP VIA WARNER VALLEY

The second trek explores the central park, a mountainous land of forests, lakes, and streams. A 19.4-mile loop, it starts and ends at Summit Lake with a stopover at Drakesbad Guest Ranch.

Day 1: Summit Lake to Warner Valley

See Transportation (page 106) for driving directions. Hike the boardwalk from the ranger station parking area to the northeast corner of Summit Lake. Follow the trail on the east side of the lake to the junction. Signage on the park's trails is generally excellent.

Turn left on the trail to Echo Lake and Twin Lakes. Hike from Summit Lake to Echo Lake.   **2.1 miles**

Continue to Upper Twin Lake.   **3.3 miles**

Follow the trail along the north shore of Upper Twin Lake to the southwest end of Lower Twin Lake. Take the right fork of the trail around the south shore of Lower Twin Lake to the PCT.   **4.2 miles**

Turn south on the PCT to Swan Lake.   **4.7 miles**

Continue to the Corral Meadow junction along Grassy Swale.   **8.7 miles**

Continue on the PCT to Warner Valley and Drakesbad Guest Ranch. Leave the PCT at the Warner Valley Campground, turn right on the park road, and continue 0.5 mile until it ends at Drakesbad.

total miles 11.1

Day 2: Warner Valley to Summit Lake

Return to the Warner Valley Campground. Pick up the PCT next to site 7, and ascend out of Warner Valley to the junction of the trail to Kings Creek Falls.   **1.5 miles**

Take the left fork, leaving the PCT, to Bench Lake.   **3.1 miles**

Continue to Kings Creek Falls.   **4.1 miles**

Follow the signs toward Corral Meadow, hiking downstream on Kings Creek Trail to the trail junction to Summit Lake.   **6.1 miles**

The junction to Summit Lake is near the confluence of Kings and Summit Creeks. Turn left and ascend to the Summit Lake South Campground. The trail enters the camp between sites E10 and E11. Hike through the campground in a northerly direction toward Summit Lake. Find the trail between sites C8 and C9. Follow the signs to the amphitheater around the east side of the lake. Follow the trail and boardwalk to the ranger station, the overnight parking area, and your car.

total miles 8.6

TRANSPORTATION

Public Transportation

UNFORTUNATELY, THERE IS NO PUBLIC TRANSPORTATION to Lassen Volcanic National Park. A Greyhound bus goes from Reno to Susanville three times a week, but a taxi ride to and from the park is prohibitively expensive. It would be much less expensive to rent a car.

Driving Directions: Butte Lake to Bumpass Hell

THIS WALKABOUT REQUIRES TWO CARS, one parked at the Bumpass Hell parking area and the other at Butte Lake. The walkabout can be made in either direction. CA 89 winds through the park's western half. The Bumpass Hell parking lot is 6.4 miles north of the southwest entrance station. After parking one car, drive north on CA 89 through the park, exiting its northwest corner. Continue on CA 89 to CA 44, and turn east. Eleven miles from the junction of CA 89 and

CA 44, turn south on Forest Service Road 32N21. Look for the sign to Butte Lake. Drive several miles on the well-graded gravel road, and proceed through the campground to the end of the road at the northwest end of the lake, where you will find the trailhead.

Driving Directions: Summit Lake Loop via Warner Valley

SUMMIT LAKE IS 17.5 MILES NORTH of the southwest entrance to the park on CA 89 and 12 miles south of the northwest entrance. To park overnight, drive 0.3 mile north of the entrance to the North Summit Lake Campground. Turn right toward the ranger station to the parking area at the end of the road.

MAPS

THE LASSEN VOLCANIC NATIONAL PARK WEBSITE (nps.gov/lavo) provides a free downloadable map that is also available at the park entrance. Wilderness Press's *Lassen Volcanic National Park* ($7.46) covers the park plus Bucks Lake, Caribou, and Thousand Lakes Wilderness. Visit wildernesspress.com to order.

The U.S. Geological Survey sells topographical hiking maps and provides free downloadable maps at store.usgs.gov, and go to the map locator. For Butte Lake to Bumpass Hell, you'll need *Prospect Peak* (Butte Lake area), *Mount Harkness* (Twin Lakes area), and *Reading Peak* (Warner Valley and west). For Summit Lake Loop via Warner Valley, you'll need *Reading Peak*.

PLACES TO STAY

LODGING COST			
$ *less than $100*	$$ *$100–$150*	$$$ *$150–$200*	$$$$ *more than $200*

DRAKESBAD GUEST RANCH $$$–$$$$ • End of Warner Valley Road • 17 miles outside Chester • 866-999-0914 (reservations) • 530-529-1512 • drakesbad.com • Three meals included. Hot-springs pool, horse rides, fly-fishing, and massage.

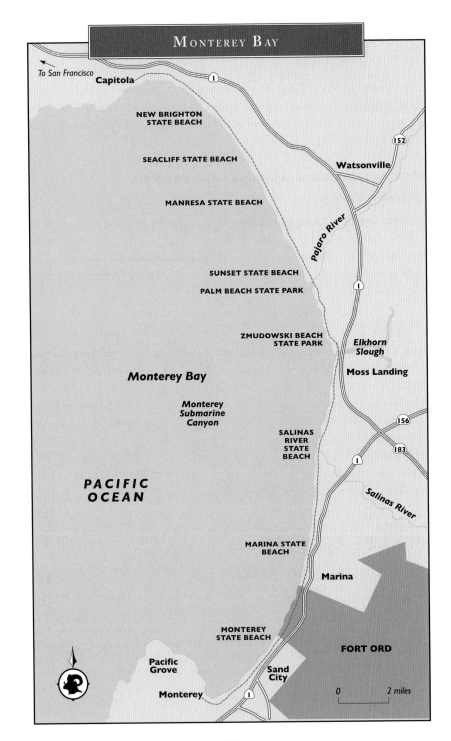

MONTEREY BAY

To San Francisco

Capitola

1

NEW BRIGHTON
STATE BEACH

SEACLIFF STATE BEACH

MANRESA STATE BEACH

152

Watsonville

Pajaro River

SUNSET STATE BEACH

PALM BEACH STATE PARK

1

ZMUDOWSKI BEACH
STATE PARK

Elkhorn
Slough

Moss Landing

Monterey Bay

Monterey
Submarine
Canyon

SALINAS
RIVER
STATE
BEACH

156

183

1

PACIFIC
OCEAN

Salinas River

MARINA STATE
BEACH

Marina

MONTEREY
STATE BEACH

FORT ORD

Pacific
Grove

Sand
City

0   2 miles

Monterey

1

Walkabout the Monterey Bay

Everybody needs beauty as well as bread, places to play in and pray in, where nature may heal and give strength to body and soul alike.

—JOHN MUIR, *The Yosemite*

New Brighton State Beach

There is more to life than increasing its speed.
—MOHANDAS K. GANDHI

WHO HAS STOOD ON A BEACH that stretches all the way to the horizon and not felt a primal longing to walk, perhaps all day, to see how far it goes, to explore that region where sea meets shore? Satisfy that yearning on this 37-mile, four-day hike on the edge of Monterey Bay. The protected waters of Monterey Bay National Marine Sanctuary teem with ocean and bird life. You'll hike pristine beaches and have miles all to yourself. Enjoy unique inns and great dining. Stop for an extra day in Moss Landing and kayak in Elkhorn Slough for some of the most spectacular wildlife viewing on California's coast. You may want to hike only part of this trek or break it into two two-day journeys. It is easy to return to Capitola at the end of any day along the route. Enjoy the great beauty and power of the Pacific by hiking its shoreline along Monterey Bay.

ITINERARY

DAY 1:	Capitola to Manresa State Beach	**8.7**
DAY 2:	Manresa State Beach to Moss Landing	**12.1**
DAY 3:	Moss Landing to Marina	**7.3**
DAY 4:	Marina to Monterey	**9.0**
TOTAL MILEAGE		**37.1**

ON A CLEAR DAY FROM THE BLUFFS above New Brighton State Beach, you can see the shoreline of Monterey Bay as it arcs south all the way to the hills of the Monterey Peninsula. It beckons you to take a long stroll.

Begin this adventure just north of New Brighton in the tourist-friendly village of Capitola. Stay at a coastal inn and enjoy Capitola's restaurants, taverns, music, and dancing. My wife, Heidi, and I stayed right in the heart of the nightlife district at the charming Capitola Hotel, which I recommend with one minor reservation. After an evening of good food and live music, we settled into bed. Heidi used the earplugs that the hotel provided, thinking they may have been put there for a reason.

I passed, but soon regretted it when I was jolted awake by loud snippets of songs every time the doors swung open from the karaoke bar across the street—first "Feelings," then "Great Balls of Fire," then "My Way." I searched for the earplugs in the dark with no luck while Heidi slept contentedly. Finally I fell into a sound sleep after last call, only to be awakened at 5 a.m. by what sounded like a

Sunset at Manresa State Beach

fleet of garbage trucks emptying dumpsters filled with bottles. The garbage men had to shout to be heard above the din. I gave up on sleep and read until Heidi awoke, well rested and ready to hike.

Day 1: Capitola to Manresa State Beach

TO START THE HIKE, choose between two routes. If the tide is very low, a passage opens, heading south below the rocky cliffs of Capitola. Otherwise, walk inland a short distance and hike 0.5 mile on a trail along the railroad tracks to the cliffs above New Brighton State Beach (see The Route, page 120, for detailed directions).

We hiked the first half of this trip, from Capitola to Moss Landing, in October and came back in the spring to finish the trek to Monterey. The fall brings an extraordinary abundance of wildlife to Monterey Bay. On our first morning, under low clouds, hundreds of California brown pelicans dotted the placid, steel-blue waters. Prehistoric in appearance, with ancestors reaching back 30 million years, one rises with a slow, powerful sweep of wings spanning 6.5 feet. The first flap splashes, the second kisses the water. She makes a sudden, arching ascent of about 3 feet, then plunges down, wings snapped back, mouth wide open, spearing the smooth waters. Floating to the surface, she throws back her head, shakes, and gulps down her breakfast.

This scene entertained us all morning as thousands of birds feasted in the protected waters of Monterey Bay National Marine Sanctuary. Established in 1992 to prevent offshore oil drilling, it covers 6,094 square miles, reaching 50 miles offshore, with 276 miles of coastline stretching from the Marin Headlands, just north of San Francisco, to Cambria, south of Big Sur. Thirty-four species of marine mammals ply these waters—humpback, blue, gray, sperm, and finback whales; seals; sea lions; porpoises; and sea otters. Ninety-four species of seabirds visit the sanctuary, and many were on hand to delight us. Marbled godwits, curlews, and willets with long, skinny beaks roamed the shore on tall, spindly legs, probing the bubbling sand behind receding waves for small mollusks and crustaceans. Groups of comical, tiny sanderlings scurried to the water's edge to pick up a morsel before racing inland to avoid the next surge. Gulls, cormorants, egrets, herons, and coots joined the party.

The tide was high when we started. The sand along the ocean's edge was soft and the walking slow. Then the tide turned and a 100-foot-wide walkway of flat, firm sand opened, a perfect surface for beach hiking. The hours before and after low tide are usually the best for finding a firm surface. Check out tide schedules at tidesandcurrents.noaa.gov/tide_predictions.

State park beaches New Brighton, Seacliff, and Manresa protect long sections of the forested coastal dunes from development and offer campgrounds. Outside the parks, houses line the beach for the first few hours of the walk. Then human structures become intermittent and steep bluffs rise a few hundred feet, cutting off any view of the rich agricultural fields to the east. Beachgoers seldom wander far from state park access. A few hours south of New Brighton, you have this enchanted coastal Eden to yourself.

Hiking along Seacliff State Beach, you will come to the extraordinary cement ship, Palo Alto. This 400-foot vessel was built in 1919, after World War I, when steel was precious, so, it was made of concrete. But it was never launched.

Towed to Seacliff and grounded, it functioned as an amusement park, dance hall, and restaurant in the 1930s. As time passed, it served as an artificial reef and fishing pier. Then a violent storm with 34-foot waves struck in January 2017, tearing off a 50-foot section and toppling it on its side. Now, the cement ship rests in pieces just offshore. There are no B&Bs or inns along the stretch of beach between Capitola and Moss Landing, but there are two interesting lodging options. The KOA, just east of Manresa Beach (8.7 miles from Capitola), offers cabins and Airstream trailers. Their deluxe cabins and trailers come with bedding and kitchens, and a small store offers limited options for dining: hot dogs, burritos, breakfast cereals. You may want to drop off food in advance.

For a more luxurious option, choose Pajaro Dunes (at 12 miles), and book a condominium. It has no restaurant, so you will need to drop off a cache of food or carry in your meals. For more about lodgings and contact information, see page 124.

We chose the KOA. About 0.7 mile south of the Manresa Beach parking lot, you will pass a row of town houses just above the beach. Continue another 0.5 mile, where you will see a sign at the top of the beach and a paved path. Climb the path, pass through the campground to its exit, and walk east on Sand Dollar

Drive, a pretty country lane passing through fields of lettuce and flowers. Turn right on San Andreas Road for a short distance to the KOA. It is a kid's paradise, with a playground, swimming pool, and miniature golf course. The night we stayed, RVs and tents crowded in, and kids ran in packs. After dark, families gathered around fires before bed, and it had the feel of a modern gypsy encampment.

Day 2: Manresa State Beach to Moss Landing

SIX-FOOT WAVES GREETED US the second day of hiking, and surfers joined the other sea creatures near the state beach access points. Schools of porpoises glided north just beyond the surf line. Harbor seals hunted offshore and stopped to stare at us walking on the long stretches of empty beaches between parks. They seemed to say, "We don't see your strange species in these parts very often." In the late fall, gray whales can be spotted migrating south, spouting far out to sea. They return in late winter and early spring for the journey north with their calves, this time much closer to shore.

With rougher seas, the pelicans change their hunting strategy. Flying high in long skeins, they spot a school of fish. One after another they dive from 20 feet with beaks closed, grabbing their prey well below the surface. Cranial air sacks

Sea lions crowd the wharf in Moss Landing Harbor.

Pelicans take a rest in Elkhorn Slough.

protect their heads from the violent collision. Gulls swarm in to grab any scraps, and a feeding frenzy commences.

Hike along the shore of the wild Pacific for two days, and nature's powerful life force fills the senses—the sound of crashing waves, the smell of the salty sea air, the cool breeze on your skin, a circus of flying and swimming creatures to delight the eyes. This home of the Ohlone people before the arrival of Europeans was described as a land of amazing abundance. Great herds of deer, elk, and pronghorn grazed the coastal hills. Migrating ducks and geese flew in such numbers that they were reported to blacken the sky. In the fall and winter, steelhead trout and coho salmon spawned in the crowded streams. The sea provided seals, sea otters, shellfish, and massive runs of smelt. Acorns, pine nuts, greens, berries, wild roots, bulbs, and seeds rounded out the rich diet.

Shamans from the coastal villages danced and sang, summoning whales to the shore. The discovery of a beached whale produced a flurry of activity. The people needed to claim this prize before the grizzly bears could congregate and devour it. Blubber was stored in woven baskets. Strips of meat were hung high in branches to dry, out of reach of the grizzlies.

Before the Europeans came, Central California was the most densely populated region north of Mexico. More than 10,000 people were estimated to live along the coast between San Francisco Bay and Big Sur. Living in small tribelets, each with its own defined territory, the Ohlone developed a rich culture of mutual support, moderation, artistic basket making, and a spirituality deeply connected to the land. Warfare was rare and brief. In *The Ohlone Way*, Malcolm Margolin describes their way of life:

Beyond doubt the Ohlones had been settled for an extremely long time before the arrival of Europeans, and it was during these many centuries that they achieved something quite rare in human history: a way of life that gave them relative peace and stability, not just for a generation or two, not just for a century, but probably for thousands of years.

The first encounter with Europeans came in 1769 when Captain Gaspar de Portolá, Spanish governor of Las Californias, led a Sacred Expedition of 62 soldiers, priests, and Indian servants, along with 200 horses and mules from Baja to Monterey Bay. Word spread in advance of their arrival, but the Indians were still stunned by the sight of men with fair skin and strange-colored eyes, dressed in long robes and armor, astride extraordinary beasts. Having suffered from bad weather, hunger, and scurvy, the Portolá party was greeted by Ohlone bringing gifts of fresh meat, fish, and seed cakes. In return, the Spanish gave wonderful gifts of beads and cloth. The Ohlone could tell these strangers were powerful and magical. Margolin explains:

Eventually the Ohlones reached a conclusion, which in later years they told to the missionaries. They believed at the beginning that the Europeans were the children of the Mule—a new, very powerful animal-god who had created the Europeans (just as Coyote had created the Ohlones) and had blessed them with stupendous magical powers.

Portolá's party continued north and became the first Europeans to see San Francisco Bay. After traveling back to Southern California, Portolá returned the next year to establish the presidio at Monterey, and the lives of the Ohlone people would forever change.

Six miles south of Manresa Beach, after Sunset State Beach and Palm Beach, you reach the Pajaro River, the border between Santa Cruz and Monterey Counties. The Pajaro Dunes condominiums lie just north. The Pajaro flows swift and deep as it approaches the sea and then fans out at its mouth to form a shifting sandbar. You can usually wade across at low tide during the summer and fall (see The Route, page 120, for directions if the river is too deep to ford). Hundreds of pelicans and gulls gather at the river's mouth. We rested and ate lunch, watching the avian theatrics and letting the tide recede. At low tide we waded across through knee-deep water and continued our stroll past Zmudowski and Moss Landing State Beaches to the mouth of the Moss Landing Harbor. Walk on Jetty Road along the north arm of the harbor to CA 1, and stroll south on the shoulder into Moss Landing.

You are entering one of the best spots for wildlife viewing on America's west coast. Outside the harbor lies the Monterey Submarine Canyon, a chasm that plunges almost 2 miles and rivals the Grand Canyon in size. Great white sharks and giant squid inhabit its depths. Upwelling currents from deep in the canyon bring nutrients to the surface each spring that kick-start the aquatic food chain, creating the bay's rich environment. Inland to the east spreads Elkhorn Slough—2,500 acres of marshlands and tidal flats, home to 400 species of invertebrates and 80 species of fish, and positioned along the Pacific Flyway. About 200 species of birds visit the slough or call it home.

You may want to stop at the Sea Harvest Fish Market and Restaurant for beer and oysters and to watch the seals that gather in the harbor. Ornery sea lions crowd the public wharf bellowing and arguing. A few dozen sea otters usually hang out sunning and floating on their backs, preening and playing. Periodically one dives and swims madly just under a lounging flotilla of back floaters, disrupting everyone. Others break off to chase the joker. Then everyone settles down for a good rest, floating on their backs with their back flippers sticking out of the water and their front paws, looking like furry mittens, folded across their chests. They have the appearance of guys who have permanently taken to the hammocks.

Moss Landing is worth a stopover for a day or two. Settle into Captain's Inn at Moss Landing, and enjoy the excellent seafood eateries. Our bed was perched high on top of a rowboat. A step was provided to climb up, and from our bed we watched birds feeding in the tidal flats outside our window.

Take a break from hiking and explore the slough by kayak. Rent a craft from Kayak Connection or Monterey Bay Kayaks, both located in the harbor. They will equip you, give you a quick lesson, and help you launch. Paddle along the 7-mile main channel, or explore side channels. But pay attention to the tides: if you can time your journey to go into the slough with the incoming tide and return to the harbor on the outgoing tide, the currents will do most of the work.

We paddled into the slough and entered a magical wildlife world. A dozen sea otters back-floated on the incoming tide, a stone's throw from our kayaks, some prying open clams on their chests. A pair started a playful tussle with a tumbling embrace. A group of harbor seals sunbathed on the mud flat. One slid into the shallow waters, raised his head to look at us, and darted under our boats. A skein of pelicans glided up the channel, almost caressing the surface. Shorebirds grazed at the water's edge, and hundreds of cormorants, egrets, herons, gulls, grebes, and murres graced the waters and skies. Red-shouldered hawks circled high above it all. Wildlife viewing in Elkhorn Slough is good any time of year. The peak season starts in mid-November, but by early October it was already spectacular. The

Elkhorn Slough Safari offers another way to explore the backwaters, with a 2-hour pontoon boat excursion.

Day 3: Moss Landing to Marina

LEAVING MOSS LANDING on the third hiking day, walk a short distance on Sandholdt Road along the harbor, past pleasure boats and the fishing fleet, to the beach. The sand can be soft on this stretch, but by paying attention to the tides, you will find mostly firm footing. Sand dunes grow larger as you head south on Salinas River State Beach. Occasionally the beach becomes narrow and steep, and hiking is harder in the soft sand. At 4 miles you come to the Salinas River. Prior to 1909 it reached the sea at Moss Landing, but to control flooding and to claim farmland from the lush riverbed, engineers dug a channel through the sand dunes to the Pacific. During the winter, the Salinas River flows freely to the sea. In the summer months, a sandbar forms to block the river's exit. In April, after a dry winter, there was no need to get our feet wet. We might have missed the Salinas altogether if we hadn't climbed the beach and looked over the dunes that block the river's egress to see its deep-blue waters winding back through fertile farmland to the green coastal hills.

South of the river, a grounded barge rusts away in the surf, covered in seaweed and barnacles. The dunes are protected by the Salinas River National Wildlife Refuge, and a small rope line stops hikers from entering the dunes, protecting the nesting grounds of the endangered snowy plover. Few people venture onto the

Miles of untrampled beach

beach between Moss Landing and Marina. It is a joy to let your pace slow and to relish the beauty and solitude along this leg of the journey.

Monterey Bay was first sighted by Juan Cabrillo when he sailed past in 1542. Three ships explored the coast in 1603, led by Sebastian Vizcaíno, who mapped the bay and gave it its name. But it was not until 1770 that Mission Carmel was established by Father Junipero Serra, president of the California missions, and Monterey became the capital of Spanish California.

Jean-François de La Pérouse, who led a French expedition that visited Monterey in 1786, described the richness of the soil, the bounty of crops, and the abundance of game. Of the harbor he wrote, "It is impossible to describe either the number of whales with which we were surrounded, or their familiarity. They spout every half minute within half a pistol shot of our frigates, and caused a most annoying stench."

The southern shore of Monterey Bay was the home of around 400 Rumsen, one of the main peoples of the Ohlone. Their religion and way of life were held in contempt by the powerful newcomers. With no immunity to European diseases—smallpox, influenza, measles—they perished in droves. Families and villages were decimated, and survivors from this deeply interdependent society were left without their natural support systems. Many gravitated to the mission, where they were imprisoned, forced to labor in the fields, and made to pray in Latin. La Pérouse described the treatment of the American Indians by the missionaries this way:

> [It] brought to our recollection a plantation at Santo Domingo or any other West Indian island. The men and women are collected by the sound of a bell; a missionary leads them to work, to the church, and to all their exercises. We observed with concern that the resemblance is so perfect that we have seen both men and women in irons, and others in the stocks. Lastly, the noise of the whip might have struck our ears, this punishment also being administered, though with little severity.

As you hike this pristine shoreline, it is easy to imagine the life of a people who lived for centuries in balance with nature along this bay.

South of Moss Landing 7.3 miles, look for rooftops and a chain-link fence on a high dune that signals your arrival in Marina, which has several inns. A short walk from the beach, Marina Dunes Resort offers a swimming pool, a spa, and rooms with fireplaces. The restaurant on the grounds, AJ Spurs, serves fire-roasted artichokes, perfect after a day of hiking on the beach. You can settle into this steakhouse or walk into town and try one of many restaurants. The English Ales Brewery is a friendly pub, and My Thai offers savory Thai cuisine.

Approaching Monterey

Day 4: Marina to Monterey

THE 9-MILE BEACH WALK FROM MARINA to the Monterey Municipal Wharf is a stretch of high dunes, steep beaches, and soft sand. The walk is slow, but the reward is miles of pristine Pacific shoreline all to yourself.

An alternative and easier route is the Monterey Peninsula Recreation Trail. A paved hiker/biker trail, it winds from Marina to Monterey through the sand dunes of the former Fort Ord Military Reservation. It goes through Marina between the main north–south street, Del Monte Boulevard, and the railroad tracks. Leaving the south end of town, it passes under the highway. At that point you can either stay on the narrow hiker/biker trail or go through a gate and take an abandoned military road south several miles. This route travels through the dunes, closer to the beach than the recreation trail, and farther from the sounds of CA 1. The old road ends, and you reunite with the recreation trail, pass El Estero Lake, and enter Monterey.

Unable to tear ourselves away from the wild beauty of the Pacific shoreline, we continued on the beach. The day started in glorious sunshine, but after a few miles, a light fog moved in, and the sea turned gray and churning. Flocks of cormorants floated beyond the 12-foot breakers. The only soul we saw on the 5.5-mile stretch from Marina to Sand City was a hang glider suspended comfortably beneath a bright-orange sail. We were hiking at a 2-miles-per-hour pace, and she must have been gliding at around 5. She sailed south, growing fainter and disappearing into the haze. Twenty minutes later she appeared out of the vapor heading north and waved as she passed 50 feet overhead. It looked so easy, like she could hang glide from inn to inn all the way to Cabo San Lucas.

The beach levels out and the hiking becomes easier south of Sand City. The Monterey Peninsula turns sharply northwest, forming the southern end of the bay. Approaching the city, the beach becomes busy with sunbathers, Frisbee players, and dog walkers—such a contrast to the solitude of a few miles north.

The beach ends at the municipal wharf, where a few restaurants await you for a relaxing lunch. The Monterey Bay Recreation Trail continues along the waterfront past Fisherman's Wharf, Cannery Row, and the Monterey Bay Aquarium, offering hotels, restaurants, and bars for grateful peregrinators. Most hotels sell same-day tickets to the extraordinary aquarium. Hiking the coast is a vivid education in the abundant shore life of the bay, and the aquarium opens a window to the bay's amazing underwater world. Enjoy the many delights of Monterey after a hike that few have ever done, hiking from inn to inn on glorious Monterey Bay.

THE ROUTE

All mileages listed for a given day are cumulative.

Day 1: Capitola to Manresa State Beach

Start the journey in Capitola's restaurant and nightlife district, where the Soquel Creek reaches the sea. If the tide is very low, a passage opens, heading south below the rocky cliffs of Capitola. Otherwise, walk inland on Monterey Avenue. Turn right on the trail adjacent to the railroad tracks, or walk on the wide shoulder of Park Avenue to New Brighton State Beach. Hike along the beach until you reach Manresa State Beach.

You can run into soft sand on this trek, which is great if you want to build up your quads. But the hours before and after low tide are usually best for finding a firm surface. For most of the first two hiking days of this trek, a 100-foot-wide walkway of flat, firm sand opens during those hours, a perfect surface for beach hiking. Check out tide schedules at tidesandcurrents.noaa.gov/tide_predictions.

Walk from Capitola to New Brighton State Beach. **0.9 mile**

Walk from New Brighton State Beach to Seacliff State Beach. **2.4 miles**

Continue to Manresa State Beach parking lot. **6.5 miles**

Look for a row of town houses 0.7 mile south of the Manresa Beach parking lot. Continue another 0.5 mile to a sign at the top of the beach and a paved path leading up to the bluffs. **7.7 miles**

Walk up the path and through the upper campground. Head east on the exit road, Sand Dollar Drive. This country lane passes through agricultural fields. Turn right on San Andreas Road and proceed a short distance to the Santa Cruz KOA.

total miles 8.7

Day 2: Manresa State Beach to Moss Landing

Start at the Santa Cruz KOA, and walk to Manresa State Beach.   **1.0 mile**

Walk from Manresa State Beach to Sunset State Beach.   **3.1 miles**

Continue to Palm Beach.   **6.4 miles**

Continue to the Pajaro River. The Pajaro forms a sandbar at its mouth, and you can usually wade across in the summer and fall at low tide. If the river is impassable, *Hiking the California Coastal Trail: Volume One* recommends, "from the Palm Beach access, follow Beach Road northeast. Then turn right and go south on Thurwachter Road. After crossing the river, Thurwachter continues as McGowan Road. Turn right and follow Trafton Road; then go left on Bluff Road, then left on Jensen Road to CA 1. Follow the highway shoulder about 1.5 miles south. Turn right and walk Struve Road to Gilberson Road, then go right on Gilberson to its end."   **7.4 miles**

Continue to Moss Landing. At the mouth of the harbor, follow its north shore on Jetty Road to CA 1. Stroll south on the shoulder into Moss Landing.

total miles 12.1

Day 3: Moss Landing to Marina

Leaving Moss Landing, walk along the southern edge of the harbor on Sandholdt Road to the beach. Continue to the Salinas River. You can usually wade across the Salinas River in the summer and fall. The river is often blocked from the sea by sand dunes, and you may not even see it. A rusting barge is grounded on the shore just south of the Salinas River's usual egress. If the river blocks your passage, return 1.1 miles to the Salinas River State Beach parking lot. Walk on Monterey Dunes Way, and turn right on Molera Road. Hike the shoulder of CA 1 across the river, and take the first right back to the beach   **4.0 miles**

Continue to Marina. Look for rooftops and a chain-link fence on a high dune that signals your arrival in Marina.

total miles 7.3

Day 4: Marina to Monterey

Walk from Marina to Sand City.   **5.4 miles**

Walk to Monterey Tides hotel.   **7.0 miles**

Walk to Monterey Municipal Wharf. The Monterey Bay Recreation Trail continues along the waterfront.

total miles 9.0

Alternate Route for Day 4

The beach on the final section of the hike has the softest sand. You may want to take the Monterey Bay Recreation Trail for an easier hike on a paved hiker/biker trail through coastal sand dunes. Pick up the trail in Marina between the main north–south street, Del Monte Boulevard, and the railroad tracks. Leaving the south end of town, it passes under the highway. At that point you can either stay on the narrow hiker/biker trail or go through a gate and take an abandoned military road south several miles. The road travels closer to the beach and farther from the highway than the recreation trail does. The road rejoins the Monterey Bay Recreation Trail, and you pass El Estero Lake and enter Monterey.

You can stay in an Airstream trailer at the Santa Cruz KOA campground.

TRANSPORTATION

Returning to Capitola from Monterey

MONTEREY SALINAS TRANSIT PROVIDES bus service between Monterey and Capitola, with stops along the way ($8). Routes vary depending on the day and time; for trip planning, go to mst.org. Amtrak also provides a combination bus and train service from Monterey to Santa Cruz ($35); visit amtrak.com for trip planning. Monterey, Salinas, and Santa Cruz all have taxi services. The fare from Monterey to Capitola should cost around $110. Your innkeeper can assist you with taxi options.

Public Transportation from the Bay Area

AMTRAK PROVIDES A COMBINATION train and bus service from its Oakland Coliseum Station to San Jose and then to the Santa Cruz Metro Center. The trip takes approximately 2 hours and costs $23; go to amtrak.com for schedules and to purchase tickets. You can reach the Oakland Coliseum Station by BART; go to 511.org to plan your trip to the Oakland Coliseum Station. The Amtrak station is a short walk from the BART station.

The Santa Cruz Metropolitan Transit District provides bus service from the Santa Cruz Metro Center to Capitola Village for $2; for schedules visit scmtd .com. You can also take a taxi from the Santa Cruz Metro Center to Capitola Village for around $18. Try Go Green Cab at 831-246-1234.

Flying into the Bay Area

IF YOU ARE PLANNING to take public transportation, flying into the Oakland Airport is more convenient than SFO. From the Oakland International Airport take the BART shuttle to the Oakland Coliseum BART Station ($1.95), and follow the public transportation directions above. From SFO, take BART to the Oakland Coliseum Station, and follow the public transportation directions above. The trip takes approximately 1 hour and costs $9.70. Go to bart.gov to plan your trip.

MAPS

THIS WALKABOUT HIKES THE SHORELINE of Monterey Bay. A road map of the region should be sufficient for identifying state beaches and coastal towns.

EXPLORING ELKHORN SLOUGH BY KAYAK AND BOAT

DURING POPULAR TIMES OF YEAR, it is best to make reservations. If possible, time your kayaking journey to paddle into the slough with the incoming tide and return to the harbor with the outgoing tide.

KAYAK CONNECTION
2370 CA 1, Moss Landing
831-724-5692
kayakconnection.com

MONTEREY BAY KAYAKS
2390 CA 1, Moss Landing
831-373-5357
montereybaykayaks.com

GUIDED PONTOON BOAT EXPLORATION
Elkhorn Slough Safari
7881 Sandholdt Road, Moss Landing
831-633-5555
elkhornslough.com

PLACES TO STAY

LODGING COST			
$ *less than $100*	$$ *$100–$150*	$$$ *$150–$200*	$$$$ *more than $200*

Capitola-by-the-Sea

CAPITOLA HOTEL $$$–$$$$ • 210 Esplanade • 831-476-1278 • capitolahotel.com

CAPITOLA VENETIAN HOTEL $$–$$$$ • 1500 Wharf Road • 831-476-6471 • 800-332-2780 • capitolavenetian.com

INN AT DEPOT HILL B&B $$$$ • 250 Monterey Ave. • 831-462-3376 • innatdepothill.com • Full breakfast.

MONARCH COVE INN $$–$$$$ • 620 El Salto Dr. • 831-464-1295 • monarchcoveinn.com • Breakfast included.

Between Capitola and Moss Landing

SANTA CRUZ KOA $$–$$$ • 1186 San Andreas Road • La Selva Beach • 8.7 miles south of Capitola • 831-722-0551 • 800-562-7701 • santacruzkoa.com for cabins • No restaurant, but a small store. Deluxe cabins and Airstream trailers come with bedding and kitchens.

PAJARO DUNES RESORT $$$$ • 101 Shell Dr. • Pajaro Dunes • 12.2 miles south of Capitola, just north of the Pajaro River • 800-564-1771 • pajarodunes.com • No restaurant; carry or drop off food. Two nights minimum.

Moss Landing

CAPTAIN'S INN AT MOSS LANDING $$$–$$$$ • 8122 Moss Landing Road • 831-633-5550 • captainsinn.com • Full breakfast. Great location on the slough. Bird-watch from your bed.

Capitola Hotel is in the heart of the nightlife district in tourist-friendly Capitola.

Marina

In addition to these lodging choices, Marina also has several motels.

SANCTUARY BEACH RESORT $$$–$$$$ • 3295 Dunes Dr. • 855-693-6583
• thesanctuarybeachresort.com

BEST WESTERN BEACH DUNES INN $–$$$ • 3290 Dunes Dr. • 831-883-0300
• bestwestern.com

Monterey

Of the many inns in Monterey, these are some that are along or near the waterfront.

HI MONTEREY HOSTEL $–$$$ • 778 Hawthorne St. • 831-649-0375 • hiusa.org
• Dorm beds or private rooms. • Great location. • Breakfast included.

MONTEREY BAY INN $$$$ • 242 Cannery Row • 831-373-6242 • 800-424-6242
• montereybayinn.com

MONTEREY PLAZA HOTEL AND SPA $$$$ • 400 Cannery Row • 877-862-7552
• montereyplazahotel.com

MARTINE INN $$$$ • 255 Ocean View Blvd. • Pacific Grove • 831-373-3388
• martineinn.com

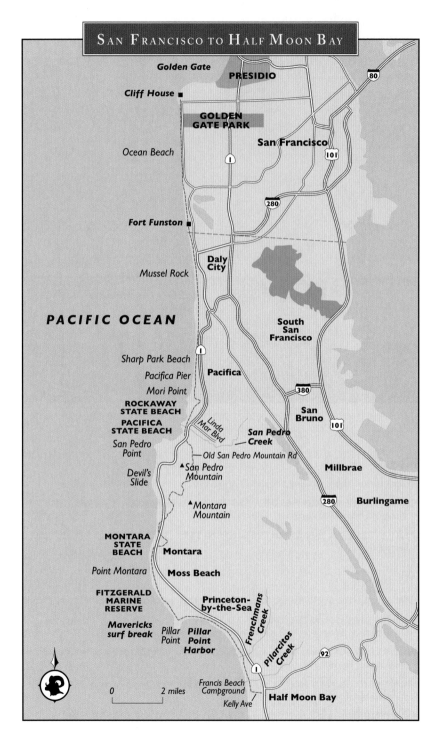

Golden Gate

PRESIDIO

Cliff House ■

GOLDEN
GATE PARK

San Francisco

Ocean Beach

80

101

280

Fort Funston ■

Daly
City

Mussel Rock

PACIFIC OCEAN

South
San
Francisco

Sharp Park Beach

Pacifica Pier

Mori Point

ROCKAWAY
STATE BEACH

PACIFICA
STATE BEACH

San Pedro
Point

Devil's
Slide

Pacifica

380

San
Bruno

101

Linda Mar Blvd

San Pedro
Creek

Old San Pedro Mountain Rd

▲ San Pedro
Mountain

Millbrae

▲ Montara
Mountain

280

Burlingame

MONTARA
STATE
BEACH

Montara

Point Montara

Moss Beach

FITZGERALD
MARINE
RESERVE

Princeton-
by-the-Sea

Frenchmans Creek

Mavericks
surf break

Pillar
Point

Pillar
Point
Harbor

Pilarcitos Creek

92

0   2 miles

Francis Beach
Campground

Kelly Ave

Half Moon Bay

San Francisco to Half Moon Bay

To me the sea is a continual miracle,
The fishes that swim—the rocks—the motion of the
waves—the ships with men in them,
What stranger miracles are there?

        —WALT WHITMAN, "Miracles"

Devil's Slide

He walked and he walked, and the earth and the holiness of the
earth came up through the soles of his feet.

—GRETEL EHRLICH, *Legacy of Light*

THIS EASY FOUR-DAY, 30-MILE WALKABOUT from Ocean Beach in San
Francisco to Half Moon Bay starts with an 8.9-mile hike along the beach, climbs
the flank of Montara Mountain, follows the cliffs above Fitzgerald Marine Reserve,
and ends with a stroll on Half Moon Bay State Beach. Along the way, you will visit
coastal villages with fine dining and entertainment. The coast of San Francisco and
San Mateo Counties is extraordinarily wild for being so close to urban centers.
Take a multiday walkabout and immerse yourself in its power and beauty.

ITINERARY

DAY 1: Ocean Beach to Rockaway State Beach	**13.6**
DAY 2: Rockaway State Beach to Montara	**7.8**
DAY 3: Montara to Pillar Point Harbor	**4.0**
DAY 4: Pillar Point Harbor to Half Moon Bay	**4.6**
TOTAL MILEAGE	**30.0**

THE VIEW FROM SUTRO HEIGHTS PARK is a classic San Francisco vista. The vast
Pacific stretches out before you, the horizon interrupted on a clear day only by the
Farallon Islands, ancient mountain peaks jutting out of the sea 27 miles offshore. To
your right, the steep, forested hills of the Marin Headlands climb abruptly from the
narrow channel of the Golden Gate. The rugged Marin Coast extends north to the
cliffs of Point Reyes. The Cliff House (in its third incarnation) lies below.

Originally a modest white clapboard house built in 1863 and then rebuilt as a
Victorian pleasure palace in 1896, it served San Franciscans who traveled from the
east side of the peninsula across empty sand dunes for a day at the beach. The first
two structures were destroyed by fire; the third was built in 1909. To the south, two
windmills rise out of the forests of Golden Gate Park. Built in 1903 and 1908, they
pumped subterranean water to irrigate the 1,017-acre park. Ocean Beach, broad
and flat, beckons, stretching as far as you can see and disappearing into the mist.

You may want to stop for breakfast at Louis', a favorite San Francisco eatery
known for its conviviality and spectacular setting on the cliffs at the edge of the
continent. Cantankerous sea lions bark from Seal Rock just offshore. Lands End
and the ruins of Sutro Baths lie below. Built in 1896 by San Francisco entrepreneur

San Francisco's Cliff House

and former mayor Adolph Sutro, it was the largest indoor swimming structure in the world, with seven fresh- and saltwater pools, an ice-skating rink, a museum, and a concert hall. Fire destroyed it in 1966. Enjoy your meal while watching massive freighters glide in and out of the Golden Gate.

Day 1: Ocean Beach to Rockaway State Beach

I STARTED THIS WALKABOUT ON A WARM, sunny October morning. Spring, from mid-April to June, and fall, from September to mid-November, are prime hiking times on the Northern California coast, offering the best chances to avoid the winter rains and the summer fog. Autumn hiking has another advantage; the ocean has had all summer to warm up. Although the waters off the coast are never balmy, this is the best season for a swim.

I arrived at Ocean Beach midmorning, 15 minutes after high tide. The sand at the shoreline was soft, but as the day progressed, the tide receded and the sand became firm. One of the best hiking beaches I know, Ocean Beach is flat with solid footing and stretches for 9 uninterrupted miles. The hours before and after low tide are usually the best for beach walking; tide schedules can be found at tidesandcurrents .noaa.gov/tide_predictions.

A very high tide will sometimes block the last section of this 9-mile beach hike. Play it safe, and plan to arrive at Mussel Rock at least 2 hours before or after high tide.

Ocean Beach can be wild on weekends, with surfers, joggers, dogs, kites, Frisbees, windsurfers, kids playing in the cool waters, and families building sand castles. Weekdays are much quieter. A concrete seawall separates the wide beach from the Great Highway, and the forests and windmills of Golden Gate Park peek over it. After a few miles, sand dunes replace the seawall, framing the eastern edge of the beach. The dunes block the view of civilization, and the only sounds are the breeze and the roar of the mighty Pacific. As you hike south, the number of people dwindles to only a few fellow walkers and a handful of people fishing for striped bass and ocean perch.

The Pacific feels immensely powerful. On this October morning, the 10-foot waves were fairly fierce. Mist spun in the air as they crested and crashed. Walking on the ocean's edge, you feel connected to its other shores. Have you strolled on a beach in Hawaii or on the west coast of Mexico or South America? Perhaps you have waded in the warm waters off Japan or Southeast Asia. The world is vast, connected, and mostly water. Walk the shoreline of the Pacific Ocean from high tide to low, and feel the ancient rhythms of pounding waves and the cyclical pull of the moon. Your pace slows. There is no hurry. With 13 miles to hike, you can take a swim, stop for lunch, have a nap, and still arrive before dinner.

Although your walk feels so calming, never turn your back on the unpredictable ocean. A rogue wave can soak your shoes, and unsuspecting beachcombers have been swept out to sea along this beach. If you swim, stay close to shore and don't swim alone. Riptides can be swift and dangerous.

After 3.6 miles, the dunes rise, the Great Highway turns inland, and a trail leads up to Fort Funston. Originally built during World War I to defend the entrance to San Francisco Bay from enemy ships, it continued its role through

Ocean Beach

World War II. A Nike missile base during the early Cold War, it was decommissioned in 1963. Today it is part of the Golden Gate National Recreation Area. You may want to leave the beach and enjoy the views from the cliffs. The Fort Funston Trail climbs and follows an old asphalt road to the Environmental Education Center, where a trail returns to the beach. The fort is a favorite spot for hang gliders, as offshore breezes strike the cliffs, causing updrafts. If you continue hiking on the shore, you are likely to see them floating on the wind and landing on the beach.

Fort Funston marks the border of San Francisco and San Mateo Counties. The worn sandstone cliffs climb to 400 feet. You can expect to have the beach pretty much to yourself south of the fort. The San Mateo County coast is mostly open space, which is extraordinary because of its proximity to San Francisco. In the early 1900s the owners of the Ocean Shore Railroad set out to build a rail line from Santa Cruz to San Francisco along the coast. The 1906 earthquake and the financial panic of 1907 prevented their dream from becoming a reality, but sections of the line operated between 1905 and 1920. Part of the dream was to develop the San Mateo County coast into "the Coney Island of the Pacific." We are fortunate they failed.

The beach ends abruptly at 8.9 miles in a jumble of large boulders just before Mussel Rock. The offshore rock with a metal structure on top is unmistakable. Scramble over boulders on an informal path, and ascend the gravel roads and trails to the Mussel Rock parking area.

Follow the directions in The Route, page 139, for the trail through Pacifica. It takes you along Esplanade Avenue where apartment buildings cling to the edge of the high cliffs. Winter storms in 2009 caused the saturated bluff to collapse. Apartment balconies once 20 feet from the cliffs were now suspended over open space. A few buildings were condemned, but apartment owners drilled long steel tubes into the sheer sandstone cliffs to shore up others and to drain excess water. El Niño storms of 2016 finished the job, and buildings were demolished. The San Andreas Fault turns out to sea just north of Pacifica and comes back to land in Marin County. It is only a matter of time before the powerful forces of winter storms and violent earthquakes send nearby apartment buildings into the sea.

Our trail returns to the shore at Sharp Park Beach, and you reach the municipal pier at 11.7 miles. The paved promenade is a great place for people-watching. The trail follows the seawall, which turns from concrete to earthen, separating the ocean from Sharp Park and Laguna Salada, a freshwater lagoon and marsh. Mori Point is a massive rock that separates Sharp Park Beach from Rockaway State Beach to the south. It rises 400 feet and extends into the sea, ending in a string of battered sea stacks.

The trail turns inland at the base of Mori Point, crosses an arm of the Laguna Salada marsh, and continues to CA 1. Follow the paved hiker/biker trail along the highway 0.2 mile until it turns to the back side of Mori Point and passes through wetlands and a pampas grass forest taking you into Rockaway State Beach, where you will find restaurants and inns.

I continued another 0.9 mile to the Pacifica Beach Hotel. A soak in their Jacuzzi bathtub with the sound of the waves pounding outside your balcony is a great way to end a day of hiking. The first day's 14.5-mile stroll along the coast took me a leisurely 7 hours.

The neighboring restaurant, Puerto 27, was quiet that evening, and I dined at the bar on a rich Peruvian paella, salad, and a glass of pinot grigio while watching the National League playoffs. The bartender, Paul, was from Thailand, slightly graying with a big smile and a gentle voice. He had been a monk before he came to California 30 years ago. As a Buddhist, he still meditates daily. I forgot about the game as we talked for a few hours about Buddhism and Christianity, the spiritual and psychic benefits of meditation and walking, and of life in Thailand and the United States. He was excited about hiking inn to inn. "Breathe deeply as you walk. If you are a Christian, breathe in thinking, 'Jesus.' Breathe out, 'Christ.' You will feel connected to the earth and to God."

Day 2: Rockaway State Beach to Montara

IN THE MORNING I RAN INTO PAUL on my way to get coffee. He said, "Remember to breathe while you walk and think, 'It is a great day to be alive.'" We stood in the parking lot and shared a few deep breaths of the cool ocean air. It was truly a great day to be alive.

Leaving Rockaway State Beach, follow the paved hiker/biker trail to Pacifica State Beach, and cross back to the east side of the highway at Linda Mar Boulevard. Montara, our destination for Day 2, has limited dining options. You can pick up supplies at the Linda Mar Shopping Center, and the Point Montara Hostel has a nice kitchen where you can prepare meals.

Walk 0.1 mile on the hiker/biker trail on the side of the highway across San Pedro Creek. The trail turns inland to skirt the next stretch of the coast, named Devil's Slide. The highway once wound along sheer cliffs, and some motorists who stopped concentrating for a moment perished on the rocks hundreds of feet below. Landslides periodically close the road. A pair of tunnels, dug through the mountain, replaced this dangerous stretch in 2013, and the old section of CA 1 has been converted to a 1.3-mile hiking trail with breathtaking views of the wild Pacific crashing on steep cliffs.

Our trail follows the San Pedro Creek Valley before ascending the flank of Montara Mountain. It was along the San Pedro where in 1769 Gaspar de Portolá encountered an Ohlone village and then made an amazing discovery. Based on journals from the Portolá expedition and the wonderful classic, *The Ohlone Way*, by Malcolm Margolin, as I hiked along San Pedro Creek, this is the way I imagine that first encounter 250 years ago:

Morning in the village began as it had for hundreds of years. The villagers rose before dawn, faced the east, and shouted greetings and exhortations to the sun, who once again listened and rose. Many of the men had beards and moustaches. They wore stone and shell amulets. Otherwise they were naked. The women wore deerskin or tule reed skirts and necklaces made of shells and feathers, their chins tattooed with lines and dots. Children played while babies were bound tightly in woven cradles near their mothers' sides.

The village of 200 was enjoying the season's bounty. Acorn gathering was just completed, and their stores held enough for the next year. The shaman's dance and song had drawn a whale to the shore, and they had feasted for days, storing blubber in baskets and drying strips of flesh on high branches beyond the reach of grizzlies. The village, near where the river meets the sea, was blessed with year-round abundance. Vast schools of smelt ran for days and filled nets to overflowing. Soon steelhead would flood the stream, and their dried and smoked flanks would be savored for months. Herds of deer, elk, and antelope roamed the hills and savannahs. And always, oysters, clams, and mussels were easily harvested.

This day would not end as others had. Word had reached the village that a party of strangers was headed their way. Captain Gaspar de Portolá, Spanish governor of Las Californias, was leading a party of 62 soldiers, priests, and Indian servants, along with 200 horses and mules. They had marched from Baja to San Diego, where Portolá left Father Junipero Serra behind to establish the first California mission. Portolá and his party then marched north to find Monterey Bay, the "protected harbor" that Sebastian Vizcaíno had discovered and praised 150 years earlier. They hiked up the coast but had to turn inland to get around the rugged Santa Lucia Mountains of Big Sur. Reaching the upper Salinas Valley in late September, they followed the Salinas River downstream and back to the coast. Failing to recognize Monterey Bay because of fog and because it was nothing like the snug harbor Vizcaíno had described, they continued north.

By the time the party reached San Pedro Creek, they had battled bad weather and were suffering from hunger and scurvy. The Ohlone greeted them with the usual hospitality of Bay Area natives—gifts of deer, elk, and shellfish. Portolá's party gratefully made camp across the river from the village.

That afternoon, Sergeant Ortega led a small hunting party into the hills. They climbed to what today is called Sweeney Ridge. Looking down to the east, they saw grassy savannahs, dark stands of oak trees, and creeks flowing into "an immense arm of the sea," with vast marshlands bordering its shore. On November 4, 1769, the entire party climbed the ridge—the first Europeans to view the San Francisco Bay. Father Juan Crespi called it "this most noble estuary." Descending to what is now Menlo Park, they explored the southwest shore of the bay for several days.

The party of strangers returned to the Ohlone village but soon departed for San Diego. The following summer, word reached the villagers that Portolá had come back to the land of the Ohlone, this time with the priest, Junipero Serra. On June 3, 1770, Portolá claimed the land for Spain. A presidio and mission were established in Monterey. The era of enslavement and destruction of the Bay Area's native peoples had begun.

Leaving San Pedro Creek, take a short walk through the Linda Mar neighborhood, and climb Higgins Road to just beyond where the houses stop. Pass through a gate onto the Old San Pedro Mountain Road. Now a wilderness trail, it was once a wagon road that climbed the mountains to avoid the impossible cliffs of Devil's Slide. Before that, it was most likely an Indian trading route. A chronicler from the Portolá party described it as "a very bad road up over a high mountain" that "though easily climbed on the way up, had a very hard abrupt descent on the opposite side."

Ascend through Monterey pine and eucalyptus forests before emerging into open coastal hills dense with sage and coyote brush and spotted with mimulus, Scotch broom, hemlock, ceanothus, sweet peas, and pampas grass—the views are spectacular. Turn a corner and see the vast blue Pacific extending to the horizon. Turn again and see the soaring coastal mountains. This trail is often the dividing line between sunshine and fog. Morning clouds gradually burn off, and you are bathed in warm sunlight. Fingers of fog return in the late afternoon, drifting in to fill valleys and then blanket the peaks.

The trail passes between San Pedro Mountain at 1,050 feet and Montara Mountain at 1,898 feet. There are benches at overlooks where you can enjoy a rest. Crossing the Montara Mountain Trail at 4.1 miles, you may want to take a side trip up the mountain to enjoy the views.

There are dozens of side trails made by mountain bikers along the descent to the coast. The main trail drops down through McNee State Park to CA 1, north of Montara. Hike 0.1 mile along the highway shoulder, cross the highway into a parking area, and take the stairs to Montara State Beach. Hike south to the end of the beach 0.5 mile and then into town.

Walk down Main Street, which becomes a footpath, to get to the Point Montara Lighthouse Hostel. Perched on a point, it is one of a series of Hostelling International USA hostels set in amazing locations along California's coast. Rooms overlook the rugged coastline and Devil's Slide to the north. There is a large communal kitchen and a small coffeehouse. A dormitory bed costs only $32 a night. My wife, Heidi, joined me that evening for the last two days of the walkabout. We had a simple private room in a truly spectacular setting for $88. That evening we cooked dinner and shared a meal with travelers from around the globe. Montara has a small convenience store and a few small restaurants if you are not preparing food at the hostel.

Day 3: Montara to Pillar Point Harbor

THE THIRD LEG OF THIS WALKABOUT is short, just 4 miles, but the coastline is beautiful, the tide pools of the Fitzgerald Marine Reserve are fascinating to explore, and a restaurant on the bluffs above the Pacific is a wonderful spot for a long lunch. You may want to combine the last two days of this walkabout and hike 8.6 miles from Montara to Half Moon Bay, but spending a leisurely day exploring the coast between Point Montara and Pillar Point is a delight.

The hike starts by leaving the south end of Montara and strolling through the coastal neighborhood of Moss Beach (see The Route, page 139, for detailed directions). After 0.5 mile you reach an open space along the bluffs with benches overlooking the crashing waves relentlessly pounding offshore rocks—a nice place to pause and take in the beautiful scene. Our route leads back to CA 1, where you take an immediate right on California Avenue and walk a few blocks until it ends at the entrance to the James V. Fitzgerald Marine Reserve. The reserve and inter-tidal reefs extend from just south of Point Montara to Pillar Point. A small ranger station at the end of California Avenue has information about the reserve. Turn right and walk one block to take a side trip to the beach.

Low tides expose an intricate web of tide pools. We saw green anemones, orange sea stars, and crabs. Harbor seals frolicked just outside the exposed reef and stopped to watch us watching them. Lines of brown pelicans glided past, almost skimming the waves. A snowy egret landed gracefully on the reef and stepped gingerly, staring into the water. Quickly her head darted and her long beak plunged into a pool, skewering a tasty morsel. Cormorants and grebes floated in the protected open water, periodically diving for a fish. Curlews probed the shoreline with long, curved beaks, searching for crustaceans and insects.

Return to the end of California Avenue to continue south on the trail. Cross the metal footbridge, and follow the path up to the coastal bluffs. The trail passes through a forest of stately Monterey cypress. As we hiked, the rays of the morning sun pierced the cypress canopy as though shining through the high windows of an ancient cathedral. Harbor seals napped below on the reef. As the tide receded, they galumphed across the rocks and into the sea to swim to a newly exposed shelf farther offshore for a peaceful snooze with greater protection.

The trail ends and you briefly stroll through the neighborhood to the Moss Beach Distillery restaurant. We stopped for the best meal of the trip, a lunch on the sunny patio of fried shrimp, steamed clams, and beer. Harbor seals played below the cliffs in the clear waters of a protected cove.

The restaurant opened in 1927 as Frank's Place, a well-known speakeasy during Prohibition. Canadian rumrunners docked below and unloaded supplies that were hauled up the cliffs and quickly transported to San Francisco. Some of the bounty stayed behind for local enjoyment. Throughout the years, "The Blue Lady," an unfortunate victim of a love triangle involving a handsome piano player and a jealous husband, has haunted the restaurant. They say her spirit remained behind to cherish the good times she had before her untimely death.

Leaving the restaurant, take Ocean Boulevard from the parking lot. The first section of the road is closed to traffic. It is a joyful hike over a roller-coaster road, tossed and buckled by shifting coastal bluffs. You soon reach open space. Take the trails along the bluffs to Pillar Point. The end of the point is fenced off for an Air Force tracking station, but a trail on the north side descends the cliffs to the beach, where you may want to enjoy more tide pooling along the reef.

The world-famous Mavericks surf break lies 0.5 mile offshore. The seafloor forms a long, sloping ramp that slows and builds the swells. Winter waves can reach heights of 50 feet. Since 1999 big-wave surfers from around the globe have gathered to ride these enormous waves in an invitation-only surfing contest, one of the most dangerous in the world.

The stormy seas north of the peninsula are in sharp contrast to the calm protected waters to the south. Pillar Point forms the northern tip of Half Moon Bay. The peaceful Pillar Point Harbor and Princeton-by-the-Sea lie below. Take the road down from the point, and stroll along the beach into town, where you will find inns, restaurants, bars, and a lively nightlife. The Half Moon Bay Brewing Company and the Old Princeton Landing offer live music and dancing on the weekends.

Hiking to Montara Mountain

Day 4: Pillar Point Harbor to Half Moon Bay

THE BAY FORMS A LONG, GRACEFUL ARC. You can walk the beach or the paved hiker/biker trail along the low bluffs. A favorite spot for a day at the beach and for surfing lies just beyond the southern breakwater of Pillar Point Harbor. Sweetwater Camp, at 2.4 miles, sits on the bluff at the edge of Frenchman's Creek, sheltered by Monterey pines. Frenchman's and Pilarcitos Creeks, the latter at 2.7 miles, may flow to the sea, depending on the winter rains. You can leave the beach and take the paved trail to cross them.

As we hiked along the bay, I thought of my Thai monk friend, Paul, who said, "You are walking the beach? You must take off your shoes when you walk and feel the connection to the earth."

We removed our shoes, forded the creek, and continued along the beach to Francis Beach Campground and the Half Moon Bay State Beach office at 3.7 miles. Turn inland and take Kelly Avenue another 0.9 mile into downtown Half Moon Bay.

This four-day hike provides a deep connection to the Pacific Ocean along its beaches, bluffs, and coastal mountains, through wilderness and small towns. Take a walkabout and breathe in the beauty, history, and wildness of the Pacific Coast from San Francisco to Half Moon Bay.

Mori Point

THE ROUTE

All mileages listed for a given day are cumulative.

Day 1: Ocean Beach to Rockaway State Beach

For directions to Ocean Beach, see Transportation, page 141. This day's hike starts with an 8.9-mile stroll on the beach. Time your hike with the outgoing tide. The hours before and after low tide are best for hiking—wide beaches with firm sand. Consult tide schedules at tidesandcurrents.noaa.gov/tide_predictions. Walk down the sidewalk from the Cliff House to Ocean Beach, and head south.

Walk along Ocean Beach to Fort Funston. **4.5 miles**

Continue on the beach to Mussel Rock. **8.9 miles**

The beach ends at a jumble of large boulders. The approach to Mussel Rock beach can be blocked by high tides, so plan to arrive at least 2 hours before or after high tide. Scramble up the informal path over rocks, and walk the gravel road that parallels the shore for 200 yards. Turn left on another gravel road, and climb. Take the path to the Mussel Rock City Park parking area. **9.1 miles**

Continue on the road south from the parking area, Westline Drive to Palmetto Avenue, and turn right. **9.5 miles**

Turn right on Esplanade Avenue. **10.0 miles**

Turn left on West Avalone Drive. **10.5 miles**

Turn right on Palmetto Avenue and right on Paloma Avenue, and walk to the paved promenade along Sharp Park Beach to the Pacifica Pier. **11.7 miles**

Continue south along the paved promenade and earthen seawall to the base of Mori Point, where the trail turns inland. Cross a marsh along a boardwalk, and turn right on Lishumsha Trail. Walk 200 yards and then turn left on Upper Mori Trail. When you reach the road, turn right and follow the paved hiker/biker trail along CA 1 for 0.2 mile until it leaves the highway and travels through a pampas grass field on the back side of Mori Point to Rockaway State Beach. **total miles 13.6**

Day 2: Rockaway State Beach to Montara

Hike south along the paved hiker/biker trail to Pacifica State Beach. **0.9 mile**

Cross CA 1 at Linda Mar Boulevard and walk the hiker/biker trail on the eastern side of the highway 0.1 mile across San Pedro Creek. Follow the trail inland along the creek as it merges with San Pedro Terrace Road. Turn right on Peralta Road, and continue until it ends. Pass through a wooden gate, and walk a short path and up Higgins Way to the gate that marks the beginning of Old San Pedro Mountain Road. **2.2 miles**

Continue to the intersection of the Montara Mountain Trail. **4.1 miles**

Continue on the Old San Pedro Mountain Road to CA 1. **6.8 miles**

Hike south along the highway shoulder 0.1 mile, cross the highway at the parking area, and take the stairs to Montara State Beach. **7.0 miles**

Hike to the end of the beach, and climb to the parking area. Cross the highway, take Second Street inland, and turn right on Main Street. To reach Point Montara Hostel, walk to the end of Main Street, and continue on the path to 16th Street. The hostel is across the highway.

total miles 7.8

Day 3: Montara to Pillar Point Harbor

Leaving the Montara Hostel, follow the frontage road along a chain-link fence until it ends. Take the path, and continue on Vallemar Street. Turn right on Juliana Avenue until it reaches CA 1 and California Avenue. Take an immediate right on California Avenue, and walk a few blocks until it ends. Cross the metal bridge, take the path through the Monterey cypress forest to the trail along the coastal cliffs, and head south. The trail ends at Beach Way. Follow it along the coast to the Moss Beach Distillery restaurant. **1.7 miles**

Take Ocean Boulevard from the restaurant parking lot until it ends. Follow the trail along the bluffs toward Pillar Point. The end of the narrow point is fenced off for an Air Force tracking station. Turn left on the road off the point, and take the path to the beach and to Pillar Point Harbor.

total miles 4.0

Day 4: Pillar Point Harbor to Half Moon Bay

Hike along the waterfront to the breakwater at the end of Pillar Point Harbor. Follow the shore on the beach or on the trail along the bluffs to Francis Beach Campground and the Half Moon Bay State Beach office. **3.7 miles**

Turn inland on Kelly Avenue. Walk to CA 1 and into downtown Half Moon Bay.

total miles 4.6

Cypress forest at Fitzgerald Marine Reserve

TRANSPORTATION

Public Transportation

TO REACH OCEAN BEACH and the start of this walkabout, take BART to the Embarcadero Station in San Francisco. Walk up Market Street two blocks to Fremont Street and take Muni Bus 38R ($2.75) to Sutro Heights at the end of the line.

To return from Half Moon Bay to downtown San Francisco, go to 511.org to plan your journey ($10.75). Go to samtrans.com for more information on Samtrans schedules.

Flying into the Bay Area

FROM SFO TAKE BART to San Francisco's Embarcadero Station ($8.95), and follow the public transportation directions above. From the Oakland International Airport, take the Oakland Airport BART to the Oakland Coliseum BART Station. Take BART to San Francisco's Embarcadero Station ($10.20), and follow the public transportation directions above.

MAPS

THE U.S. GEOLOGICAL SURVEY sells topographical hiking maps and provides free downloadable maps; visit store.usgs.gov, and go to the map locator for the following: San Francisco South, 2015 ($15); Montara Mountain, 1997 ($8); Half Moon Bay, 2015 ($15), all 7.5-minute. A good road map of the Bay Area might also be sufficient.

PLACES TO STAY

LODGING COST			
$ *less than $100*	$$ *$100–$150*	$$$ *$150–$200*	$$$$ *more than $200*

San Francisco

There are scores of hotels in San Francisco. This one is very close to the start of the walkabout.

SEAL ROCK INN $$–$$$ • 545 Point Lobos Ave. • 415-752-8000 • sealrockinn.com

Pacifica: Rockaway Beach

INN AT ROCKAWAY $$–$$$ • 200 Rockaway Beach Ave. • 650-359-7700 • 800-522-3772 • innatrockaway.com

NICK'S RESTAURANT AND SEA BREEZE MOTEL $$ • 100 Rockaway Beach Ave. • 650-359-3903 • nicksrestaurant.net • Live music in the restaurant on the weekends.

LIGHTHOUSE HOTEL $$$–$$$$ • 105 Rockaway Beach Ave. • 650-355-6300 • pacificalighthouse.com • Live music in restaurant on weekends.

Pacifica: Pacifica State Beach

PACIFICA BEACH HOTEL $$–$$$$ • 525 Crespi Dr. • 650-355-9999 • pacificabeachhotel.com • Jacuzzi bathtubs.

Montara

POINT MONTARA LIGHTHOUSE HOSTEL $ • 16th St. and CA 1 • 650-728-7177 • hiusa.org

Moss Beach

If you wish to hike 1.5 miles beyond Montara, follow The Route (page 139) south into the Fitzgerald Marine Reserve. The bluff trail through the Monterey cypress grove ends at Cypress Ave. Turn left, and continue two blocks to reach this lovely, secluded inn.

SEAL COVE INN $$$–$$$$ • 221 Cypress Ave. • 650-728-4114 • sealcoveinn.com

Pillar Point Harbor

OCEANO HOTEL AND SPA $$$$ • 280 Capistrano Road • 650-726-5400
• oceanohalfmoonbay.com

INN AT MAVERICKS $$$$ • 346 Princeton Ave. • 650-421-5300 • innatmavericks.com

Half Moon Bay

NANTUCKET WHALE INN $$$–$$$$ • 779 Main St. • 650-726-1616
• nantucketwhaleinn.com

COASTSIDE INN $$–$$$$ • 230 Cabrillo Hwy. • 650-726-3400 • coastsideinn.com

HALF MOON BAY INN $$–$$$$ • 401 Main St. • 650-726-1177
• halfmoonbayinn.com

Point Montara Lighthouse Hostel

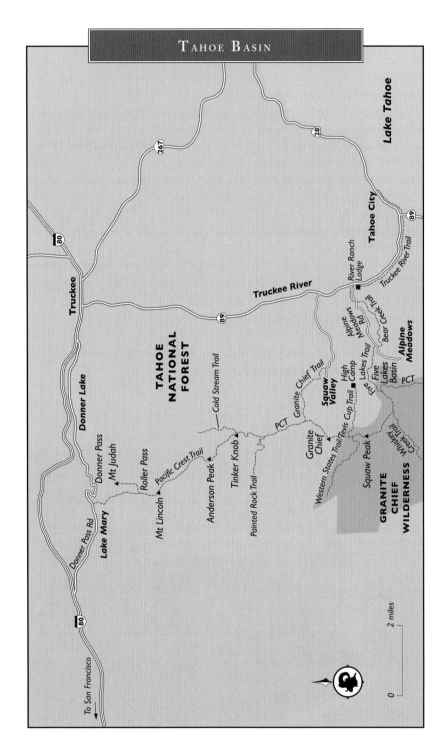

TAHOE BASIN

Lake Tahoe

28

267

80

Tahoe City

89

Truckee

River Ranch Lodge

Truckee River Trail

Truckee River

89

Alpine Meadows Rd

Bear Creek Trail

TAHOE NATIONAL FOREST

Cold Stream Trail

Granite Chief Trail

Squaw Valley

High Camp

Five Lakes Trail

Alpine Meadows

Donner Lake

Donner Pass

Mt Judah

Roller Pass

PCT

Granite Chief

Five Lakes Basin

PCT

Donner Pass Rd

Mt Lincoln

Pacific Crest Trail

Anderson Peak

Tinker Knob

Painted Rock Trail

Western States Trail/Tevis Cup Trail

Whiskey Creek Trail

Squaw Peak

GRANITE CHIEF WILDERNESS

Lake Mary

To San Francisco

80

0

2 miles

HIKING THE TAHOE BASIN

Donner Pass to Lake Tahoe

Each day is a journey, the journey itself home.

—MATSUO BASHO,
The Narrow Road to the Deep North

Hiking the Sierra Crest

The earth never tires,
The earth is rude, silent, incomprehensible at first,
Nature is rude and incomprehensible at first,
Be not discouraged, keep on, there are divine things well envelop'd,
I swear to you there are divine things more beautiful than words can tell.

—WALT WHITMAN, "Song of the Open Road"

WITH THE TRUCKEE RIVER VALLEY TO THE EAST, the deep gorge of the American River Canyon plunging to the west, and Lake Tahoe shimmering in the distance, this walkabout follows the spine of the High Sierra along the Pacific Crest Trail (PCT). A challenging 30-mile trek spread over three hiking days, it has two steep descents and one ascent of 1,900 feet. You'll be rewarded with stopovers at mountain resorts in spectacular settings and the solitude and pristine beauty of the Sierra Nevada.

Traverse 18.5 miles of the Pacific Crest Trail on this walkabout.

ITINERARY

DAY 1:	Donner Pass to Squaw Valley	**13.4**
DAY 2:	Squaw Valley to Truckee River at Alpine Meadows Road	**12.6**
DAY 3:	Alpine Meadows Road to Lake Tahoe	**4.0**
TOTAL MILEAGE		**30.0**

Day 1: Donner Pass to Squaw Valley

THE TRAIL STARTS AT DONNER PASS (7,100') and climbs sharply along a series of rocky switchbacks, but soon it levels off for a long, gradual ascent. You are hiking on the PCT. Stretching 2,650 miles from the US–Mexico border near Campo, California, to 9 miles into British Columbia's Manning Provincial Park, it follows the crest of the Sierra Nevada and the Cascade Range. On this walkabout you will hike 18.5 spectacular miles of the PCT.

My friend Scott and I set out at dawn in the first week of October. With only 11.5 hours of daylight, we wanted to get an early start. A storm had swept through the Northern Sierra the week before, the remnants of a typhoon that had hammered the Philippines. It dropped several inches of snow, but most of it had melted. Patches of ice and snow remained in the shadows. Frozen earth crunched underfoot, and snow graced the high peaks. The air was crisp and fragrant with the smell of pines.

The trail rises along the west side of the ridge, shaded from the early morning sun. Lake Mary lies below, and soon the high mountains that form Sugar Bowl Ski Resort come into view. Hike below a chairlift and past the turnoff to Mount Judah at 2.1 miles. With a short side trip, you can easily reach its summit of 8,243 feet. Continue on the PCT, ascending until you reach Roller Pass, an open ridge at 2.4 miles. A metal sign marks the spot where a portion of the ill-fated Donner Party crossed this pass: WE MADE A ROLLER AND FASTENED CHANS TO GETHER [SIC] AND PULLED THE WAGONS UP WITH 12 YOKE OXEN ON THE TOP AND THE SAME AT THE BOTTOM. —NICHOLAS CARRIGER, SEP 22, 1846.

Roller Pass marks the most difficult barrier that the party faced on its journey to California. Emigrant Canyon plunges 1,500 feet, and they had to winch their wagons up the final ascent. Spectacular views of Donner Lake and the meadows north of Truckee now open to the east. To the southeast the PCT snakes along the rolling ridgeline for several miles on its way to Anderson Peak.

The first wagon train to cross these mountains, the Stevens Party, came in 1844, two years before the Donner Party and five before the gold rush. For each of the next four years, only a few hundred brave pioneers traveled overland to California. Mostly middle-class farm families, they fled malaria and the economic hard times of the Mississippi Valley for the promise of fertile land and a gentle climate. Pulled by teams of four to eight oxen, their prairie schooners were loaded with 1,500 pounds of supplies, enough for the 2,000-mile, four- to six-month journey. The wagons had no brakes or springs, and rather than endure the bone-jarring ride, most adults walked. Traveling at the speed of oxen, they averaged 14 miles per day across the plains and 10 miles in the mountains.

Leaving the Iowa or Missouri territories, wagon trains followed fur-trapper and Indian trading routes, crossing the prairie along the Platte River. There were vast herds of buffalo, and progress was easy across the open grasslands. As one early pioneer diarist described it:

> Our camp this evening presents a most cheerful appearance. The prairie, miles around us, is enlivened with groups of cattle, numbering six or seven hundred, feeding upon the fresh green grass. The numerous white tents and wagon-covers before which the campfires are blazing brightly, represent a rustic village; and men, women, and children are talking, playing, and singing around them with all the glee of light and careless hearts. While I am writing, a party at the lower end of the camp is engaged in singing hymns and sacred songs.

Hearts became less "light and careless" as weeks passed and the wagons finally reached the Rockies, but this crossing was easy compared to the Sierra. Leaving the Platte, they followed the Sweetwater River in Wyoming, and after 900 miles, the trail rose gradually through a broad valley named South Pass. Early pioneers realized they had crossed the Continental Divide only when they noticed that streams now flowed west.

The trail divided, with some wagon trains heading north to Fort Hall in what today is Idaho, and others traveling south to the Great Salt Lake. Heading south-west, they converged along the Humboldt River. In 1844 the Stevens Party followed the Humboldt through the Great Basin until it ended abruptly, swallowed by the desert at the Humboldt Sink. They were uncertain which way to turn until they met an elderly Indian who drew a map in the sand and told them to head due west across 50 miles of desert. They would come to a great river with trees and good grass. His name was Truckee, and out of gratitude, they gave the river his name.

The Pacific Crest as seen from Roller Pass

After climbing the Truckee River Canyon and coming to Donner Lake, the wagon trains reached the Sierra Nevada and faced what looked like an impassable, ragged 1,200-foot granite wall. Finding passages for a man and a single ox, they coaxed the oxen to a plateau and yoked them into teams. Another team was assembled below. Long chains ran over large logs, or rollers, that worked as pulleys to haul up empty wagons—backbreaking work for man and beast.

A small book published in 1845, *The Emigrants' Guide to Oregon and California* by Lansford W. Hastings, inspired the early pioneers to brave the uncertain journey. He described California as a paradise:

> *There is no country, in the known world, possessing a soil so fertile and productive, with such varied and inexhaustible resources, and a climate of such mildness, uniformity and salubrity; nor is there a country, in my opinion, now known, which is so eminently calculated, by nature herself, in all respects, to promote the unbounded happiness and prosperity, of civilized and enlightened man.*

Hastings was an ambitious adventurer and opportunist who encouraged the United States to wrestle California from the weak and unstable control of Mexico. The Donner Party followed Hastings's route in 1846, a "shortcut" to the Great Salt Lake that proved disastrous—impassable canyons and dense thickets of trees and brush that they had to laboriously clear with axes. A combination of incompetent leadership, poor decisions, and bad luck led the party to near starvation in the Nevada desert, every family fending for itself. When they reached the lake now called Donner, they confronted deep snow. Eighty members built cabins to wait for a break in the weather that never came. After eating the oxen and then the dogs, they reluctantly turned to cannibalism of those who had perished. Only 40 made it across the Sierra.

Hastings and his route were discredited. His "shortcut" was 120 miles longer and more treacherous than the earlier trail. Today a creek, pass, mountain, and lake bear the name of the Donner Party. The PCT now follows the crest, and it is one of the most beautiful trails I have hiked in the Sierra—exposed volcanic ridges, snowcapped peaks, scattered fir and pine forests, and deep gorges and canyons to the west and east. The bright-yellow flowers of mule's ears cover mountain slopes in the spring. Now, in October, brown and brittle, they wait for their winter blanket of snow.

The PCT rambles along the rolling crest past Mount Lincoln (8,383') to Anderson Peak (8,683') at 5.1 miles. The path divides, with the left fork climbing to the peak and to the Benson Hut, a Sierra Club shelter for backpackers and skiers. Take the right fork, and circle the west side of Anderson Peak on a rocky trail carved out of boulders and scree. To the south and west lies the deep canyon of the North Fork of the American River.

Patches of snow settled in the trail's depressions. We saw deer, rabbit, and bird tracks. For a 2-mile stretch, we followed the tracks of a lone coyote. There were no bootprints except ours.

View of Tinker Knob

The trail turns southeast and climbs a narrow ridge to the base of Tinker Knob (8,979'), the highest point on this walkabout. Here you can stop for a break with a view of the northern bay of Lake Tahoe, the town of Truckee to the northeast, and the American River Canyon to the southwest.

Scott said, "We are the only hikers to come here since last week's storm, and another is headed this way on Sunday. I feel like we are putting this part of the Sierra and the Pacific Crest Trail to bed for the winter."

Lake Tahoe, pale blue, sparkled in the autumn sunlight. Ten million years ago the immense pressure of the North American Continental Plate grinding over the Pacific Ocean Plate caused uplifts and folds, forming the Sierra Nevada and the Carson Range. The Tahoe Basin dropped between the two folds. Volcanic flows dammed the basin, and the great lake was formed. The Truckee River eventually cut through the volcanic deposits, giving the lake its only outlet.

At a depth of 1,645 feet, it is the second-deepest lake in the United States, after Crater Lake in Oregon. Glaciers dammed the Truckee both 2 million and 20,000 years ago, and the lake level rose 800 feet higher than it is today. When the glaciers receded the second time, the Truckee broke through and flowed again. Earthquake faults underlie the depths of the lake, and scientists predict tsunamis that can cross it in a few minutes. While you are enjoying a piña colada in one of Tahoe's shoreline bars after your walkabout, you may want to consider the quake that formed McKinney Bay on the west side of the lake 50,000 years ago and set off a 330-foot tsunami. Cheers!

Cold Stream Trail meets the PCT under Tinker Knob at 7.8 miles. The Aram Party of 1846 spent three days searching for a better route over the Sierra than the cruel wall of granite at the west end of Donner Lake. They followed Cold Stream and discovered that, even though the pass was 700 feet higher, oxen teams could pull their wagons to within 100 feet of the ridge. Then, using rollers, they reached this junction. There was still a difficult week of mountain travel ahead of them before they would arrive at Sutter's Fort, but they had conquered the most difficult barrier of their 2,000-mile journey.

Gold was discovered in 1848, and by 1849 the rush was on. Now, rather than a few hundred wagons a year, there were thousands. Pioneer diarists reported an uninterrupted line of wagons stretching 1,000 miles across the prairie. In 1849, 21,000 forty-niners made the journey, crossing the Sierra in fairly equal portions between the Lassen Route to the north, the Carson River Route to the south, and the Truckee River Route. Most emigrants on the Truckee took their wagons up Cold Stream Canyon.

The quest for gold and the mass migration continued through the early 1850s. Up to 50,000 people made the overland journey each year from 1850 to 1852. Most chose the Carson River Route 50 miles to the south, avoiding the dozen or so hazardous crossings of the Truckee River and the brutal granite wall that stood between them and their fortunes.

The PCT descends 1,150 feet over the next 1.5 miles into the American River Canyon. After a mile of steep switchbacks, the descent becomes more gradual. You drop to 7,600 feet and cross a 4-foot-wide creek that flows out of Meadow Lake. It joins other small streams to form the American River and carve its magnificent canyon.

The trail climbs, passing Painted Rock Trail at 9.3 miles. After another 1.2 miles and an ascent of 560 feet through dense forests, you reach the junction with Granite Chief Trail at 10.5 miles. Turn left on the Granite Chief Trail, and continue another 2.9 miles to Squaw Valley, a descent of 1,900 feet.

The trail alternates between pleasant switchbacks and scrambles over granite shelves. Giant ponderosa and Jeffrey pines now appear as you lose elevation. Ancient, gnarled western juniper with reddish bark and blueberry-like cones grow in impossible rock crevasses, seeming to have chosen the most difficult spot to live for a millennium or perhaps three. Approaching the valley floor, we were greeted by stands of aspen dressed in their brightest golden-yellow autumn colors.

The trail reaches Squaw Creek and diffuses into several small trails that end at the valley's north parking lot near the Olympic Village Inn. After 8.5 hours on the trail, we checked into PlumpJack's. It was the slowest season of the year. With the Jacuzzi to ourselves, we soaked our weary muscles under the towering mountain peaks and star-filled sky. Then we headed off to Suko Yama's for a sushi feast.

Day 2: Squaw Valley to Truckee River at Alpine Meadows Road

DAY 2 STARTS BY RETRACING YOUR STEPS up the Granite Chief Trail, the steepest sustained ascent of the walkabout with a 1,900-foot climb over 2.9 miles. You may want to skip this section and shorten the hike by taking the aerial tram to Squaw Valley Resort's High Camp. It costs $46 and usually runs in summer and during ski season. Follow The Route, page 156, to return to the PCT. For tram information, call 800-403-0206 or go to squawalpine.com.

The cable car was not running in October, so we headed back up the Granite Chief Trail. Finding the trailhead out of Squaw Valley can be confusing because it

You can take the aerial tram from Squaw Valley to Squaw's High Camp.

fans out into several minitrails as it approaches the valley. Consult The Route for detailed directions.

The trail climbs steadily through gradual switchbacks past sturdy junipers and stately Jeffrey and ponderosa pines. It scrambles over granite shelves with views of Squaw Valley and the surrounding peaks. As we methodically climbed, four young women ran past us. "Where are you headed?" we asked. "Donner Pass," they cheerfully replied.

We watched them quickly disappear into the fir and pine forest of the higher elevations on their 13.4-mile jog. Scott said, "Ours might be the last bootprints of the season, but it looks like there will also be four sets of running shoes."

It took us 2 hours to climb the 2.9 miles back to the PCT. Turn left, head south, and continue a gradual ascent toward Granite Chief. You pass a marshy meadow, the headwaters of Squaw Creek, and then climb a short series of switchbacks. After passing under a chairlift, you reach the junction of the Western States Trail in a saddle between the back of Squaw Peak and Granite Chief.

To our astonishment, three young men came running up the trail. They asked, "Which way to Donner Pass?" Members of a Nordic ski team from Vermont, they had come to the Sierra to train. They hoped to catch up to the four women, who were their teammates. Nothing like a brisk 20-mile jog in the mountains to get the heart pumping. We pointed them in the right direction, and they waved and pranced off like gazelles. Scott said, "Make that seven sets of running-shoe tracks in the snow covering our bootprints."

The PCT descends right. A hundred yards down from the junction is a sign marked GRANITE CHIEF WILDERNESS, 4.2 miles from the trailhead. Here a Steller's jay taunted us from the branch of a mountain hemlock, and two chipmunks busily gnawed on pinecones, fattening up for the long winter.

The Western States Trail follows the PCT 0.2 mile and then breaks off to the west. After another 0.8 mile you come to the northwest-heading Tevis Cup Trail, the route of the annual Tevis Cup Ride, a 100-mile, one-day horse race from Tahoe to Auburn. Between the two trails, you cross a small stream, the headwaters of the North Fork of the mighty American River.

The PCT descends through a series of switchbacks, dropping into the Whiskey Creek watershed. You reach Whiskey Creek Trail at 7 miles after dropping 1,330 feet from the Western States Trail junction. Now the PCT climbs gradually northeast 0.9 mile to the Five Lakes Trail.

Turning onto Five Lakes Trail, you leave the PCT after hiking it for the better part of two days through some of the most spectacular scenery in the Sierra. A taste of the PCT leaves the hiker yearning to come back next season to explore it again; you might consider the two other walkabouts in this book that visit the PCT (see "Crossing the Sierra on the Emigrant Trail," page 28, and "Exploring Lassen Volcanic National Park," page 90).

The trail climbs gradually 0.3 mile, crossing Five Lakes Creek. It levels off as you enter Five Lakes Basin. Easy access and crystal-clear alpine lakes surrounded by granite walls and fir forests make this a popular destination in the summer. A side trail branches off to the lakes 0.9 mile from the PCT junction.

The small lakes had been warming up all summer, but apparently a few subfreezing autumn nights were enough to cool them back down. Drying in the sun on a warm granite ledge after a brief and energizing swim, I thought of the words of George R. Stewart, writing about the pioneers in his book, *The California Trail*:

> *The psychology would have been that of the traveler—and there is no more pleasant state of mind for most people. When anyone is traveling, life is reduced to a simple and solvable daily problem: to make the required distance. If the people in a wagon train totaled their fifteen miles westward, they could sleep peacefully.*

The psychology is just as true for today's inn-to-inn hiker. The hectic demands of modern life melt away, and you are left with the joy of a deep encounter with nature. Your only "daily problem" is to make the required distance to your next inn and then to enjoy the pleasures of dining by a roaring fireplace and sleeping under a down comforter.

Five Lakes Trail descends steadily, dropping 1,000 feet over 1.4 miles to Alpine Meadows at 6,560 feet. As you lose elevation, the Alpine Meadows Ski Resort comes into view. Giant Jeffrey pines and then aspens appear as you reach the valley at 10.2 miles. The trail ends at Alpine Meadows Road. The ski resort is to your right, but it is closed in the summer.

Take the Bear Creek Trail downvalley 1.9 miles. Finding the trail is a bit tricky; see The Route, page 156, for directions. This lovely trail passes through dense pine and fir forests along the south side of the canyon. Countless springs, seeps, and creeks flow across the trail and into Bear Creek as it races to the Truckee.

The trail drops back down to Alpine Meadows Road. Turn right, and walk the broad shoulder of the road 0.5 mile until you reach the Truckee River and River Ranch Lodge.

The lodge sits on the river's edge. The rooms are small and comfortable, and the Truckee flowed below our balcony. We dined on portobello napoleon and a delicious rack of lamb with a mustard-rosemary glaze. The river takes a turn and forms a large pool below the lodge's deck. Kayakers and inner tubers gather here in the summer after floating down from Lake Tahoe. There is live music and an outdoor bar on the deck on summer weekends.

The Pacific Crest Trail in late autumn

Truckee River

Day 3: Alpine Meadows Road to Lake Tahoe

THE LAST LEG OF THE JOURNEY is a brief 4-mile stroll on the hiker/biker path along the river to Lake Tahoe, a gradual reintroduction to civilization. A noisy flock of Canada geese honked loudly as they flew up the valley and landed in a deep pool. We lingered, not wanting to rush, savoring the beauty of the Truckee and then the grandeur of Lake Tahoe. This 30-mile walkabout is a stroll through pioneer and geological history and a hike through the spectacular beauty of the Sierra Nevada Mountains.

THE ROUTE

All mileages listed for a given day are cumulative.

Day 1: Donner Pass to Squaw Valley

See Transportation (page 158) for driving directions to the trailhead. The PCT starts to the left of the trailhead sign. You will stay on the PCT, heading south, for the next 10.5 miles

Hike the PCT to the Mount Judah Trail. **2.1 miles**

Continue to Anderson Peak Trail. At an unmarked fork in the trail, turn right. The PCT circles the west side of Anderson Peak. **5.1 miles**

Continue to Cold Stream Trail. **7.8 miles**

Continue on the PCT to Painted Rock Trail. **9.3 miles**

Continue to the junction of Granite Chief Trail, and turn left. **10.5 miles**

The Granite Chief Trail splits into several branches as you approach Squaw Valley, but all the branches lead to the parking lot adjacent to the Olympic Village Lodge in Squaw Valley.

total miles 13.4

Alternate Route for End of Day 1

You can take the Squaw Valley Aerial Tramway to the valley and avoid 1,200 feet of descent on Granite Chief Trail. Continue south on the PCT past the Granite Chief junction 2.3 miles to Tevis Cup Trail, and turn left. Follow the Tevis Cup Trail 0.3 mile. The trail then angles south up to the ridgeline. A stone monument commemorating the Emigrant Road stands where the trail crosses the ridge. Descend on gravel roads past the Gold Coast Express ski lift, turning left at the T junction, and descend past the Shirley Lake and Big Blue ski lifts. Stay left at the Y intersection, and hike into Squaw's High Camp. Take the aerial tram to the valley. The last tram leaves at 5 p.m. It may be closed between Labor Day and the opening of ski season. For more information, go to squawalpine.com or call 800-403-0206.

Day 2: Squaw Valley to Truckee River at Alpine Meadows Road

You may want to take the Squaw Valley Aerial Tramway from Squaw Valley to Squaw's High Camp ($46 for an all-day pass). For information, go to squawalpine .com or call 800-403-0206. Pick up a Squaw Valley Hiking Guide when you purchase the pass. Hike Ridge Road out of High Camp. Take Siberia Ridge Road past the Big Blue and Shirley Lake ski lifts. Turn right on Emigrant Peak Road at the Gold Coast Express ski lift, and hike to the ridge and a stone monument commemorating the Emigrant Road. Descend to a junction. Take Tevis Cup Trail left 0.3 mile to the PCT, and turn left.

The Granite Chief Trailhead is found at the northwest end of Squaw Valley's north parking lot. Cross a small bridge to the right of the Olympic Village Lodge, and walk up 100 feet. Turn left on unmarked Granite Chief Trail, which runs through the ropes course. Follow the trail along Squaw Creek. Shirley Canyon Trail continues along the creek. Granite Chief Trail turns right and starts climbing. Continue to the junction of the PCT. **2.9 miles**

Turn left and hike south on the PCT 5 miles. The trail reaches a saddle between Squaw Peak and Granite Chief Trail and an unnamed trail. Take the right fork. The sign marking the boundary of the Granite Chief Wilderness is 100 yards beyond the fork. **4.2 miles**

Continue to Whiskey Creek Trail. **7.0 miles**

Reach the junction of Five Lakes Trail, and turn left, leaving the PCT. **7.9 miles**

Follow Five Lakes Trail to Alpine Meadows Road. **10.2 miles**

Cross Alpine Meadows Road, and walk right 100 yards. Take the unmarked, unpaved road to the left, the start of the Bear Creek Trail. After 50 feet take the unmarked trail to the left, descending three stone steps, and hike toward the sound of rushing water to a bridge over Bear Creek. The trail climbs a series of switchbacks to a paved road. Make a short jog right, cross the road, and find the trail, marked by two metal posts. The trail briefly turns southwest, the opposite of the way you want to go, but don't despair—it climbs, turning back northeast. The trail briefly joins a rocky road. After a short distance the road crests, and you will see a large green water tank. The trail turns off to the right, marked with a metal diamond nailed to a post. After a short distance, you will reach a junction marked with a metal post. Take the trail to the left. Ascend a small hillock, and angle to the right on the narrow trail. Continue straight, crossing a dirt road. The trail is marked by a post with a diamond. Continue on Bear Creek Trail along the south slope above Bear Creek Valley until it descends back to Alpine Meadows Road. **12.1 miles**

Turn right on Alpine Meadows Road, and walk along the shoulder to the Truckee River and the River Ranch Lodge.

total miles 12.6

Day 3: Alpine Meadows Road to Lake Tahoe

Walk to Lake Tahoe and Tahoe City on the Truckee River hiker/biker trail.

total miles 4.0

TRANSPORTATION

Driving with Two Cars

LEAVE ONE CAR IN TAHOE CITY, and drive the other to the Donner Summit and Pacific Crest Trailhead. Take the Soda Springs and Norden exit off I-80 and drive east on the old Donner Pass Road 3.6 miles. Turn right on the road across from the Donner Ski Ranch; a sign at the intersection reads SUGAR BOWL SINCE

1939—MT. JUDAH PARKING. After 0.1 mile, take the first left and go another 0.2 mile to a small parking area on the left. The trail starts 100 feet beyond the parking area on the right. If the parking area is full, return to Donner Pass Road, and park in a turnout.

Driving with One Car

DRIVE TO THE DONNER SUMMIT and Pacific Crest Trailhead. Follow the directions above. To return to your car, Tahoe Area Regional Transit (TART) buses run from Tahoe City to Truckee regularly during daylight hours; go to placer.ca.gov /departments/works/transit/tart.aspx. There are several taxi companies serving the Truckee area. Try High Sierra Taxi (530-412-1927). The ride back to the trailhead and your car should cost $20–$30.

Headwaters of the mighty American River

By Train

TAKE A BEAUTIFUL AND RELAXING train trip from the Bay Area, Sacramento, Los Angeles, or Reno to Truckee on Amtrak (amtrak.com). The trip from the Bay Area to Truckee costs $49–$53 and should take anywhere from 5 to 6 hours. See Driving with One Car, previous page, for information on taxis from Truckee to the trailhead to start the hike and on public transportation from Tahoe City back to Truckee at the trip's end.

Flying into the Bay Area

FOR TRIP PLANNING from the airport to Amtrak, visit 511.org. From SFO take BART to the Oakland Coliseum Station ($9.70), and walk a few minutes to the Amtrak Station. From the Oakland International Airport take the AirBART Shuttle to Oakland Coliseum BART Station ($6), and walk a few minutes to the Amtrak Station. Take an Amtrak train to Truckee, and follow the By Train directions (above).

MAPS

NATIONAL GEOGRAPHIC'S *Lake Tahoe Basin* (#803) is a great recreational topo map that covers this entire route. It can be purchased for $11.95 at shop.national geographic.com.

PLACES TO STAY

LODGING COST			
$ less than $100	$$ $100–$150	$$$ $150–$200	$$$$ more than $200

Squaw Valley

PLUMPJACK SQUAW VALLEY INN $$$$ • 1920 Squaw Valley Road • 530-583-1576 • plumpjacksquawvalleyinn.com • Full breakfast included.

OLYMPIC VILLAGE INN AT SQUAW VALLEY $$$$ • 1909 Chamonix Place • 800-989-1387 • 530-581-6000 • olympicvillageinn.com

THE VILLAGE AT SQUAW VALLEY $$$$ • 1750 Village East Road • 530-583-4264 • squawalpine.com • Vacation rental condominiums.

Snow-dusted peaks along the Pacific Crest Trail

Alpine Meadows
RIVER RANCH LODGE $$–$$$$ • At CA 89 and Alpine Meadows Road • 4 miles north of Lake Tahoe • 530-583-4264 • riverranchlodge.com

Truckee
TRUCKEE HOTEL $–$$$$ • 10007 Bridge St. • 530-587-4444 • truckeehotel.com

RIVER STREET INN $$–$$$ • 10009 E. River St. • 530-550-9290 • riverstreetinntruckee.com • Continental breakfast included.

CEDAR HOUSE SPORT HOTEL OF TRUCKEE $$$–$$$$ • 10918 Brockway Road • 530-582-5655 • cedarhousesporthotel.com

Tahoe City
MOTHER NATURE'S INN $–$$ • 551 N. Lake Blvd. • 530-581-4278 • 800-558-4278 • mothernaturesinn.com

AMERICA'S BEST VALUE INN $$ • 455 N. Lake Blvd. • 530-583-3766 • 866-588-8247 • redlion.com/tahoe-city • Continental breakfast included.

BASECAMP HOTEL $$–$$$ • 955 N. Lake Blvd. • 530-580-8430 • basecamptahoecity.com • Continental breakfast included.

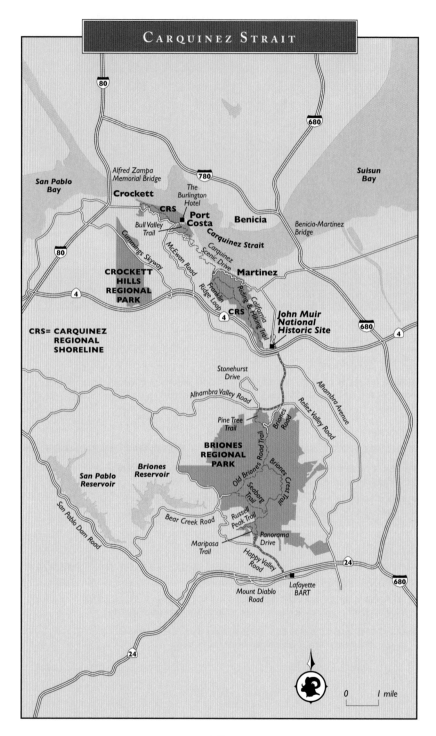

CARQUINEZ STRAIT

San Pablo Bay

Suisun Bay

Alfred Zampa Memorial Bridge

Crockett

The Burlington Hotel

CRS

Port Costa

Benicia

Bull Valley Trail

Carquinez Strait

Benicia-Martinez Bridge

Cummings Skyway

McEwan Road

Carquinez Scenic Drive

Martinez

CROCKETT HILLS REGIONAL PARK

Franklin Ridge Loop

California Riding & Hiking Trail

CRS

John Muir National Historic Site

CRS= CARQUINEZ REGIONAL SHORELINE

Stonehurst Drive

Alhambra Valley Road

Alhambra Avenue

Pine Tree Trail

Briones Road

Reliez Valley Road

BRIONES REGIONAL PARK

San Pablo Reservoir

Briones Reservoir

Old Briones Road Trail

Briones Crest Trail

Seaborg Trail

San Pablo Dam Road

Bear Creek Road

Russell Peak Trail

Panorama Drive

Mariposa Trail

Happy Valley Road

Lafayette BART

Mount Diablo Road

0   1 mile

Walkabout Carquinez Strait

For those who find their pleasure out-of-doors . . .
All the years of existence represent a long love affair
with the earth, this earth, the only earth we know.

—EDWIN WAY TEALE,
A Naturalist Buys an Old Farm

Briones Regional Park

The sun shines and the stars, and new beauty meets us at every step in all our wanderings.

—JOHN MUIR, *John of the Mountains*

HIKE THE ROLLING GRASSLANDS AND FORESTS along Carquinez Strait on this moderate 21-mile, three-day walkabout. Hiking the northern fringe of the Bay Area, you will feel transported to a bygone era, walking the lands of the Karkin Ohlone and visiting hamlets rich with California history. Take public transportation to start and end this journey. It makes a nice weekend vacation for Bay Area residents. Leave work on Friday, take a short evening stroll to Port Costa, and enjoy fine dining and a charming Victorian hotel. Hike to Martinez Saturday, and return home Sunday either directly from Martinez or after a final day of traversing the rolling hills and valleys of Briones Regional Park. You will feel rejuvenated by the peace and beauty of hiking the wilds of California.

ITINERARY

DAY 1:	Crockett to Port Costa	**2.5**
DAY 2:	Port Costa to Martinez	**7.9**
DAY 3:	Martinez to Lafayette	**10.3**
TOTAL MILEAGE		**20.7**

Hiking above the Carquinez Strait

Day 1: Crockett to Port Costa

WINTER STORMS ROLL IN from the Pacific, saturating California's parched land and rejuvenating her rivers. Blocked by the peaks of the Sierra Nevada Mountains, the storms drop snow that will replenish those rivers for months. Into the Sacramento River, streams flow from as far north as Mount Shasta. As far south as Bakersfield, they flow into the San Joaquin. These two great rivers converge, draining 40% of California, a 62,500-square-mile watershed. The waters then surge into San Francisco Bay through a narrow, 8-mile break in the Coastal Range: the Carquinez Strait.

Our walkabout begins in Crockett, near the mouth of the strait where it meets San Pablo Bay, the northern extension of San Francisco Bay. My wife, Heidi, our friends Scott and Mary Jo, and I set out on a summer afternoon. We'd taken BART to the end of the Richmond Line. Five minutes later, a ride-hail driver picked us up and dropped us at the trailhead. It is very convenient to use the BART system to start and end this walkabout. If you are walking only the first two days, Amtrak's Capitol Corridor train will return you from Martinez to East Bay stations and BART connections.

The trail begins with a descent through a eucalyptus grove and then climbs through woodlands of oak, buckeye, and coastal chaparral. This land is protected, part of Carquinez Regional Shoreline. Views open to the narrow strait, the towns of Vallejo and Benicia, the rolling grassy hills on the north side of the channel, and the Carquinez Bridge.

After 0.5 mile, the trail reaches a park at the base of Eckley Pier with picnic tables and restrooms. We were in no hurry; this first day's hike is only 2.5 miles. We walked out on the fishing pier and felt the power of the waterway. The tide was rising, surging through the narrow passage, racing miles inland before it would reverse its flow.

The trail ascends to open grasslands where you will find a sign commemorating the 1776 visit of Lieutenant Colonel Juan Bautista de Anza. In the early 1770s, Spain had established tenuous control over Alta California, but English ships off the California coast had begun preying on Spanish galleons returning from the Philippines, and Spain feared England would attempt to stake a claim.

The viceroy of New Spain ordered Anza to undertake two overland expeditions, the first in 1774 to establish a route from Mexico to Monterey. The second, in 1775–1776, would bring settlers and establish a new colony near the "River of San Francisco."

The second expedition set out on September 29, 1775, with 34 soldiers; 123 family members and settlers; 20 mule drivers; and more than 1,000 horses, mules, and cattle. After exploring the San Francisco Bay region, Anza took a small group to scout the north bay. Along the strait, they encountered the Karkin Ohlone. Father Pedro Font wrote that as the sun rose on April 2, 1776, "ten gentiles wearing feathers and garlands of flowers" came into camp dancing, singing, and bringing gifts. They invited the expedition to their rancheria for a day of food, music, and dance.

The Karkin, for whom the strait is named, lived in this region for thousands of years. Hiking these hills, we could sense the bounty of their land, which was rich with deer and other game. These early inhabitants harvested plants and seeds from the forests and grassland. From reed kayaks, they fished for salmon and sturgeon. Anza wrote, "We have noticed that since the mouth of the bay the most abundant fish is salmon—deep red, tender and large. Of the ones we have seen none was less than five hands." In less than 25 years, the Karkin's land would be appropriated.

Hike Bull Valley Trail as it winds along the grassy hillsides and passes through eucalyptus groves. It hadn't rained for months when we took this walkabout, and the hills were covered with long dried grass. This hike is beautiful any time of year. Rains return in October and November, and the grass quickly turns lush and green. April and May bring a riot of wildflowers. In June the hills will start to turn brown. Check the forecasted temperatures in the summer: it can be brutally hot, with temperatures in the 90s.

Rounding a curve, you come to an overview with a bench and picnic table. We stopped to take in the view. A freighter cruised below us, headed inland for the ports of Sacramento or Stockton, and a lone windsurfer zipped across the strait. The remains of rotting wharfs gave an indication of a time when these waters were bustling with trade. The Capitol Corridor Amtrak train passed by on tracks winding along the shoreline. To the east, the channel widens into Suisun Bay. At 3,849 feet, the double pyramid peaks of Mount Diablo dominate the skyline.

The trail descends, turning left at two more intersections, and enters the back streets of Port Costa. Stroll down the main street, Canyon Lake Drive, and you feel like you have stepped into a bygone era. Small wooden houses with gardens line the street. After a short while, you reach "downtown": a hotel, two bars, and a restaurant.

The 2010 census shows a Port Costa population of 190. It is hard to believe it was once a major transportation hub and the busiest wheat shipping port in the nation. From 1879 to 1930 the Central Pacific Railroad used giant ferries to transport trains across the strait between Benicia and Port Costa, where they were reassembled and sent on to Oakland. The wharfs were crowded with ships from Europe, Asia, and Africa carrying Central Valley grain to the world. Eighteen saloons, seven hotels, a dance hall, and several bordellos served workers from Spain, Portugal, Ireland, and China.

In 1930 a bridge was built across the strait, and trains no longer needed to be ferried. Channels to Sacramento and Stockton opened in 1932, and ocean-going ships could now dock closer to the source of grain. A 1941 fire raged through town for a week, leaving only a hotel, a warehouse, and a few other commercial buildings near the water.

Over the years, Port Costa reemerged as a quiet backwater on the fringe of the Bay Area. Surrounded by East Bay Regional Park, it is being rediscovered by hikers, bikers, motorcyclists, and a few tourists as a destination for fine dining, convivial nightlife, and an escape from the modern urban ramble.

Earl Flewellen checked us into the Burlington Hotel. The major entrepreneur in town, he owns the hotel and the Bull Valley Roadhouse restaurant. Built in 1883, the Burlington is a Victorian beauty that Earl is methodically restoring to be "rustic but comfortable."

We climbed the creaking stairway to the third floor, past walls with velvet-flocked wallpaper, old photos, and oil paintings. It is still debated whether or not the Burlington was once a bordello, but each of her 19 rooms is named after a "lady

Burlington Hotel

of the night." The bay windows of our room overlooked the strait, and we realized why there were a few packets of earplugs when the Amtrak roared by.

Visit the Warehouse Café across the street. Housed in a former granary with giant redwood beams and an eclectic ornate décor that includes a stuffed Cape Horn buffalo and a huge polar bear, it claims to serve more than 250 beers.

It took a while to study the long beer menu. After a few questions, the friendly bartender invited me to visit the walk-in cooler, where she showed me racks of beers from all over the world.

Although I wanted to stay and work my way through the IPAs, I settled on one that was new to me. Taking our drinks out back to the shady veranda in the late afternoon, we washed away the trail dust. We ordered sandwiches for lunch the next day and marveled at our good fortune to have settled in this peaceful spot after a beautiful hike.

We dined that evening at the Bull Valley Roadhouse. The bar specializes in Prohibition-era cocktails with names like Missionary Downfall and Islay Paralysis. Patrons at the Warehouse told us to be sure to try the beer-battered green beans with aioli, and we were grateful for the local tip. We worked our way through small plates of steamed mussels, halibut ceviche, and fresh garden salads. Then we feasted on a delicately fried buttermilk chicken, a slow-roasted pork stew, and a light risotto with garden vegetables. Strolling back to the Burlington in the cool starry night, we looked forward to another day of hiking.

Day 2: Port Costa to Martinez

LEAVING PORT COSTA, our trail returns to Carquinez Strait Regional Shoreline Park, climbing grassy hills to Carquinez Scenic Drive. The narrow road winds along the hillside between Port Costa and Martinez overlooking the strait and meanders through oak forest and open grassland. There are virtually no cars because the middle section of road is closed to traffic.

Pass through one gate that blocks traffic from the west and another blocking traffic from the east. Shortly after the second gate, you will see another gate on the right leading to a wide trail. Leave the road and follow this trail as it angles left, climbing into oak forest.

After 0.2 mile you reach the intersection of Franklin Ridge Loop Trail. Both forks will lead to our destination, but the left fork has more spectacular vistas. The trail initially climbs steeply. Then the ascent along the ridge becomes more gradual.

Hike 4 miles through rolling grasslands. There is very little shade, so be sure to carry plenty of water. If it is a very hot day, you may want to follow the alternate route described on page 174.

Hiking the ridge, you can look to the west and see San Francisco Bay and the mouth of Carquinez Strait as it meets San Pablo Bay. To the east you see Suisun Bay, Mount Diablo, the Sacramento–San Joaquin River Delta, and into California's Central Valley.

The formation of these great waterways began about 560,000 years ago, when the planet was colder. Glaciers covered much of the Sierra Nevada, and sea levels were 400 feet lower than they are today. The coastline extended west beyond the Farallon Islands, now 27 miles offshore, and San Francisco Bay was a valley of grassland and forest. Lake Corcoran, an immense inland sea, filled San Joaquin Valley.

The planet warmed, and glaciers began to melt. Tectonic forces uplifted the Coastal Range, and the waters of Lake Corcoran rose. They finally burst through a narrow breach in the Coastal Range with a torrent that drained the lake and carved Carquinez Strait.

The narrow strait creates a bottleneck, slowing outflow of Sierra rivers, and sediment deposits have formed the vast Sacramento–San Joaquin River Delta. Only the Pearl River Delta in China stretches as far inland. The Sacramento–San Joaquin is also a rare inverted river delta: Almost all the world's great rivers end with a fan-shaped delta of sediment that spreads outward into a body of water. The backed-up sediment of the Sacramento and San Joaquin Rivers spreads inland, creating an inward-facing, fan-shaped delta extending over 1,100 square miles, forming a fertile labyrinth of marshes, sloughs, meandering rivers, islands, and backwater hamlets.

It is said that the political history of modern California is the battle for water. Great water projects export delta water south and supply 1.1 million acres of farmland and 23 million people in Southern and Central California. As a result, fisheries and water quality have suffered. More projects are on the agenda, and the water wars continue.

After a mile on Franklin Ridge Loop Trail, it meets and joins California Riding and Hiking Trail and Hulet Hornbeck Trail. A short walk later, you reach the intersection with the other arm of Franklin Ridge Loop Trail. Turn left on California Riding and Hiking Trail.

The trail follows the rolling ridge through pastureland and then descends to a fenceline bordering private property. It arcs along the hillside above CA 4. The blue cupola of John Muir's house comes into view as you make a quick descent to an asphalt path adjacent to the John Muir National Historic Site. Take a short walk through the residential streets of Martinez to your motel.

Martinez is a fun town. Unfortunately, its three motels are 1.6 miles from the best bars and restaurants. You may be able to find an Airbnb or VRBO closer to downtown. The motels are close to the John Muir National Historic Site. This is where the naturalist and conservation crusader lived from 1890 until his death in 1914. It was while he was living here that he cofounded the Sierra Club and wrote articles and books advocating preservation of our nation's natural treasures.

His 17-room Victorian house is worth a visit. John and his wife, Louisa, raised their family here and managed a 2,600-acre fruit farm. The National Park Service acquired the house and 325 surrounding acres in 1964 and restored it to its original condition. You can explore the house and grounds, watch a brief film, or take a formal tour to get a sense of the great man's life and times.

We used a ride-hailing service to travel into central Martinez and explored the marshland and trails of Martinez Regional Shoreline Park. Willets and sandpipers grazed along the shore, while egrets waded in narrow channels intent on spearing a meal.

Martinez evenings are usually balmy. Check out Creek Monkey Tap House for interesting brews and bar food served in a tranquil outdoor setting along the creek. Or try La Tapatia, an award-winning Mexican restaurant with sidewalk seating. If you still have energy, Armando's offers live bluegrass, blues, folk, jazz, or zydeco most nights.

You can end your walkabout in Martinez by taking Amtrak's Capitol Corridor train to East Bay stations, where you can take BART to Bay Area destinations.

Day 3: Martinez to Lafayette

SPEND MOST OF TODAY'S JOURNEY hiking the rolling hills and valleys of Briones Regional Park, but start with a stroll on rural-suburban lanes along with joggers, dog walkers, and bicyclists. (Half of our party decided to skip the walk along the roads and hailed a ride to the park entrance.) Hike south on Alhambra Avenue, and pick up bagel sandwiches at Alhambra Donuts and Deli. Then pass by John Muir National Historic Site and under CA 4. There is a walking path on the left.

You will come to a small park with a statue of Muir. We are hiking in his footsteps through Alhambra Valley and into the hills where he roamed.

After 0.6 mile, turn right on Alhambra Valley Road, where there are sporadic walking paths but traffic is light. Look for the park entrance 0.4 mile beyond Briones Road. You will see a regional park sign and a parking area on the left, opposite Stonehurst Drive.

Take Pine Tree Trail from the parking area. It passes by park buildings and climbs a short slope past a small pond and through a gate, where it makes a right turn. After a short distance, you come to a grove of pines with huge cones. These are Coulter pines. They thrive in Baja and Southern California, but some have strayed as far north as the Bay Area. This cluster may be one of the most northern. The Coulter's cones are the heaviest of any pine in the world, weighing up to 11 pounds! Stay on your toes. The cones are also called widow-makers.

The trail climbs through grassy hillsides and oak woods. Leave Pine Tree Trail, following the sign to Old Briones. Join Old Briones Road Trail when you reach a parking area with bathrooms and water. Continue to ascend through woodlands

Mount Diablo

Descent to the corrals on Old Briones Road Trail

of oak, madrone, and buckeye. Pass through a gate and hike into rolling grasslands. These hills are graced with an abundance of wildflowers in April and May.

In 1829 Maria Manuela Valencia Briones and her husband, Felipe, built a home and raised cattle in what is now the southwest end of the park near Bear Creek Staging Area. Felipe, a soldier at San Francisco Presidio, was killed in 1840. Maria petitioned for a land grant, and Governor Juan Alvarado granted her 3 square leagues, about 17,000 acres in 1842. Most of Briones Regional Park lies within her land, Rancho Boca de la Cañada del Pinole.

Our trail merges with Briones Crest Trail for 0.2 mile. They separate at the crest, and we pass through a gate and continue on Old Briones Road Trail. After ascending through the hills since entering the park, our trail now snakes steeply downhill.

Turn right at the corrals, continuing on Old Briones Road as it winds on a level path. South-facing hills on the right side are grassy open slopes. On the left, the north-facing hills are densely forested with oak, madrone, and bay.

Take a sharp left on Seaborg Trail as it ascends along a seasonal creek where big-leaf maples, willows, and alders fill the creekbed. Seaborg gradually climbs through a lovely valley and then rises steeply 0.2 mile until it ends at a T junction.

Turn right on Briones Crest Trail, which becomes Russell Peak Trail. Views open to Mount Diablo to the east. To the west, you can see Mount Tamalpais and the Golden Gate in the distance. The blue waters of Briones Reservoir snake through hills of grasslands and oak forests, and the white dome of UC Berkeley's Leuschner Observatory perches on a hilltop.

Descend through oak woods to an asphalt path, and turn right. Pass through a gate onto Panorama Drive, and walk through a quiet residential neighborhood to Happy Valley Road.

We strolled the tree-lined path to the Lafayette BART Station, each of us lost in thought. With a short journey, we had left our busy urban lives and hiked through beautiful countryside and what felt like a bygone era. Then we hopped on BART and headed back to civilization.

THE ROUTE

All mileages listed for a given day are cumulative.

Day 1: Crockett to Port Costa

Start the hike across the street from 189 Winslow St. in Crockett. Pass through the iron gate with a FIRE TRAIL sign and onto Bull Valley Trail. The trail descends and takes a sharp left. After a short distance, turn right on the trail in front of the ELKHORN CREEK HABITAT RESTORATION sign. Continue to Eckley Pier parking and picnic area.   **0.5 mile**

Take the fire road located on the far side of the loop between two parking lots, and continue on Bull Valley Trail. Take the left forks at the next two intersections, continuing on the wide trail. Stay on the main trail as it winds along the hills. Pass an overlook of Suisun Bay and Mount Diablo with a bench and picnic table. Descend from the overlook and take the left fork at the Y. Continue left at the next Y, and pass through a gate. Follow the trail to Prospect Ave., and descend to Canyon Lake Dr. Turn left and walk into "downtown" Port Costa.   **total miles 2.5**

Day 2: Port Costa to Martinez

Leaving Port Costa, walk up Canyon Lake Dr., and turn left on Reservoir St. As Reservoir makes a sharp curve right, turn left on the trail in front of 11 Reservoir St. Ascend the trail to Carquinez Scenic Dr., and turn left.   **0.7 mile**

Continue on Carquinez Scenic Dr. through a gate that blocks traffic from the west and another gate that blocks traffic from the east. Leave the asphalt road a short distance after the second gate, and turn right through a gate and onto a wide trail.   **3.5 miles**

Angle left, ascending a short distance to the intersection of Franklin Ridge Loop. Turn left. Stay on the main trail, passing unmarked trails to the left. Stay right at the intersection with Hulet Hornbeck Trail. After a short distance, leave Franklin Ridge Loop, and turn left on California Riding and Hiking Trail.   **4.9 miles**

Continue on the main trail, passing Rankin Park Trail and an unnamed trail with a windmill. Pass a cattle shed, and continue straight. The trail descends through pastureland and follows the park's boundary along a fence. Pass through a gate. The trail goes along the hillside above CA 4. It descends to a paved path adjacent to the John Muir Historic Site. Turn left and onto Canyon Way, a Martinez residential street. Take the second right, Arroyo Dr. Turn left on Rapp Ave., and take the second right onto K St. to Alhambra Ave. The motels of Martinez are a short distance to the right.

total miles 7.9

Alternate Route

If it is a hot summer day, you may want to avoid the open hills and take a shadier route. At 3.5 miles, continue on Carquinez Scenic Dr. into Martinez.   **5.0 miles**

Carquinez Scenic Dr. ends at Foster St. Walk on Foster to Talbart St., and turn right. Turn left on Buckley St. and right on Alhambra Ave. You will pass through downtown Martinez. Walk down Alhambra Ave. to the motels of Martinez.

total miles 7.5

Day 3: Martinez to Lafayette

Leaving Martinez, walk south on Alhambra Ave. 0.6 mile, and turn right on Alhambra Valley Road. Enter Briones Regional Park, turning left on a short road to a parking area opposite Stonehurst Dr.   **2.4 miles**

Take Pine Tree Trail from the parking area. Pass through a gate, and bypass Toyon Canyon Trail. Take the right fork at the next intersection, following the sign to Old Briones to a parking area with bathrooms.   **3.4 miles**

Hike Old Briones Road Trail. Pass through a gate, and stay right. Pass through another gate where Briones Crest Trail branches off to the left, and descend on Old Briones Road Trail to the corrals.   **5.1 miles**

Turn right at the corrals, continuing on Old Briones Road Trail. Turn left on Seaborg Trail, and hike until it ends at a T junction. Turn right on Briones Crest Trail. Continue on the wide trail that becomes Russell Peak Trail. Continue on Mariposa Trail as Russell Peak Trail peels off to the right. Turn right when you reach the paved path and stay on this path to the gate at the park boundary.   **8.8 miles**

Descend through the neighborhood on Panorama Dr. Turn left on Happy Valley Road, walking on the path on the left side to Lafayette BART Station.

total miles 10.3

TRANSPORTATION

Flying into the Bay Area

FROM SFO TAKE BART to El Cerrito del Norte Station on the Richmond Line ($9.35). This may require a transfer. From Oakland International Airport take BART to the Coliseum Station and then to El Cerrito del Norte Station on the Richmond Line ($9.20). A transfer may be required. Follow the public transportation directions below.

Public Transportation

TAKE BART TO EL CERRITO DEL NORTE STATION on the Richmond Line. Take a taxi or ride-hailing service to the trailhead across the street from 189 Winslow St. in Crockett. Our Lyft price was $23.30, but ride-hailing pricing is dynamic.

Returning by Public Transportation

IF YOU ARE HIKING only the first two days, take Amtrak from Martinez to return to East Bay stations, where you can take BART to Bay Area destinations. The fare from Martinez to Oakland's Coliseum Station is $14. If you complete the three-day walkabout, take BART from the Lafayette Station to Bay Area destinations.

View of San Francisco Bay and Mount Tamalpais

MAPS

THE EAST BAY REGIONAL PARK WEBSITE provides maps of Carquinez Strait Regional Shoreline Park and Briones Regional Park in PDF format at ebparks.org /parks/maps#B. The Briones brochure and map should also be available at the entrance sign to the park.

PLACES TO STAY

LODGING COST			
$ *less than $100*	$$ *$100–$150*	$$$ *$150–$200*	$$$$ *more than $200*

Port Costa

BURLINGTON HOTEL $$–$$$ • 2 Canyon Lake Dr. • 510-787-6795 • thehotelburlington.com • Fun, historic Victorian hotel. Continental breakfast included.

Martinez

All lodging is located near the John Muir National Historic Site.

QUALITY INN $$ • 3999 Alhambra Ave. • 925-228-7471 • choicehotel.com/california /martinez/quality-inn-hotels

MUIR LODGE MOTEL $$ • 3930 Alhambra Ave. • 925-228-3308 • muirlodgemotel.com

SUPER 8 $$ • 4015 Alhambra Ave. • 925-372-5500 • wyndhamhotels.com

Lafayette

You may want to end your walkabout with an evening in Lafayette.

LAFAYETTE PARK HOTEL AND SPA $$$–$$$$ • 3287 Mount Diablo Blvd. • 855-382-8632 • lafayetteparkhotel.com • 1.7 miles from Lafayette BART Station

John Muir's house

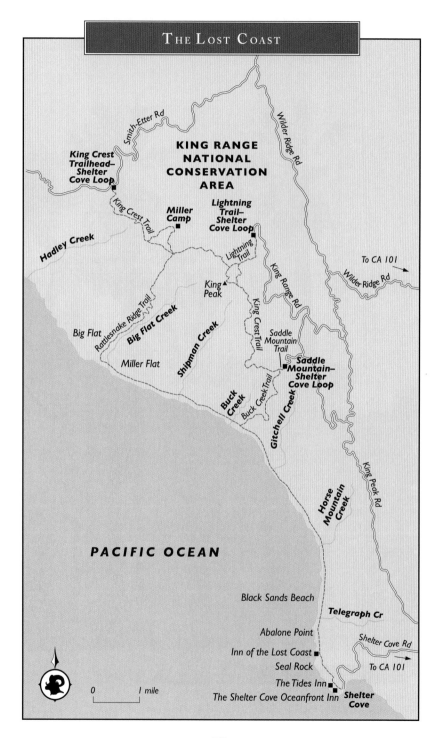

KING RANGE
NATIONAL
CONSERVATION
AREA

Smith-Etter Rd

Wilder Ridge Rd

King Crest
Trailhead–
Shelter
Cove Loop

King Crest Trail

Miller
Camp

Lightning
Trail–
Shelter
Cove Loop

Hadley Creek

Lightning Trail

To CA 101

Wilder Ridge Rd

King
Peak

King Range Rd

Rattlesnake Ridge Trail

Big Flat

Big Flat Creek

Shipman Creek

King Crest Trail

Saddle
Mountain
Trail

Miller Flat

Saddle
Mountain–
Shelter
Cove Loop

Buck
Creek

Buck Creek Trail

Gitchell Creek

Horse
Mountain
Creek

King Peak Rd

PACIFIC OCEAN

Black Sands Beach

Telegraph Cr

Abalone Point

Shelter Cove Rd

Inn of the Lost Coast

To CA 101

Seal Rock

The Tides Inn

The Shelter Cove Oceanfront Inn

Shelter
Cove

0   1 mile

The Lost Coast

There is a pleasure in the pathless woods,
There is a rapture on the lonely shore,
There is society where none intrudes,
By the deep Sea, and music in its roar.
—LORD BYRON, *Childe Harold's Pilgrimage*

Lost Coast shoreline

O for the voices of animals—O for the swiftness and balance of fishes!
O for the droppings of raindrops in a song!
O for the sunshine and motion of waves in a song!

—WALT WHITMAN, "A Song of Joys"

PENETRATED BY ONLY A FEW NARROW, WINDING ROADS, the Lost Coast is the most remote and inaccessible section of the California coastline. The wild, rugged shore and the soaring peaks of the King Range are visited only by backpackers, ambitious day hikers, and walkabout adventurers. This chapter features three two-day loop hikes, ranging from 21 to 39 miles, all stopping over at the picturesque fishing village of Shelter Cove. Because of the distances and challenging trails with climbs and descents of more than 3,000 feet, these are the most difficult walkabouts in this guide. Your reward is to be among the few brave explorers to really experience the spectacular and wild beauty of the Lost Coast.

ITINERARIES

Of these three routes, the King Crest Trailhead–Shelter Cove Loop is the longest. An all-wheel-drive vehicle is recommended for this route and for the Saddle Mountain–Shelter Cove Loop, the shortest of the three. Lightning Trail–Shelter Cove Loop is the most easily accessed by car; an all-wheel-drive vehicle is not needed. The route is 2 miles shorter than the King Crest Trailhead–Shelter Cove Loop. See Transportation (page 94) for driving information.

King Crest Trailhead–Shelter Cove Loop

DAY 1: King Crest Trailhead to Shelter Cove via Buck Creek Trail   **20.3**
DAY 2: Shelter Cove to King Crest Trailhead via
Rattlesnake Ridge Trail   **18.7**

TOTAL MILEAGE   **39.0**

Lightning Trail–Shelter Cove Loop

DAY 1: Lightning Trailhead to Shelter Cove via Buck Creek Trail   **16.8**
DAY 2: Shelter Cove to Lightning Trailhead via
Rattlesnake Ridge Trail   **20.2**

TOTAL MILEAGE   **37.0**

Saddle Mountain–Shelter Cove Loop

DAY 1:	Saddle Mountain Trailhead to Shelter Cove via Buck Creek Trail	**10.5**
DAY 2:	Shelter Cove to Saddle Mountain Trailhead via Buck Creek Trail	**10.5**
TOTAL MILEAGE		**21.0**

KING CREST TRAILHEAD–SHELTER COVE LOOP

CA 1 SNAKES NORTH from San Francisco, hugging the coastline for more than 200 miles, but its tenacious builders gave up in the 1930s when they encountered the impenetrable King Range and turned inland. The coast was declared "lost," and it remains so today. The rugged coastline and towering mountains still limit most human encroachment, but walkabout hikers can join backpackers in exploring the Lost Coast from the crest of the King Range to the wild Pacific shore.

This walkabout starts at the north end of the King Crest Trail and follows the ridge south 10.5 miles before plunging 3.6 miles to the sea. Hiking the shore another 6.2 miles brings you to the comforts of Shelter Cove. The return trip follows the coast 10 miles north before climbing 3,500 feet over 5.7 miles back to the mountaintops, finishing with a 3-mile stroll along the crest to your car. This difficult hike is a wonderful way to deeply experience the Lost Coast.

Day 1: King Crest Trailhead to Shelter Cove via Buck Creek Trail

THE KING CREST TRAIL BEGINS at the parking area for North Slide Peak. Starting at 3,000 feet, it climbs gradually 5.5 miles to King Peak, passing through forests of madrone, tan oak, manzanita, and Douglas-fir. Much of the trail travels the knife-edge ridgeline.

My wife, Heidi, and I hiked this walkabout in September during the dry season. Rain falls in this area from October to April, and the Lost Coast is one of the wettest spots on the Pacific Coast. Storms blowing in from the ocean crash into the King Range, dropping more than 200 inches of rain in a wet year.

The morning fog gradually lifted as we approached the peak, revealing miles of forested mountains to the east. To the west, steep cliffs drop precipitously thousands of feet to the Pacific. Only Big Sur is comparable in California, and few

Morning fog on the Lost Coast

other spots in the world match the abrupt ascent from ocean shore to mountain summit. King Peak, the highest pinnacle in the range, soars to 4,087 feet, less than 3 miles from the coast. A 1990 fire burned large swaths of the approach to King Peak, leaving forests of charred tree trunks, but also opening extraordinary vistas.

At the intersection with Lightning Trail, you can take the left fork and then turn right through Maple Camp, where water is available, but this would be a missed opportunity. Take the right fork at the Lightning Trail intersection, and ascend to the summit for a spectacular 360-degree view of the King Range to the north and south and the vast Pacific stretching to the western horizon. Deep canyons carved into the watershed of Big Flat Creek start almost at your feet and drop abruptly to the sea.

The King Range National Conservation Area, established by Congress in 1970, covers 60,000 acres spreading 6 miles inland and 35 miles north and south. The protected lands of Sinkyone Wilderness State Park, adjacent to the conservation area, cover another 7,400 acres, extending 20 miles south. The steep, winding road to Shelter Cove is the only paved road that penetrates the parks and reaches the coast. Prior to state and federal protection, logging of Douglas-fir forests denuded mountain slopes, causing large-scale mudslides. Sediment choked watersheds, and some rivers are still recovering.

The crest trail gently rolls south for another 5 miles, gradually descending 800 feet to the Buck Creek Trail. Forests of stately madrones, reaching 50 feet in height, thrive along this section. Their twisted trunks and branches intertwine, and reddish-brown bark peels away, revealing a shiny, beautiful cinnamon skin. The trail becomes an unpaved fire road for the last few miles before Buck Creek Trail.

Signage is good along the entire route of this walkabout, and the Buck Creek sign points you west for a 3.6-mile, 3,300-foot drop to the sea. A former gravel road, it descends through Douglas-fir forests. Gardens of irises and sword ferns line the lower section of the trail where it steepens as it approaches the coast. The trail meets the shore at the mouth of Buck Creek. Slightly upstream you will find a few inviting campsites.

Wandering the crest and descending to the sea gives you a visceral sense of the powerful natural forces that are shaping the Lost Coast, a Lord Shiva dance of creation and destruction. The San Andreas Fault runs offshore, reaching land just north of Shelter Cove. It is essentially underfoot at the mouth of Buck Creek. The Gorda, North American, and Pacific Plates meet just offshore, forming the Mendocino Triple Junction, one of the world's most geologically unstable areas. Around 80 earthquakes, measuring more than 3.0 on the Richter scale, shake the Lost Coast every year. Radiocarbon dating shows that over the last 6,000 years, the shoreline has risen 66 feet.

On April 25, 1992, the 6.9 Ferndale earthquake jolted the region. In the days that followed, residents of Petrolia noticed a powerful odor blowing in from the west. When they went to inspect, they found that what once had been offshore tide pools were now high and dry, the tidal animals and plants rotting in the open air. The King Range had bolted upward 3–4 feet in a few seconds from the powerful quake.

Archaeologists have unearthed coastal Indian villages in this area dating back thousands of years. While excavating middens (mounds of discarded shells, bones, and tools), scientists noted that the older ones were farther from the shore than the more recent ones. You might wonder whether the more ancient native peoples preferred a longer stroll to the beach. But, no, scientists have determined that seismic uplift over millennia moved the shell mounds farther from the coast.

As the mountains rise, the deluge of rain, sometimes as much as 2 feet over two days, tears them down. Much of the soil is brittle, a crumbling combination of compressed shale and graywacke, a dark sandstone. Fires periodically sweep through the forests, leaving the soil unprotected and hastening erosion. Short, powerful streams start a few miles inland, high in the mountains. They quickly tumble to the sea, carving deep canyons, leaving immense talus piles at their bases, and creating black sand beaches. Winter storms with massive waves pound the shore, dragging sand out to sea. Smaller summer waves push the sand back up, rebuilding the beach.

Hike south on the shore 5.2 miles to Black Sands Beach at the north edge of Shelter Cove. The first 3 miles are not easy hiking, with a surface that varies among soft sand, pebbles, and rocks, but the beach widens over the last 2 miles. If the tide is out, this wider section becomes a fine, firm surface for hiking.

If the tide is low, round the point at the end of the beach, walk a short distance to Abalone Point, and stroll into town on the roads along the coast. If the tide is high, turn inland at the south end of Black Sands Beach (see The Routes, page 190, for directions).

Shelter Cove

Shelter Cove sits on the beautiful, flat terrace of Point Delgada. Marine shelves along the shore host bountiful tide pools rich with crabs and anemones. Sea lions and harbor seals lounge on the rocks just offshore. At its south end, the point curves into a crescent cove, sheltering the fishing fleet from Pacific storms that rage in from the northwest.

Houses along the coast are a jumble of pleasure palaces, each pitching and stretching to maximize its vista, an eclectic assortment of architectural visions, the anti–Sea Ranch. Climbing up the mountains from the terrace, houses are hugged by the forest and then completely lost in its embrace. There are four interesting inns, a few restaurants, a small airfield, a nine-hole golf course, and a campground. Perched on the point with spacious rooms and balconies overlooking rocky outcroppings and the Pacific, the Oceanfront Inn is a great place to rest and recuperate for a day or two before resuming your hike. Nights in Shelter Cove are quiet, and with no streetlights, the star shows are brilliant.

Point Delgada

Native Americans dwelled on Point Delgada for more than 8,000 years. The Tahng-i-keah band of the Sinkyone Indians made summer camps here, feasting on shellfish and sea mammals. With abundant game and bountiful sea life, the Lost Coast region was one of the most densely populated Native American territories in North America. The Sinkyone lived in villages with cone-shaped, plank houses made of redwood bark. Every year great runs of steelhead trout and coho and Chinook salmon returned to the rivers of their birth. Smoked fish provided food for months. The Sinkyone also hunted Roosevelt elk, deer, rabbits, raccoons, game birds and even bears. Acorns, mostly from tan oaks, were the staple of the Sinkyone diet.

In the mid-1800s, within a generation, they were decimated and dispersed. European diseases swept through villages. Soldiers from Fort Bragg hunted them down and slaughtered the survivors or marched them to the Round Valley Indian Reservation near Covello.

Ranchers started settling the Lost Coast in the 1860s, grazing cattle and sheep. The tan oak industry peeled the bark from the trees and shipped it to San Francisco for leather processing. Commercial fishing boomed in the early 1900s, and lumbering thrived in the 1950s and '60s. Today the fishing industry has at least temporarily played out. Construction of new houses has ground to a halt. Tourism and marijuana-growing have become the main industries.

Day 2: Shelter Cove to the King Crest Trailhead via Rattlesnake Ridge Trail

AFTER A DAY OF REST and a little tide pooling in Shelter Cove, we were on the trail at 7 a.m. With 13 hours of daylight in mid-September and a 19-mile hike ahead of us, we wanted to get an early start. Pulling on her boots, Heidi said, "I think you should recommend a two-day rest in Shelter Cove." My still-aching muscles had to agree.

It is crucial to time this day's hike with the tides. The beach narrows and can be blocked at high tide, especially around rocky points from just north of Buck Creek at 6.5 miles to Miller Flat at 8.5 miles. Consult tide tables at tidesandcurrents .noaa.gov. The best hiking conditions on the beach are the hours before and after low tide, but always keep an eye on the sea. Rogue waves can crash far up the beach without warning.

The trail north retraces your steps along the beach to Buck Creek. It was a glorious, sunny day when we set out. Black sand beaches stretched out before us, and forested mountains dropped steeply to the coast. Small creeks tumbled out of canyons, and most sunk into the sand before they reached the sea—be prepared for several stream crossings if you hike earlier in the season. Seeps and springs percolated from the cliffs, creating vertical wildflower gardens of lavender asters and yellow mustard. Seals lounged on offshore rocks. A group of Steller sea lions feasted in a frenzy on a school of fish just beyond the breakers, the water roiling and fins flying. The frigid waters off the coast are a rich feeding ground: northerly currents churn the sea, bringing deep, cold, nutrient-rich waters to the surface, boosting the food chain for plants, fish, sea mammals, and birds.

Soft sand and rocks make this a challenging beach hike. Shipman Creek at 7.9 miles is 1.7 miles beyond Buck Creek. North of Shipman Creek, the beach narrows, bordered by steep cliffs, and is impassable during high tides greater than 4 feet. We arrived at noon, more than 2 hours before high tide, but the tide was scheduled to reach 6.5 feet. We had to race around points between surges. If we had arrived a half hour later, we would have had to wait 4 hours until the tide receded.

At 8.5 miles the trail climbs to Miller Flat, a broad, grassy terrace. After the long beach hike, it is a joy to stroll on firm, level ground. The trail gradually descends to another terrace, Big Flat, which forms a promontory. The point creates one of the best surfing spots in the world, especially during the high winter seas. Several campsites and driftwood shelters dot the terrace. With only 12-pound day packs, we found it hard to imagine hiking this trail with a backpack and a surfboard!

The trail crosses Big Flat Creek. Watch out for timber rattlesnakes that dwell in driftwood piles and the creekbed. The trail passes several Sinkyone shell middens. With abundant sea life and a freshwater creek, Big Flat was an excellent spot for a summer camp.

Just beyond the creek the trail comes to a crude landing strip and a private residence at the back of the terrace. A few private landholdings were grandfathered in when the conservation area was established. The sign for the Rattlesnake Ridge Trail is near the southeastern corner of the landing strip.

The mountains climb steeply along Big Flat Creek. Three miles east, majestic King Peak towers over the willows, sword ferns, and alders that line the creekbed. Rattlesnake Ridge Trail crosses Big Flat Creek several times as it starts its ascent, climbing 3,500 feet over the next 5.7 miles back to King Crest Trail. Stop for a rest and a swim in one of the many inviting pools.

The trail climbs gradually 1.5 miles until it leaves the creek and starts a series of long switchbacks up to fire-scorched Rattlesnake Ridge. It burned hot through this forest, leaving stands of charred Douglas-fir trunks and opening panoramic

View from Miller Flat

views of the densely forested coastal mountains that rise right from the ocean's edge. The firs have been replaced by a thriving forest of manzanita and madrone.

The switchbacks are fairly gradual until the final 1.5 miles of the climb, where the trail gets steep. Stop for a rest a mile from the top at Bear Hollow Camp and fill up with water before you start the final climb. The Rattlesnake Ridge Trail meets the King Crest Trail only 3 miles from your car. Turn left and hike the undulating spine of the King Range as it gradually descends 500 feet to the trailhead. You arrive back at your car undoubtedly tired but content knowing that you are among the few souls who have explored this rugged wilderness, hiking both the mountain peaks and the wild shoreline of the Lost Coast.

LIGHTNING TRAIL–SHELTER COVE LOOP

Day 1: Lightning Trailhead to Shelter Cove via Buck Creek Trail

THIS HIKE IS SLIGHTLY shorter than the North Slide Peak trip. Of the three routes, this trailhead is the most easily accessed by car because it does not require an all-wheel-drive vehicle (see page 194 for details about the drive).

The Lightning Trail starts at 2,270 feet and climbs 1,800 feet over 2 miles to King Peak. It ascends along the ridge through forests of madrone, tan oak, and Douglas-fir. Windows open periodically through the trees with dramatic views to the west of sheer mountain slopes plunging toward the sea.

You meet the King Crest Trail after 1.6 miles. Maple Camp is to the left, where you can fill up with water and continue south on the King Crest Trail.

Better yet, take the right fork and follow the signs to King Peak. As you approach the summit, the forest thins, replaced by dense chaparral. The stunning 360-degree view from King Peak, at 4,087 feet, stretches from the King Range to the north and south to the vast Pacific out to the western horizon.

Head south from the peak along the King Crest Trail. The trail follows the crest 5 miles to Buck Creek Trail. You descend 3,300 feet to the sea and head south along the shore 6.2 miles to Shelter Cove. For the rest of this day's journey and a description of Shelter Cove, see pages 182–185, starting at "The King Range National Conservation Area . . ."

Day 2: Shelter Cove to Lightning Trailhead via Rattlesnake Ridge Trail

THIS HIKE RETURNS TO THE BEACH and travels 10 miles along the shore to Big Flat, where it turns inland for a 3,500-foot ascent over 5.7 miles along Rattlesnake Ridge Trail to King Crest Trail. After hiking 2.5 miles on King Crest Trail, return to Lightning Trail for an 1,800-foot, 2-mile descent to your car.

It is crucial to time the shoreline section of this day's hike with the tides. The beach narrows and can be blocked at high tide, especially around rocky points from just north of Buck Creek at 6.5 miles to Miller Flat at 8.5 miles. Consult the tide tables at tidesandcurrents.noaa.gov/tide_predictions. The best hiking conditions on the beach are the hours before and after low tide, but keep an eye on the sea. Rogue waves can crash far up the beach without warning.

Rock shelves off Shelter Cove

For a description of the first 15.7 miles of this day's hike from Shelter Cove to King Crest Trail, see pages 185–187, starting at "Shelter Cove to the King Crest Trailhead via Rattlesnake Ridge Trail."

Rattlesnake Ridge Trail meets the King Crest Trail where you turn right. A 1990 fire burned large swaths of the approach to King Peak, leaving charred tree trunks but also opening extraordinary vistas. From the knife-edge spine of the King Range, the mountain slopes drop precipitously to the sea. Turn left on Lightning Trail for a 2-mile descent along another ridge to your car.

SADDLE MOUNTAIN–SHELTER COVE LOOP

THIS SHORTEST OF THE THREE LOST COAST WALKABOUTS, 10.5 miles in each direction, gives a taste of the King Range's crest before descending to the sea for a nice beach hike to Shelter Cove. The return trip retraces your steps back to your car.

Day 1: Saddle Mountain Trailhead to Shelter Cove via Buck Creek Trail

AFTER HIKING 0.7 MILE from the Saddle Mountain Trailhead through a Douglas-fir and madrone forest, you reach the intersection of the King Crest and Buck Creek Trails. Your route turns left, down Buck Creek Trail, but if you get an early start, you may want to explore the crest trail before descending to the sea.

Follow the sign to the Buck Creek Trail for a 3,300-foot descent over 3.6 miles. The trail reaches the shore at the mouth of Buck Creek. Turn left and hike 6.2 miles along the beach to Shelter Cove. For the rest of this day's journey and a description of Shelter Cove, see pages 183–185, starting at "Signage is good along the entire route . . ."

Day 2: Shelter Cove to Saddle Mountain Trailhead via Buck Creek Trail

THE TRAIL NORTH RETRACES YOUR STEPS along the beach to Buck Creek. Black sand beaches stretch out before you, and forested mountains drop steeply to the coast. Small creeks tumble out of canyons, and most sink into the sand before they reach the sea. Be prepared for several stream crossings if you hike early in the season. Seeps and springs percolate from the cliffs, creating vertical wildflower gardens of lavender asters, orange paintbrush, and yellow mustard. Heidi and I hiked this section on a glorious, sunny September day. Seals lounged on offshore rocks. A group of Steller sea lions feasted in a frenzy on a school of fish just beyond the breakers, the water roiling and fins flying. The frigid waters off the coast are a rich feeding ground: northerly currents churn the sea, bringing deep, cold, nutrient-rich waters to the surface, boosting the food chain for plants, fish, sea mammals, and birds.

Turn right on Buck Creek Trail for the steep climb back to the ridge. Each switchback of this 3.6-mile, 3,300-foot ascent opens new views of the Pacific and of densely forested mountains plunging to the sea. When you reach the King Crest Trail, turn right for a 0.7-mile stroll to your car.

THE ROUTES

All mileages listed for a given day are cumulative.

KING CREST TRAILHEAD–SHELTER COVE LOOP

Day 1: King Crest Trailhead to Shelter Cove via Buck Creek Trail

Hike 10.5 miles on the King Crest Trail before descending to the beach. If you need water, turn left at the Lightning Trail intersection to Maple Camp.

From King Crest Trailhead, hike to Rattlesnake Ridge Trail. **3.0 miles**

Continue on the King Crest Trail to King Peak. **5.5 miles**

Hike from King Peak to Buck Creek Trail. **10.5 miles**

Turn right on Buck Creek Trail, and descend 3,300 feet over 3.6 miles to the coast. **14.1 miles**

Turn left at the shore, and walk to Black Sands Beach. **19.3 miles**

From Black Sands Beach, walk to Shelter Cove. Continue beyond Black Sands Beach to Abalone Point. Leave the beach where it ends, and take the paved lanes along the coast to your inn. If the passage to Abalone Point is blocked by the tide, take the path up to the Black Sands Beach staging area. A large boulder marks the south end of beach. The path follows the bed of Telegraph Creek. Walk up the road a short distance, and turn right on Humboldt Loop Road, which climbs and descends over the next 0.6 mile to where you turn right on Upper Pacific Drive. Turn right at Albatross Road and Wave Drive. You reach the Inn of the Lost Coast 1 mile from Black Sands Beach. Turn right on Lower Pacific Drive and go another 0.6 mile to reach both the Oceanfront and Tides Inns.

total miles 20.3

Day 2: Shelter Cove to King Crest Trailhead via
Rattlesnake Ridge Trail

Hike 10 miles along the beach to Rattlesnake Ridge Trail, then climb back to King Crest Trail. The rocky points north of Buck Creek (6.5 miles) to Miller Flat (8.5 miles) may be impassable at high tide. The section beyond Shipman Creek (7.9 miles) is the most hazardous. Find tide schedules at tidesandcurrents.noaa .gov/tide_predictions. The hours before and after low tide are also the times when you will find the best hiking conditions—wider beaches with firm sand.

Hike from Shelter Cove to Black Sands Beach.   **1.0 mile**

Continue to Buck Creek.   **6.2 miles**

Hike from Buck Creek to Shipman Creek.   **7.9 miles**

Your route leaves the beach and climbs to a trail along Miller Flat.   **8.5 miles**

Continue on the bluff trail to Big Flat and Rattlesnake Ridge Trail.   **10.0 miles**

After crossing Big Flat Creek, you will see a crude landing strip and a private cabin at the back of the terrace. Turn right on Rattlesnake Ridge Trail (near the southeast corner of the landing strip), and ascend 3,500 feet over 5.7 miles to King Crest Trail.   **15.7 miles**

Turn left on King Crest Trail, and head back to the trailhead.
                                                        total miles 18.7

LIGHTNING TRAIL–SHELTER COVE LOOP

Day 1: Lightning Trailhead to Shelter Cove via Buck Creek Trail

Lightning Trail climbs 1,800 feet from the trailhead to King Peak. If you need water, turn left after 1.6 miles to Maple Camp. Otherwise, stay right on the Lightning Trail to the King Crest Trail. Turn left, and follow the signs to the peak.   **2.0 miles**

Continue south on King Crest Trail to Buck Creek Trail.   **7.0 miles**

Turn right on Buck Creek Trail, and descend 3,300 feet over 3.6 miles to the coast.   **10.6 miles**

Turn left at the shore, and walk to Black Sands Beach.   **15.8 miles**

Continue beyond Black Sands Beach to Abalone Point. Leave the beach where it ends, and take the paved lanes along the coast to your inn. If the passage to Abalone Point is blocked by the tide, take the path up to the Black Sands Beach staging area. A large boulder marks the south end of beach. The path follows the bed of Telegraph

Creek. Walk up the road a short distance and turn right on Humboldt Loop Road, which climbs and descends over the next 0.6 mile to where you turn right on Upper Pacific Drive. Turn right at Albatross Road and Wave Drive. You reach the Inn of the Lost Coast 1 mile from Black Sands Beach. Turn right on Lower Pacific Drive and walk another 0.6 mile to reach the Oceanfront and Tides Inns.

total miles 16.8

Day 2: Shelter Cove to Lightning Trailhead via Rattlesnake Ridge Trail

Hike 10 miles along the beach to Rattlesnake Ridge Trail, and then climb back to King Crest Trail. The rocky points north of Buck Creek (6.5 miles) to Miller Flat (8.5 miles) may be impassable at high tide. The section beyond Shipman Creek (7.9 miles) is the most hazardous. Tide schedules are available at tidesandcurrents .noaa.gov/tide_predictions. The hours before and after low tide are also the times when you will find the best hiking conditions—wider beaches with firm sand.

Hike from Shelter Cove to Black Sands Beach.   **1.0 mile**

Continue to Buck Creek.   **6.2 miles**

Hike from Buck Creek to Shipman Creek.   **7.9 miles**

Leave the beach and climb to a trail along Miller Flat.   **8.5 miles**

Continue on the bluff trail to Big Flat and Rattlesnake Ridge Trail.   **10.0 miles**

After crossing Big Flat Creek, you will see a crude landing strip and a private cabin at the back of the terrace. Turn right on Rattlesnake Ridge Trail (near the southeast corner of the landing strip), and ascend 3,500 feet over 5.7 miles to King Crest Trail.   **15.7 miles**

Turn right on King Crest Trail to Lightning Trail.   **18.2 miles**

Turn left on Lightning Trail to return to the trailhead.

total miles 20.2

SADDLE MOUNTAIN–SHELTER COVE LOOP

Day 1: Saddle Mountain Trailhead to Shelter Cove via Buck Creek Trail

Hike to Buck Creek Trail.   **0.7 mile**

Take Buck Creek Trail, and descend 3,300 feet over 3.6 miles to the coast.   **4.3 miles**

Turn left at the shore, and walk to Black Sands Beach. **9.5 miles**

Continue beyond Black Sands Beach to Abalone Point. Leave the beach where it ends, and take the paved lanes along the coast to your inn. If the passage to Abalone Point is blocked by the tide, take the path up to the Black Sands Beach staging area. A large boulder marks the south end of beach. The path follows the bed of Telegraph Creek. Walk up the road a short distance and turn right on Humboldt Loop Road, which climbs and descends over the next 0.6 mile to where you turn right on Upper Pacific Drive. Turn right at Albatross Road and Wave Drive. You reach the Inn of the Lost Coast 1 mile from Black Sands Beach. Turn right on Lower Pacific Drive, and walk another 0.6 mile to reach both the Oceanfront and Tides Inns.

total miles 10.5

Day 2: Shelter Cove to Saddle Mountain Trailhead via Buck Creek Trail

Return along the same route. Hike from Shelter Cove to Black Sands Beach. **1.0 mile**

Continue to Buck Creek Trail. **6.2 miles**

Turn right on Buck Creek Trail for a steep ascent of 3,300 feet over 3.6 miles to King Crest Trail. **9.8 miles**

Turn right on King Crest Trail to Saddle Mountain Trailhead.

total miles 10.5

Seagulls over Black Sands Beach

TRANSPORTATION

GARBERVILLE IS 200 MILES north of San Francisco on US 101.

Driving to King Crest Trailhead

TO REACH THE TRAILHEAD from Garberville, drive north on US 101 for 25 miles to Humboldt Redwoods State Park. Take the South Fork and Honeydew exit, and turn west on Mattole Road. Drive 24 winding, very beautiful miles to Honeydew. Turn left on the Wilder Ridge Road. Drive 1.5 miles, then turn right on the Smith-Etter Road, a rocky, gravel road that climbs into the King Range. All-wheel-drive vehicles are recommended. King Crest Trailhead, another 7.5 miles, is well marked at the north Slide Peak parking area.

Expect the drive from Garberville to take around an hour and a half on winding roads. Smith-Etter Road is usually closed November–April. Check in with the BLM (707-986-5400) for road conditions and to let them know your hiking schedule.

Driving to Lightning Trailhead

TO REACH THE TRAILHEAD from Garberville, take the road to Redway, and continue west toward Shelter Cove. At 20 miles, 3.5 miles short of Shelter Cove, turn right on King Peak Road, a well-graded gravel road. Pass a turnoff to Saddle Mountain 10 miles from the start of King Peak Road, continue another 4 miles, and turn left on King Range Road. Follow the signs to the Lightning Trailhead. Pass another turnoff to Saddle Mountain, and continue on King Range Road to its end and a parking area for the trailhead.

Expect the drive from Garberville to take around 2 hours on winding roads. Check in with the BLM (707-986-5400) for road conditions and to let them know your hiking schedule.

Driving to Saddle Mountain Trailhead

FOLLOW THE DIRECTIONS for the drive to Lightning Trailhead, but turn left on either of the well-marked turnoffs to Saddle Mountain. Both roads are steep, and all-wheel-drive vehicles are recommended. Expect the drive from Garberville to take 1.5–2 hours on winding roads. Check in with the BLM (707-986-5400) for road conditions and to let them know your hiking schedule.

MAPS

WILDERNESS PRESS PUBLISHES a map of the King Range National Conservation Area and Sinkyone Wilderness State Park, titled *California's Lost Coast,* ($7.46). Visit wildernesspress.com.

The BLM also publishes an excellent map, *King Range National Conservation Area: The Lost Coast,* which can be purchased through the mail by check for $5 by writing to Bureau of Land Management, 2800 Cottage Way, Ste. W-1623, Sacramento, CA 95825-1886. To use a credit card, call 916-978-4400.

PLACES TO STAY

LODGING COST			
$ *less than $100*	$$ *$100–$150*	$$$ *$150–$200*	$$$$ *more than $200*

Garberville Area

BENBOW HISTORIC INN $$–$$$$ • 445 Lake Benbow Dr. • 707-923-2124 • 800-355-3301 • benbowinn.com • Historic resort that once catered to the stars.

HUMBOLDT REDWOODS INN $$ • 987 Redwood Dr. • Garberville • 707-623-2451 • humboldtredwoodsinn.com

MIRANDA GARDENS RESORT $–$$$ • 6766 Avenue of the Giants, Miranda • 10 miles north of Garberville • 707-943-3011 • mirandagardens.com • A good jumping-off point for the King Crest Trailhead–Shelter Cove Loop.

MYERS COUNTRY INN $$$$ • 12913 Avenue of the Giants, Myers Flat • 15 miles north of Garberville • 707-943-3259 • 800-500-6464 • myersinn.com • Breakfast included. Another good jumping-off point for the King Crest Trailhead–Shelter Cove Loop.

Shelter Cove

OCEANFRONT INN $$$–$$$$ • 26 Seal Court • 707-986-7002 • sheltercoveoceanfrontinn.com • Superb location.

INN OF THE LOST COAST $$$–$$$$ • 205 Wave Dr. • 707-986-7521 • 888-570-9676 • innofthelostcoast.com

THE TIDES INN $$$–$$$$ • 59 Surf Point • 707-986-7900 • 888-998-4337 • sheltercovetidesinn.com

SPYGLASS INN AT SHELTER COVE $$$$ • 118 Dolphin Dr. • 707-502-1900 • 707-986-4030 • spyglassinnatsheltercove.com

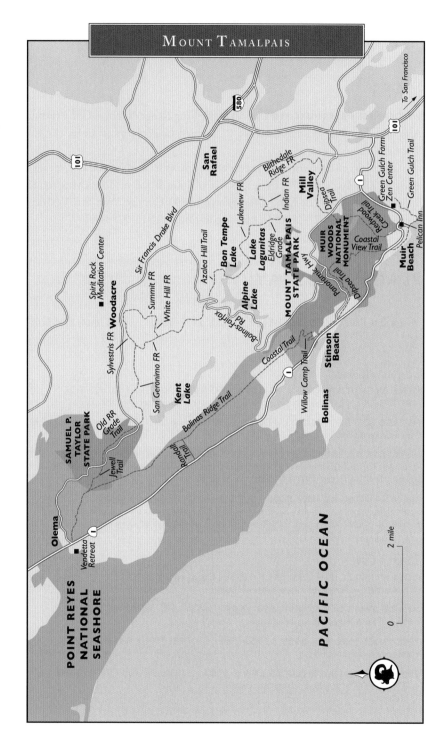

MOUNT TAMALPAIS

To San Francisco

101

San Rafael

580

Blithedale Ridge FR

Mill Valley

Indian FR

Lakeview FR

101

Green Gulch Farm
Zen Center

Green Gulch Trail

Sir Francis Drake Blvd

Azalea Hill Trail

Bon Tempe Lake

Lake Lagunitas

Eldridge Grade

Redwood Creek Trail

Dipsea Trail

Coastal View Trail

Pelican Inn

Spirit Rock
Meditation Center

Woodacre

Summit FR

White Hill FR

Alpine Lake

MUIR WOODS NATIONAL MONUMENT

Muir Beach

Sylvestris FR

San Geronimo FR

Bolinas-Fairfax Rd

MOUNT TAMALPAIS STATE PARK

Panoramic Hwy

Dipsea Trail

Kent Lake

Coastal Trail

Stinson Beach

SAMUEL P. TAYLOR STATE PARK

Old RR Grade Trail

Bolinas Ridge Trail

Willow Camp Trail

Bolinas

Jewell Trail

Randall Trail

Olema

Vendetta Retreat

POINT REYES NATIONAL SEASHORE

PACIFIC OCEAN

0   2 mile

CIRCUMTAMBULATION

A Pilgrimage Around Mount Tamalpais

Today is like no day that
Came before
I'll walk the roads and trails to Tamalpais.

—GARY SNYDER, "Hills of Home"

View south to Muir Beach, the Marin Headlands, and San Francisco

There is no place on earth so beautiful as Tamalpais.

—ROBERT LOUIS STEVENSON,
declared from the top of Mount Tam

MOUNT TAMALPAIS, THE HIGHEST PEAK FOR 250 MILES along the Central California coast, beckons hikers to explore its trails and to marvel at its extraordinary vistas. This 56-mile walkabout travels around the mountain, a circumambulation, over five hiking days. A moderate to challenging hike with days as short as 6 miles and as long as 16, it climbs up and down the mountain's flanks from sea level to 1,900 feet. Along the way you visit villages with interesting restaurants, taverns, and inns. The trail also passes three meditation centers. You may want to include a stop for a class or a few days of personal retreat. Take a long pilgrimage around the revered Mount Tamalpais—a "circumtambulation."

ITINERARY

DAY 1:	Mill Valley to Muir Beach	**5.8**
DAY 2:	Muir Beach to Stinson Beach	**6.8**
DAY 3:	Stinson Beach to Olema	**16.4**
DAY 4:	Olema to Woodacre	**12.5**
DAY 5:	Woodacre to Mill Valley	**15.0**
TOTAL MILEAGE		**56.5**

SITTING IN THE LIBRARY of the Vedanta Society Temple in the Pacific Heights district of San Francisco, surrounded by books on religion and philosophy, I waited for my appointment. An elderly nun in a midcalf-length beige-orange skirt, a beige-orange sweater, and sensible shoes came to the door and said, "The Swami will see you now."

We climbed the stairs and stopped to view the interior garden, lush with primrose and petunias. "The rain has made the flowers happy," she said, "but we are getting a little tired of it."

The air was sweet with incense. She escorted me to the book-lined office of Swami Prabuddhananda, a round, balding Indian man in beige-orange robes and a sweater sitting behind a desk. I bowed with a namaste, and he returned the gesture.

"Please sit down," he said. "You wish to visit our retreat center."

"Yes," I said. "I would like to go on a personal retreat."

"How long would you like to stay?"

On the Dipsea Trail, 676 steps climb from Old Mill Park to Panoramic Highway.

"Only two nights."

He said, "Tell me about your spiritual practice."

I'd been warned he would ask this question. "I meditate. I belong to a weekly meditation group." Thankfully he didn't inquire about my shabby attendance record. "My main practice is walking. I am walking around Mount Tamalpais, a pilgrimage, and I'd like to spend a few nights at the Vedanta Retreat."

He seemed unimpressed. "What do you plan to do there?"

"I'd like to sit and read. I'd like to practice walking meditation, walking the land."

"No, you mustn't hike," he said in earnest. "You can take short walks around the grounds. You are there to meditate and pray. And besides, there are mountain lions. Three years ago a woman on retreat got lost and was out in the woods overnight. One hundred and thirty volunteers searched for her until she was found. Please, short walks only. Stay on the trails."

"I will stay on the trails."

"All right, you may stay at the retreat center," he said, rising to escort me down the hall.

I had passed the test, but it must have been a low bar on the spiritual evolutionary scale. He left me with a nun who would record my information on an alphabetized index card.

"Thank you very much," I said to him and bowed again, hands folded at the forehead. As he returned to his office, I noticed his socks were bright orange.

The last piece of the puzzle had fallen into place. I would make a 56.5-mile circumambulation of Mount Tamalpais with visits to three meditation centers:

Green Gulch Farm, Vedanta Society Retreat, and Spirit Rock Meditation Center. They all lie at the base of Mount Tam to the south, west, and north, respectively. My plan was to take eight days, stopping for two nights at each center, but walkers can also choose to stay at inns and B&Bs around the mountain.

Mount Tam was revered by the Coast Miwok and is held as sacred by many Bay Area pagans and nature lovers. In 1989, the year he was awarded the Nobel Peace Prize, the Dalai Lama prayed for environmental peace on the eastern slope of Mount Tam. Monks in maroon and saffron robes chanted, accompanied by horns and cymbals, under the white smoke of burning juniper. The three retreat centers at the mountain's base have been blessed by the visits of holy men and women and by the intentions of thousands of visitors over the years.

Mount Tamalpais climbs to 2,547 feet, straight from the Pacific shore, the highest peak for 250 miles along the coast between Big Sur and the King Range in Mendocino County. Mostly preserved as open space, her silhouette, often called "The Sleeping Maiden," can be seen for miles from distant parts of the Bay Area. She has long beckoned hikers and pilgrims, certainly since shortly after the gold rush, and probably for millennia.

Day 1: Mill Valley to Muir Beach

MILL VALLEY SITS AT THE BASE of Mount Tam. Its streets follow the contours of the mountain, and redwood groves shade what once were summer cottages of wealthy San Franciscans. You may want to spend the first night at the peaceful and

Mill Creek

cozy Mill Valley Inn. Its cottages and rooms are built around a redwood grove, and Old Mill Creek flows through the property. Step out the front door, and walk a block into central Mill Valley to enjoy restaurants, a deli, coffee shops, a bookstore, or a movie theater. This first section begins on the Dipsea Trail. The annual Dipsea Race, the second-oldest footrace in the United States (after the Boston Marathon), started in 1905. It starts in Mill Valley and runs 7.1 miles to the Pacific Ocean in Stinson Beach. Your route follows the Dipsea Trail 2.2 miles to Muir Woods.

Leaving Old Mill Park, the trail climbs 650 feet and three flights of stairs with 676 steps to Panoramic Highway. Cross the highway, and descend the steep trail to the overflow parking lot of Muir Woods National Monument.

This day's hike is short, so you may want to take a side trip into Muir Woods. The coast redwood *(Sequoia sempervirens)* grows along a narrow strip of the Pacific Coast. Two hundred years ago, old-growth redwoods grew on 2 million acres of coastal forests. Today, redwoods are still common, but old-growth groves are rare.

Step into Muir Woods, a cathedral of ancient giants, some 1,200 years old. Their canopy reaches for the sunshine, 250 feet above a soft forest floor. Big-leaf maples, tan oaks, and California bay laurels thrive in the dappled sunlight of the forest's undergrowth. The air is fragrant from the bays and damp from heavy winter rains that drop an average of 39 inches in the valley and 47 inches on the mountain slopes. Coastal fog creeps up Redwood Creek in the summer, and the dense redwood foliage harvests water droplets that can "rain" another 55 inches of precipitation each year on the forest floor.

Redwood Creek flows through Muir Woods to the sea at Muir Beach. Coastal cutthroat and steelhead trout and coho salmon spawn in the creek. During the dry season, a sandbar forms at Muir Beach and blocks the creek's exit to the sea. Winter rains come, the creek swells, breaching the sandbar, and the fish move upstream to spawn. Where the creek passes below the Muir Woods overflow parking lot is the start of the most famous mountain circumambulation in the United States.

Members of Asian religions practice the ancient ritual of circumambulating holy sites, such as shrines, stupas, and sacred mountains. In Sanskrit the practice is known as *pradakshina*. Perhaps the most famous circumambulation is that of Mount Kailash. For thousands of years pilgrims have circled this 22,000-foot peak—consider sacred by practitioners of Buddhism, Hinduism, Jainism, Ayyavazhi, and Bon—in the Gangdise Mountains of Tibet. Climbing it would be a sacrilege. The followers of the Jain and Bon religions hike the 32-mile route in a counterclockwise direction. Hindus and Buddhists circle clockwise, with the mountain on their right.

Beat poets Allen Ginsberg and Gary Snyder became friends in the 1950s. When they met up in India in 1962, they hatched a plan to bring ritual circumambulation to America. On October 22, 1965, joined by Philip Whalen in the Muir Woods overflow parking lot, they climbed west on the Dipsea Trail. According to Snyder, they stopped to chant at spots "with a strong sense of power." Whalen wrote, "We marched around the mountain, west to east / top to bottom—from sea-level (chanting dark stream bed / Muir Woods) to bright summit sun victory of gods and / buddhas, conversion of demons, liberation of all sentient / beings in all worlds past present and future." Circling Mount Tam's east peak, they returned to Muir Woods at the end of the day. Inspired mostly by the writings of Gary Snyder, others followed their original route. Today, public one-day circumambulations of Mount Tam still happen four times a year on Sundays closest to the solstices and equinoxes.

Your route leaves the Dipsea, turns left, and follows the shoulder of Muir Woods Road 0.4 mile before taking Redwood Creek Trail. The trail crosses and follows Redwood Creek 2.2 miles to CA 1. Turn left and hike to Muir Beach and the Pelican Inn or Green Gulch Farm.

Green Gulch Farm

In Buddhism, there is a word, apranibita. It means wishlessness or aimlessness. The idea is that we do not put anything ahead of ourselves and run after it. When we practice walking meditation, we walk in the spirit. We just enjoy the walking, with no particular aim or destination. Our walking is not a means to an end. We walk for the sake of walking.

—THICH NHAT HANH, *The Long Road Turns to Joy*

Stroll up Green Gulch Trail from Muir Beach. Entering the farm from the west, you walk through broad fertile fields of lettuce, chard, broccoli, cabbage, cauliflower, kale, spinach, potatoes, and squash in long rows, planted in rich, dark, loamy soil. Rows of mighty Monterey pines and cypresses running north and south separate the fields, protecting them from gales off the Pacific. Zen students toil on the farm, planting, harvesting, or working in the greenhouses, preparing crops for the residents and guests, Greens Restaurant, and the farmers markets in Mill Valley and the San Francisco Ferry Plaza. Continue through the flower gardens. Foxgloves, poppies, dahlias, columbines, and roses blaze with color. Statues of Buddha and Quan Yin are tucked into garden corners. Benches invite the weary peregrinator to stop and rest.

Statue of Quan Yin at Green Gulch Farm

Suzuki-roshi, a major force in bringing Zen Buddhism to the West, founded the San Francisco Zen Center. Part of his dream was to establish a farming community where serious students could train in Buddhism. In 1972, less than two years after his death, the Zen Center acquired Green Gulch Farm. It has been transformed into an organic farming community with 30–40 residents who work the land and practice Buddhism. Great teachers such as the Dalai Lama, Thich Nhat Hanh, Pema Chodron, and Robert Thurman have visited the farm to share their wisdom with residents and guests.

Continue up-valley to the cluster of houses, meeting rooms, dining hall, and Green Dragon Temple, sheltered by eucalyptus, oaks, and redwoods. Guests are welcome to stay in the Lindisfarne Guest House, an octagonal building with 12 guest rooms, each with a balcony. It was exquisitely built with traditional Japanese joinery methods, using hand-planed and pegged timbers.

Accommodations include three delicious vegetarian meals. Forty of us lined up for dinner in silence. A bell rang, and we bowed and started serving ourselves millet, West African groundnut stew, and collards from large trays. Dinner was silent for the first 10 minutes; then another bell rang, and animated conversations started. Residents and guests from around the world shared stories of their travels and life at the farm.

To stay in one of the most spectacular lodgings in California, book the Hope Cottage. A 25-minute hike up a steep trail, it perches high on a rock outcropping in a grove of Monterey pines overlooking Muir Beach and the Pacific. Lichens grow on its outer stone walls, and a wood-burning stove warms the cottage. The kitchen is stocked with basic foods to fortify you between long walks down to the dining hall for meals. You can enjoy the view from the high bed next to a wall of picture windows.

Guests are invited to sit with the community for morning and evening meditation. I slept through the 5 a.m. sessions, but I joined the evening sitting. As I entered the temple, a nun gave me brief instructions on where to sit. There was a large statue of Buddha at the end of the long hall, and black meditation cushions were lined up in four straight rows. A few chairs were provided for those not comfortable on a cushion. We sat in blissful silence, facing the wall for 40 minutes. A bell rang, and I followed the students in a series of bows and chants. Then we exited into the bright sunlight and walked to the dining hall.

Most of the rest of my time was spent wandering the coastal hills and reading in the gardens. My mind and my pace slowed. The busy schedule of my everyday life seemed more remote, and I felt more alive in the present moment—a wonderful way to start a long pilgrimage.

Day 2: Muir Beach to Stinson Beach

LEAVING GREEN GULCH, return to the shore. See The Route (page 213) for directions through the village of Muir Beach. In the village, houses on stilts cling to the steep cliffs, their picture windows and decks overlooking the Pacific. The best seasons for hiking this coast are spring, from mid-April through June, or autumn, during September and October, to avoid the winter rains and the summer fog. On the sunny June day I hiked through the area, lush coastal gardens of calla lilies, pride of Madeira, and poppies spilled over their beds.

Take a short detour to the Muir Beach Overlook, where a path leads to the end of a knife-edge peninsula 300 feet above the crashing waves of the Pacific. Looking south you can see Muir Beach, the Marin Headlands, and San Francisco. To the north, the rugged coastline extends to Point Reyes. Mount Tamalpais towers above it all.

After a short walk along CA 1, the Coast View Trail starts its gradual ascent up Mount Tam through grasslands and coyote brush. It climbs over 3 miles to 1,200 feet and meets the Dipsea Trail. Below, CA 1 winds along the coast, small boats fish the coastal waters, and massive freighters enter and depart through the Golden Gate. On a clear day you can see the rocky Farallon Islands on the horizon, jutting out of the Pacific 27 miles to the west.

The Dipsea descends another 3 miles to Stinson Beach, first traversing grassy hillsides and then dropping down into the cool redwood and bay forest of Steep Ravine. Steps have been laid to form the trail that drops into the deep canyon to Webb Creek. Emerging from the woods, the trail opens to the first view of

View north to Point Reyes

Stinson Beach. Houses poke through the trees climbing up the flank of Mount Tam, and the long beach extends for miles, almost to Bolinas, sheltering broad Bolinas Lagoon to the east. After another short trip through the woods, the trail spills out onto CA 1 at the edge of town.

I stayed at the Redwoods Haus B&B, an establishment that has received mixed reviews from the Walkabout community. I enjoy its eclectic decor and weird vibe. When I called to make a reservation, the host encouraged me to upgrade to the Crows Nest Room.

"It's the only room in town where you can see the beach," he said. "It was packed last weekend. All kinds of girls in bikinis."

"I'll take it," I said. There are many paths.

Sitting out on the deck of the Sand Dollar Restaurant in the early evening sunlight, I dined leisurely on raw oysters, a salad with sliced pears and blue cheese, a crispy mushroom and Parmesan polenta cake, and a pint of Lagunitas IPA. Then I strolled down to the beach to watch the sun sink into the Pacific.

Day 3: Stinson Beach to Olema

THIS DAY ENDS IN OLEMA. If you are staying at one of the inns, you can dine at the Olema Farmhouse Restaurant and Bar or Sir and Star at the Olema. If you are staying at the Vedanta Retreat, you will need to prepare your own meals. The deli in Olema sells sandwiches, cheese, and microwavable burritos. You may want to stop at the Stinson Beach Market, on the corner of CA 1 and Calle Del Mar, for more substantial supplies.

After a short walk through the neighborhoods of Stinson Beach, you reach Willow Camp Trail. It climbs 2.5 miles to 1,900 feet to reach Bolinas Ridge. On a clear day, breathtaking views of the coast and the vast Pacific unfold with each switchback.

Turn left at the crest, and rejoin the Coastal Trail. It traverses rolling grasslands just below the ridgeline and West Ridgecrest Boulevard. Wonderful views of the coast continue until you enter a redwood forest and cross Bolinas-Fairfax Road at 5.3 miles. Continue straight on Bolinas Ridge Fire Road for the next 9.7 miles. The wide hiker/biker trail travels the rolling crest of Bolinas Ridge through redwood and oak forests. Views of Bolinas Lagoon and the ocean open periodically through breaks in the trees. You pass McCurdy Trail 8.8 miles from Stinson Beach and Randall Trail at 10.4 miles. Soon after that, the trail descends through open, grassy slopes toward Olema. Pass Jewell Trail on the right at 14.8 miles.

After another 0.2 mile you pass through a fence and under power lines that follow the fenceline. Turn left on an informal path, and descend to Olema. The path may be indiscernible at first, but it follows the fence and the power lines and

Stinson Beach, Bolinas Lagoon, and Bolinas Peninsula

is maintained by cow traffic for the first 0.8 mile. Then it passes through an informal gate and continues along the fenceline until it approaches CA 1, where it veers to the right, arcs behind some houses, and ends at the highway in Olema. The inns and restaurants of Olema are to the right. If you are going to the Vedanta Retreat, turn left at the highway, and walk 0.1 mile to the entrance.

Vedanta Retreat

Towering, regal eucalyptus lines the entry road to the Vedanta Retreat. I checked in at the monastery barn and met Vimukta, who would show me the ropes.

Walking to the large white Colonial-style house, Vimukta said, "Tom, that is the men's retreat house. It was built during the gold rush."

"As a ranch house?"

"Yes. Just about everything has been changed: new electricity, central heating, a new foundation."

"Vimukta, it sounds like you may have worked on those changes."

"Yes," he said with a soft laugh.

Dressed in a sweater, jacket, and a bright handknit hat on this warm day, he was a thin, frail-looking man who walked slowly and mindfully. His voice was gentle and full of kindness. I'm not sure why he said my name every time he spoke to me. Perhaps it was a memory device or perhaps a method for being completely present with his partner in conversation. Reaching the entrance of the men's retreat house, he moved the welcome mat over an inch to line up with the doorframe, and we went into the kitchen.

"Tom, here is the cutlery." Opening the drawer labeled CUTLERY, he moved a spoon from the fork tray to its rightful place.

"Tom, this is the refrigerator. You can store your perishables here."

He showed me the meditation room with pictures of Jesus, Buddha, and Sri Ramakrishna. "Three great souls," he said, stooping to pick a piece of lint off the carpet and straightening a picture of Swami Vivekananda in the hall. He took me to my room on the second floor, one of four available for male retreatants. People of all faiths are welcome at the retreat center, but they must first interview with the Swami, as I did, in San Francisco.

"The fellow that was here before you moved things where they shouldn't be. Tom, help me move this desk."

We moved it 2 feet to the left and then 2 inches back, centered between two tall windows.

Leaving me to settle in, he said, "We don't practice silence, but we keep it pretty quiet around here."

Vedanta is based on the Upanishads, the concluding portions of the Vedas, ancient Indo-Aryan scriptures. A brochure in the library titled "What is Vedanta" described its guiding tenets:

> The basic teaching of Vedanta is that the essence of all beings and all things—from a blade of grass to the Personal God—is Spirit, infinite and eternal, unchanging and indivisible. Vedanta emphasizes that a person in his or her true nature is this divine Spirit, identical with the inmost being and reality of the universe.

Sri Ramakrishna was a great modern Vedanta saint and teacher. His chief disciple, Swami Vivekananda, brought Vedanta to the West and founded the Vedanta Society of Northern California in 1900. Sri Ramakrishna encouraged us to take time for quiet personal retreats: "Whenever you have leisure, go into solitude for a day or two. At that time refrain from having relations with the outside world and avoid engaging in conversations with worldly people on worldly affairs."

There were only a few of us enjoying this beautiful setting and place of quiet contemplation. Tall Monterey pines and eucalyptus tower above the central pastures. Groves of oak, buckeye, and Douglas-fir snake through the grassy hillsides. I spent my time sitting, reading, and wandering aimlessly. Wild turkeys and deer roamed the pastures and woodlands. I felt fortunate to be enjoying the most peaceful place I had ever been.

Walking along a valley path, I met Vimukta strolling and bird-watching with binoculars. "Vimukta, when did the Society acquire this land?"

"They bought the 2,000 acres in 1946. It is surrounded by Point Reyes National Seashore. The women's residence was built, and we opened it up as a retreat center in 1973."

"Vimukta, how long have you lived here?"

"Oh, since Hector was a pup," he said with a small laugh. The last time I heard this saying was decades ago from my Irish grandmother.

When I left the next morning, I stopped at the monastery to tell Vimukta of my departure.

"Vimukta, I'd like to make a contribution." The society does not ask for payment from retreatants.

"Tom, let me ask you one question. Are you sure you can afford it? Some men make a contribution that they can't afford."

"Yes, I can afford it," I said.

"Tom, please come back anytime, even if just for part of a day."

"Thank you, Vimukta."

Day 4: Olema to Woodacre

RETURN TO CA 1, and retrace your steps back up to Bolinas Ridge Fire Road. As I climbed along the fenceline on this beautiful June day, the sun was shining, and a light fog hung over Tomales Bay. Most of the grasslands on Mount Tam were already turning brown, but this section of her northwest slope was green and lush. Ascending, I walked into late spring. Blue lupines, yellow daisies, white margaritas, blue-eyed grass, golden California poppies, and a half dozen other wildflowers grew in profusion. As I kept climbing, one species would diminish and another would join the bouquet.

Turn right on Bolinas Ridge Fire Road and walk 0.2 mile to Jewell Trail. Turn left, and descend into the Lagunitas Creek valley. Starting high in rolling pastures, the trail descends into forests. Oaks and bays line the high arroyos. Redwoods and Douglas-firs fill the watershed's depths.

Near the crest, a grove of live oaks bows to the east, bending from the force of the winds off the Pacific. As I passed, the grove exploded with the frightened flight of a dozen quail. I jumped and was as startled as they were. After flying

Bon Tempe Lake

20 feet, they quickly realized there was no danger. Brown, black, and spotted gray, with extravagant top tassels, the plump creatures wandered through the tall grass, pecking and cooing. My heart returned to my chest, and I descended into Samuel P. Taylor State Park.

Turn right on Old Railroad Grade Trail (Cross Marin Trail). This wide, flat path runs along Lagunitas Creek and follows the former bed of the Northwest Pacific Railroad. The creek begins high on the northern flank of Mount Tam, and its three forks flow into Lake Lagunitas, then Bon Tempe Lake, Alpine Lake, and finally Kent Lake, all reservoirs providing water to thirsty Marin County. Released from Kent Lake, it flows through the park and into Tomales Bay.

Before the dams, vast runs of coho salmon filled the creek from November through February. Though greatly reduced, the wild coho runs in the Lagunitas Creek watershed are still the largest in Central California. The young salmon spend their first year in their natal stream before venturing out to the ocean. After one to three more years, they return from the sea to the stream of their birth, leaping waterfalls and rapids to spawn. Entering freshwater, the females turn bronze, and the males turn a deep red. Their upper jaws elongate and form a downward-curving hook. After spawning, the salmon's life cycle is complete and they perish.

Old Railroad Grade Trail winds through second-growth redwood forest. It passes by the Creekside Campground, crosses the creek and Sir Francis Drake Boulevard on a bridge, and ends at the eastern edge of the park. Cross Sir Francis Drake Boulevard again, and walk on Peter's Dam Road 0.2 mile. Turn left on San Geronimo Ridge Trail, and climb to the crest. The trail passes through forests of redwoods and Douglas-fir. Turn left on Sylvestris Fire Road, and descend through moist canyons of oak and fern forests. Long manes of Spanish moss cling to the branches and wave in the breeze. The fire road ends at East Sylvestris Road. Continue down to San Geronimo Road. Turn right toward Woodacre and Spirit Rock Meditation Center. If you are not staying at Spirit Rock, their website, spiritrock.org, lists nearby B&Bs in private homes.

Spirit Rock Meditation Center

Located on 420 acres of rolling grassland, the Spirit Rock Meditation Center is nonsectarian but grounded in the Buddhist Vipassana tradition. There is no overnight lodging for individuals on personal retreats, but there are classes and daylong events. You can stay overnight on longer retreats that last from two days to several weeks. The Dalai Lama visited Spirit Rock for a conference in 2000. Alice Walker, Thich Nhat Hanh, Ram Dass, and Huston Smith have all led retreats and classes at the center. Spirit Rock's self-described purpose is "to help each individual find within himself or herself peace, compassion, and wisdom, through the practice of mindfulness and insight meditation (vipassana), and to support the individual in taking those qualities into the world."

Live oaks cluster in the washes and the central valley. Bay laurels crowd the banks of a stream that flows through the property, shading the offices, a sweat lodge, a large yurt, and the meditation hall, where about 100 of us gathered, sitting on cushions and chairs. Our teacher was Ajahn Jumniam, a Thai forest monk and a master of insight meditation. A short, stout man in orange robes with a buzz cut and a continuous smile, he had two narrow wooden boxes and a dozen sacred amulets hanging from his waist on a sash. He had just turned 70, and thousands of devotees came to his monastery in Thailand for the celebration. Now, he had come to the United States to lead a series of retreats.

We spent the day practicing sitting and walking meditation between his teachings on the true nature of our mind-body process. He took us on inward journeys through guided meditations. As we sat, the fluted chortle of wild turkeys called from outside the meditation hall. A black-tailed fawn stopped to look through the window, tail twitching, ears turning independently, attentive but unafraid.

I strolled along the stream and into the bay forest during a walking meditation session. A doe rested in the shade, out of the midday heat. Her two fawns explored, visiting three wild turkeys that grazed in the woods. The youngsters came over to look at me. Small and spotted, with moist black noses, they studied me from a dozen feet away. Then quickly they turned, bounding 6 feet at a leap, back to check in with mom before heading off to explore some more. This was a wonderful day of peace and meditation in a beautiful natural setting.

Day 5: Woodacre to Mill Valley

THE FINAL DAY'S 15-MILE HIKE climbs back to San Geronimo Ridge, descends to Bon Tempe Lake and Lake Lagunitas, and ascends to Blithedale Ridge before dropping back down to Mill Valley. Climbing out of the lush forests of Woodacre, you return to open San Geronimo Fire Road. Dense, low-growing manzanita and coyote brush line the trail, along with a pygmy forest of stunted Sargent cypress trees. The cypress can grow to 25 feet, but mature trees grow only 3–5 feet in the thin soil of the ridge. After reaching the Cascade Canyon Fire Road at 1,550 feet, the trail descends and joins Pine Mountain Fire Road, ending at Bolinas-Fairfax Road. San Francisco Bay, spreading north toward Novato and the Sacramento River Delta, comes into view.

Lake Lagunitas

Cross the road to Azalea Hill Trail, and continue to descend to Bon Tempe Lake. Your trail crosses the dam and takes the "Shadyside" of the Bon Tempe Trail on the south shore of the lake. It crosses three bridges as it travels through a deep redwood and Douglas-fir forest. In mid-June, spring runoff had filled the lake to its brim. When you reach the Lake Lagunitas parking lot, continue along the north side of the lake, and start a steep ascent on Lakeview Fire Road. The trail enters a madrone forest and ends at the Eldridge Grade.

The terrain alternates between oak and madrone forests, grassy hillsides, redwood groves, and chaparral as you climb to Blithedale Ridge Fire Road. The eastern side of Mount Tam was already warm and dry this late spring afternoon. Bright-yellow French broom and monkeyflower bloomed along the edge of the trail. Dragonflies and butterflies danced, and the air was filled with a sweet chorus of songbirds. Red-shouldered hawks and turkey vultures soared high above on warm updrafts.

Your journey ends with a final descent on Blithedale Ridge Fire Road and a stroll through the neighborhoods of Mill Valley, a return to urban civilization after a long walk visiting the rural hamlets that lie at the edge of the great mountain. Mount Tam attracts hikers from the Bay Area and around the world to explore her trails, marvel at her incomparable vistas, and bask in her majesty. Three meditation centers draw from her power and add to her serenity. What better way to explore this magnificent mountain than a long inn-to-inn pilgrimage, a "circumambulation."

THE ROUTE

All mileages listed for a given day are cumulative.

Day 1: Mill Valley to Muir Beach

Leaving Mill Valley, take the Dipsea Trail to Muir Woods. Walk from central Mill Valley on Throckmorton Avenue, and turn left on Cascade into Old Mill Park. Cross the bridge over Old Mill Creek, and continue straight on Cascade Way 100 yards to a stairway at the end of the lane. The Dipsea Trail climbs three flights of steps to Panoramic Highway. Turn right at the top of the first flight, continue 100 feet, and take the first left. Watch for the DIPSEA sign. Climb to the top of the second set of steps, turn left, continue 100 feet, and turn right onto the final steps. You emerge at the intersection of Sequoia Valley Road and Edgewood Avenue. Go right on the path that parallels Sequoia Valley Road 100 yards. Turn right on Walsh Drive, and continue until it ends. Go around a gate with a DIPSEA TRAIL sign, and continue on the path. You emerge on Bayview Drive. Continue to Panoramic Highway. **1.3 miles**

Cross Panoramic Highway, turn right, continue 100 feet to a well-marked trail, enter Mount Tamalpais State Park, and start your descent. The Dipsea Trail crosses Muir Woods Road, passing through the park's maintenance yard and crossing the road into the Muir Woods National Monument's overflow parking lot. **2.2 miles**

Turn left on Muir Woods Road, and walk the shoulder 0.4 mile to Redwood Creek Trail on the left. **2.6 miles**

Take Redwood Creek Trail to CA 1. **4.8 miles**

Turn left and walk the highway shoulder to the Pelican Inn. **5.0 miles**

If you are going on to the Green Gulch Farm, turn right at Pelican Inn, and walk to the Muir Beach parking lot. Cross Redwood Creek on the bridge at the south end of the parking lot, and hike inland, following the signs for the Middle Green Gulch Trail. Pass through a gate and into the Zen farm.

total miles 5.8

Day 2: Muir Beach to Stinson Beach

Walk west on the beach entrance road, and take the road that angles to the right just before the parking lot. Continue past the PRIVATE ROAD sign. This road is open to walkers. Opposite the first house on the left, there is a paved driveway on the right leading to a cluster of houses with a stairway at the top. Walk up the driveway (a public pathway), and take the stairs. Cross the first street, and continue on the stairs and path past the Muir Beach Community Center. Walk left on Seascape Drive to the Muir Beach Overlook and CA 1. Walk north on the broad shoulder of CA 1 for 0.5 mile.

The wide Coast View Trail is on the right side of the road. Ascend on the Coast View Trail to the Dipsea Trail. **4.1 miles**

Turn left on the Dipsea Trail to Stinson Beach.

total miles 6.8

Day 3: Stinson Beach to Olema

To reach the Willow Camp Trailhead from CA 1, turn east on Calle Del Mar, left on Buena Vista, left on Lincoln Avenue, left on Belvedere Avenue, and right on Avenida Farralone to the trailhead. Ascend Willow Camp Trail to Coastal Trail. **2.1 miles**

Turn left on Coastal Trail to Bolinas-Fairfax Road. **5.3 miles**

Cross the road, and continue straight on wide Bolinas Ridge Trail for the next 9.7 miles. Pass McCurdy Trail. **8.8 miles**

Pass Randall Trail. **10.4 miles**

Pass Jewell Trail. **14.8 miles**

Pass through a distinct fence with accompanying power lines 0.2 mile after the Jewell Trail intersection. Turn left, and take an informal trail along the fence. As it approaches Olema, the trail turns right, goes behind some houses, and ends at CA 1. If you are staying at an Olema inn, turn right. The entrance to the Vedanta Retreat is 0.1 mile to the left.

total miles 16.4

Day 4: Olema to Woodacre

Leaving Olema, retrace your steps to Bolinas Ridge Trail. The entrance to the path is 100 yards south of the intersection of CA 1 and Sir Francis Drake Boulevard. Wooden steps lead up to a house. At the top of the first set of steps, stay left and follow the path around the back of a few houses to the fence. Ascend to Bolinas Ridge Trail. **1.4 miles**

Turn right to Jewell Trail. **1.6 miles**

Turn left on Jewell Trail to Old Railroad Grade Trail (Cross Marin Trail). **2.5 miles**

Turn right and stay on Old Railroad Grade Trail through Samuel P. Taylor State Park. The trail follows Lagunitas Creek, passes over Sir Francis Drake Boulevard, and ends at the park's eastern border. Cross a metal bridge to Sir Francis Drake Boulevard. **6.6 miles**

Cross Sir Francis Drake, and walk Peter's Dam Road on the east side of Lagunitas Creek to San Geronimo Fire Road, on the left with a metal gate. Peter's Dam Road becomes paved and divides just beyond this. Turn left on San Geronimo Fire Road. **6.8 miles**

Stay on San Geronimo Fire Road until the second fire road, Hunt Camp, and turn left. **9.5 miles**

The Hunt Camp Fire Road passes a watering trough and picnic tables. Turn left on the next gravel road, Sylvestris Fire Road. **9.9 miles**

Descend to paved East Sylvestris Road. **10.7 miles**

Continue to San Geronimo Valley Drive. **11.1 miles**

Turn right on San Geronimo Valley Drive to Railroad Avenue. **12.1 miles**

Turn left on Railroad Avenue and right on Sir Francis Drake Boulevard to the entrance of Spirit Rock Meditation Center.

total miles 12.5

Day 5: Woodacre to Mill Valley

Return to Railroad Avenue, turn right on Carson Road, left on Redwood Drive, and left on Edgewood Drive. Stay right when Edgewood Drive meets Buckeye Circle to Summit Fire Road. **2.0 miles**

Turn right on Summit Fire Road until it ends at White Hill Fire Road. **2.4 miles**

Turn right on White Hill Fire Road, and continue until it ends at San Geronimo Fire Road. **3.3 miles**

Turn left on San Geronimo Fire Road. It merges with Pine Mountain Fire Road. Continue to the Bolinas-Fairfax Road. **6.1 miles**

Cross the road to the parking area, pass through a gate, and descend on the Azalea Hill Trail to Bull Frog Fire Road. **7.0 miles**

Turn right to the north end of the Bon Tempe Lake Spillway. **7.4 miles**

Cross the spillway and take the Bon Tempe Shadyside Trail around the south shore of the lake to the Lake Lagunitas parking lot. **8.9 miles**

From the Lake Lagunitas Spillway, take the Lake Lagunitas Trail around the north side of the lake to the Lakeview Fire Road. **9.3 miles**

Turn right on Lakeview Fire Road, and ascend until it ends at Eldridge Grade. **9.9 miles**

Turn right on Eldridge Grade to Indian Fire Road. **11.0 miles**

Turn left on Indian Fire Road to Blithedale Ridge Fire Road. **11.6 miles**

Right on Blithedale Ridge Fire Road to Maytag Trail. **13.4 miles**

Turn left on Maytag to Elinor Fire Road, and turn right to paved Elinor Avenue. **13.9 miles**

Turn left on Elinor Avenue. Descend to Oakdale Avenue, and turn left. Turn right on Carmeleta Avenue, right on Sunnyside Avenue to East Blithedale Avenue and downtown Mill Valley.

total miles 15.0

TRANSPORTATION

Public Transportation from San Francisco

TRAVELING TO MILL VALLEY by public transit from almost anywhere in the Bay Area is efficient and inexpensive. Visit 511.org for easy trip planning. Bus schedules vary depending upon the day of the week and time of day.

Flying into the Bay Area

FOR PUBLIC TRANSPORTATION ROUTES and fares from SFO and Oakland International Airport, go to 511.org to plan your trip.

MAPS

TOM HARRISON MAPS PUBLISHES maps that cover all 56.5 miles of this walkabout for $9.95–$10.95 each; visit tomharrisonmaps.com. The maps you'll need for this journey include *Mount Tam, Point Reyes National Seashore, and Pine Mountain*.

Map Adventures publishes an outstanding map of Mount Tam, *Mount Tam Hiking and Biking Trail Map* ($10.95), that includes all but the northwest section of this walkabout. Add Point Reyes Hiking and Biking Trail Map ($9.95) for the remainder of the route Visit mapadventures.com.

PLACES TO STAY

LODGING COST			
$ *less than $100*	$$ *$100–$150*	$$$ *$150–$200*	$$$$ *more than $200*

Mill Valley

MILL VALLEY INN $$$$ • 165 Throckmorton Ave. • 415-389-6608 • millvalleyinn.com
• Continental breakfast and evening wine included.

Muir Beach

PELICAN INN $$$$ • 10 Pacific Way at CA 1 • 415-383-6000 • pelicaninn.com
• Includes a hearty breakfast. 16th-century English country–style inn. Nice pub and restaurant.

GREEN GULCH FARM ZEN CENTER $–$$$$ • 1601 Shoreline Hwy.
• 415-383-3134 • sfzc.org/green-gulch • Three delicious vegetarian meals included. Single and double rooms in a beautiful, contemplative setting. A short walk up the valley from Muir Beach.

Stinson Beach

SANDPIPER LODGING AT THE BEACH $$–$$$$ • 1 Marine Way • 415-868-1632 • sandpiperstinsonbeach.com

REDWOODS HAUS B&B $$–$$$ • 1 Belvedere and CA 1 • 415-868-1034
• redwoodhaus.com • Breakfast included.

Olema

OLEMA HOUSE (formerly The Lodge at Point Reyes) **$$$$** • 10021 CA 1
• 415-663-9000 • olemahouse.com

ROBIN'S RETREAT AND HONEYBEE COTTAGE $$-$$$ • 10210 Shoreline Hwy.
• 415-663-1288 • robinsretreat.com

INN AT ROUNDSTONE FARM $$ • 9940 Sir Francis Drake Blvd. • 415-663-1020
• roundstonefarm.com

BEAR VALLEY COTTAGE $$$$ • 88 Bear Valley Road • 415-663-1777
• bearvalleycottage.com • 15% discount for those hiking in.

VEDANTA RETREAT • Donations accepted. • 415-922-2323 • sfvedanta.org • A place for meditation and study. Overnight stays are possible after an interview with the Swami.

Woodacre

SPIRIT ROCK MEDITATION CENTER $–$$$$ • 5000 Sir Francis Drake Blvd.
• 415-488-0164 • spiritrock.org • Accommodations are available only for participants in multiday retreats. Recommendations for accommodations in Woodacre, mostly B&Bs in private residences, are available on the website

Spring in the High Sierra (see "Hiking the Tahoe Basin," page 144)

Bibliography

This is a partial bibliography of the key sources that helped guide this book.

HIKING AND WALKING

Amato, Joseph A. *A History of Walking.* New York: New York University Press, 2004.

Cousineau, Phil. *The Art of Pilgrimage: The Seeker's Guide to Making Travel Sacred.* Berkeley: Conari Press, 1998. *An inspiration for the traveler.*

Fermor, Patrick Leigh. *A Time of Gifts.* New York: The New York Review of Books, 1977. *One of England's great travel writers, Leigh Fermor writes of his 1933 walk to Constantinople. He was 18, and he crossed a continent that was soon to change forever.*

Fletcher, Colin, and Chip Rawlins. *The Complete Walker IV.* New York: Alfred A. Knopf, 2002. *An 850-page tome by the cranky patriarch of California hiking. A thorough guide intended for backpackers, with lots of information on equipment and hiking strategies. Inspirational writing on hiking.*

Hanh, Thich Nhat. *The Long Road Turns to Joy: A Guide to Walking Meditation.* Berkeley: Parallax Press, 1996. *Peace activist and Zen monk Thich Nhat Hanh writes about mindful walking on the earth.*

Solnit, Rebecca. *Wanderlust: A History of Walking.* New York: Penguin Books, 2000. *We have walked for thousands of millennia. It is only recently that we have taken to riding horses, carriages, and now motorized vehicles. Solnit traces our bipedal history and its impact on the human psyche.*

Thoreau, Henry David. *Walking: A Little Book of Wisdom.* San Francisco: Harper Collins, 1994. *Selected writings of Thoreau, an American icon, who gained inspiration from a good walk.*

CALIFORNIA HISTORY

Brands, H. W. *The Age of Gold.* New York: Anchor Books, 2002. *The dramatic story of the California gold rush.*

Brown, Vinson, and Douglas Andrews. *The Pomo Indians of California and Their Neighbors.* Happy Camp, CA: Naturegraph Publishers, 1969.

Cole, Tom. *A Short History of San Francisco.* San Francisco: Lexikos, 1981.

Conradson, Diane R., ed. *The Natural History of the Fitzgerald Marine Reserve.* Friends of Fitzgerald Marine Life Refuge, 1999.

Frank, Phil, Kendrick Rand, and Tamae Agnoli. *Bolinas and Stinson Beach.* San Francisco: Arcadia Publishing, 2004.

Goerke, Betty. *Chief Marin: Leader, Rebel, and Legend.* Berkeley: Heyday Books, 2007. *The story of the Coast Miwok and life in the Bay Area at the time of contact with Europeans.*

Guerrero, Vladimir. *The Anza Trail and the Settling of California.* Berkeley: Heyday Books, 2006. *The account of two expeditions in 1774 and 1775–1776 through Spain's unexplored frontier, from Mexico to Monterey.*

Hastings, Lansford W. *The Emigrants' Guide to Oregon and California.* Bedford, MA: Applewood Books, 1845. *Hastings was an adventurer, an opportunist, and a relentless advocate for western migration and manifest destiny. His descriptions of California before the gold rush are extraordinary. Unfortunately, they were not always accurate. The Donner Party followed his "shortcut." It was one of many mistakes that led to tragedy.*

Kelley, Charles. *Old Greenwood.* Reno: Jack Bacon & Co., 2005. *The story of Caleb Greenwood, mountain man and guide to early California pioneers.*

Kroeber, Theodora. *Ishi: In Two Worlds.* Berkeley: University of California Press, 1961. *The extraordinary story of the Yahi Indians of Lassen and their final survivor.*

La Pérouse, Jean-François de. *Monterey in 1786: Life in a California Mission.* Berkeley: Heyday Books, 1989. *Three French ships, led by La Pérouse, set out on a scientific voyage around the world. This is his account of their visit to Spain's most remote New World outpost.* Introduction by Malcolm Margolin.

Margolin, Malcolm. *The Ohlone Way: Indian Life in the San Francisco–Monterey Bay Area.* Berkeley: Heyday Books, 1978. *A masterpiece on life in the extended Bay Area before Europeans.*

Mullen, Frank, Jr. *The Donner Party Chronicles.* Nevada Humanities Committee, 1997. *A day-by-day account of the journey of the ill-fated Donner Party.*

Schulz, Paul E. *Indians of Lassen.* Mineral, CA: Loomis Museum Association, 1988.

Stewart, George R. *The California Trail.* Lincoln: University of Nebraska Press, 1983. *The story of the overland migration to California, first a trickle in the early 1840s, then a flood when the rush for gold began.*

Strong, Douglas H. *Footprints in Time: A History of Lassen Volcanic National Park.* Lassen Loomis Museum Association, 1973.

Thalman, Sylvia Barker. *The Coast Miwok Indians of the Point Reyes Area.* Point Reyes National Seashore Association, 1993.

Tortorich, Frank, Jr. *Gold Rush Trail: A Guide to the Carson River Route of the Emigrant Trail.* Pine Grove, CA: Wagon Wheel Tours, 1998.

————. *Hiking the Gold Rush Trail: A Hiking Guide over West Pass.* Pine Grove, CA: Wagon Wheel Tours, 2004.

Tucker, Wilma, and Don Tucker. *Mendocino: From the Beginning.* Mendocino: Mendocino Historical Research Inc., 1992.

PARK AND TRAIL GUIDES

DeCoster, Miles, Mark Klett, Mike Mandel, Paul Metcalf, and Larry Sultan. *Headlands: The Marin Coast at the Golden Gate.* Albuquerque: The University of New Mexico Press, 1989.

Lorentzen, Bob, and Richard Nichols. *Hiking the California Coastal Trail: Volumes 1 and 2.* Mendocino: Bored Feet Press, 2002 and 2000. *The California Legislature established the California Coastal Trail in 2001. It runs from Oregon to Mexico, 1,200 miles in total with approximately 750 miles on trails and beaches, 250 miles on back roads, and 200 miles on highway shoulders. This is a wonderful guide for backpackers and day-trippers.*

Morey, Kathy. *Hot Showers, Soft Beds, and Dayhikes in the Sierra.* Berkeley: Wilderness Press, 2008. *Day hikes in the Sierra Nevada that are near lodgings.*

Spits, Barry. *Tamalpais Trails.* San Anselmo, CA: Potrero Meadow Publishing, 2004. *A thorough guide to the trails, flora, fauna, geology, and history of Mount Tam, along with a great map.*

White, Mike. *Afoot & Afield, Reno–Tahoe: A Comprehensive Hiking Guide.* Birmingham, AL: Wilderness Press, 2015.

———. *Lassen Volcanic National Park: A Complete Hiker's Guide.* Berkeley: Wilderness Press, 2008.

Point Reyes (see "Exploring Point Reyes National Seashore," page 76)

NATURE, ECOLOGICAL, AND OUTDOOR WRITING

Basho, Matsuo. *Basho's Journey: The Literary Prose of Matsuo Basho.* Translated by David Landis Barnhill. Albany: State University of New York Press, 2005. *Almost all Japanese schoolchildren can quote Basho, a 17th-century mystic, poet, and distance walker.*

Davis, Matthew, and Michail Farrel Scott. *Opening the Mountain: Circumambulating Mount Tamalpais, A Ritual Walk.* Emeryville, CA: Avalon Publishing, 2006. *The story of the 1965 circumambulation of Mount Tam by Allen Ginsberg, Gary Snyder, and Philip Whalen and its subsequent uninterrupted practice for more than 40 years.*

Highland, Chris, ed. *Meditations of John Muir: Nature's Temple.* Berkeley: Wilderness Press, 2009. *A compilation of the poetic writings of John Muir.*

Killion, Tom, and Gary Snyder. *Tamalpais Walking: Poetry, History, and Prints.* Berkeley: Heyday Books, 2009. *A beautiful book that explores the mountain's history, culture, and spirit with Snyder's poetry and Killion's extraordinary block prints.*

Muir, John. *My First Summer in the Sierra.* Boston and London: Houghton Mifflin Co., 1911. *Anything by John Muir is still worth reading. The fresh account of a young man's ecstatic adventure, hiking from California's Central Valley to Yosemite. He was a man of his time and for all time.*

———. *The Mountains of California.* New York: Century, 1894. *A dense and poetic description of the Sierra and Cascades by a scientist, adventurer, romantic, and ecstatic.*

Snyder, Gary. *Mountains and Rivers Without End.* Washington, DC: Counterpoint, 1996. *Gary Snyder's epic poem celebrating nature and humanity.*

index

ABOUT THE AUTHOR

AFTER COLLEGE, TOM COURTNEY moved from Minnesota to California, where he discovered the Pacific Ocean and the Sierra Nevada Mountains. He has been exploring the California wilderness ever since. Tom has retired from teaching at UC Berkeley and from his financial-management consulting practice working with nonprofit organizations. He lives in Oakland with his wife, Heidi. Most weekends you will find them on a walkabout or hiking the parklands of the Bay Area.

STAY IN TOUCH

THE WALKABOUT CALIFORNIA COMMUNITY is growing, and there are so many more inn-to-inn hikes to be discovered. We continue to explore, and so do others. Visit WalkaboutCalifornia.com to share your ideas about inn-to-inn hiking in California and around the world, your reviews of restaurants and inns that you enjoyed along the trail, photos, and any questions you have about the hikes. Find out about other amazing outdoor adventures on the Walkabout California blogs.